THE SPIRAL PATH

THE SPIRAL PATH

Explorations in Women's Spirituality

EDITED BY
THERESA KING

Yes International Publishers
Saint Paul, Minnesota

Yes International Publishers
1317 Summit Avenue
Saint Paul, MN 55105
612-645-6808

Printed in the United States of America

The Spiral path: explorations in women's spirituality / edited by Theresa King

    p.   cm.

  ISBN 0-936663-07-3 : $15.95

  1. Women—Religious life. 2. Spirituality. I. King, Theresa

  [BL625.7.S65 1992]

  291.4' 082—dc20   92-20291

                                                        CIP

*For my Mother
and all women who seek their own truth.*

Contents

Appreciation

My deep appreciation is proffered to all those who assisted in the birth of this collection, particularly all those women who shared their innermost gifts of insight in their writings or interviews. I am indebted to the invaluable assistance of my dear friends, Mahya Saitoh and Charles Thorpe of Tokyo for their translations and to Mike McColl, Jean Fideler, and Jennifer Nollan for their technical skills, so generously given. Gratitude to Dr. James Wray who offered his remarkable photo of the spiral galaxy. Of course, there would be no book without Charles and Justin. Blessings and gratitude to all of you.

Preface

*A*ll my life I have been purposefully engaged on a spiritual path. I have studied and practiced various spiritual disciplines, read stacks of classic tomes on spiritual growth, attended innumerable seminars and retreats. Truths abound; I have been deeply touched. Yet I have always been aware that something was missing; some connection to an integral part of myself was not being made. Others felt it as well. After retreats and lectures, a few women tentatively asked, "Are there any women spiritual teachers?"

Slowly other questions grew: Why are all the scriptures written by men? Why are the naves of churches filled with women while the sanctuaries are peopled with men? Why are women excluded from the lawmaking bodies of religions? Over the last decades courageous women have publicly explored these political-religious issues and wrestled out positive change from organized religions, corporations, national and international law. They have set us all on a course of discovery—enough of a discovery for the questions to continue. What can we learn from the ancient worship of the Goddess? Do women image God in a different way than men? Do the great male and female saints tread the same spiritual paths? Do they speak about enlightenment and mysticism in the same terms? Is there a difference between women's spirituality and men's?

In asking the questions I was early met with amusement, and then with definite annoyance. The chief librarian at London's Kensington library was at first perplexed when I requested the section on women's spirituality, but it was anger that slammed his wheeled chair into the wall in a sputtering of refusals when offered a free stack of the so-called 'non-existent subject matter.' Priests and teachers were unanimous in their steely assurance: "The spiritual path is the same for men and women!"

But how could it be the same? If female history is different, if female biology is different, if female psychology is different, if all the hundreds of little responses to life's daily occurrences are different, how can the spirituality be the same? Is it the same because males say that it is? I was reminded of the woman in the audience of the great eighth-century Indian Vedantist, Shankara, who challenged him to prove his statements about women through experience rather than rhetoric.

Women have been given their steps to spirituality by the same patriarchal groups that have given them their place in society, in politics, in the arts, in the workplace. Their spirituality was developed for them alongside their subjugation and invalidation. Masculine values have been taught as the norm in spirituality as well as in every other art and science in our culture. Women have so internalized these concepts that they themselves have guided young women into those same male norms. The most elemental reading in feminist literature will overwhelm the reader with staggering evidence of the determined and successful efforts of the male system to invent a place for women and keep them in it at all costs. Philosophy, psychology, and medicine have studied men and boys to develop a universal norm and then measured women against it with the result that women question their own feelings and responses, doubting their experiences and altering their judgments in the effort to force themselves into the masculine norm. Religions, meant to be vessels for the celebration of life, have told women that they are inferior, the origin of humankind's fall, the temptation to man's purity, the source of his sin. Her own body, in its life-giving cycles, is called 'unclean.'

The resultant pain of women throughout the ages and across the world, the loss of their gifts in science, art, spiritual literature, and service that might have been given to humankind can only be mourned. But after our mourning, we must begin again the process of discovery.

We have done much discovering over the last decades. Female exegetes have reexamined sacred texts to find their original, female-affirming meanings. Female historians have uncovered patriarchal plots to hide the role of women in salvation history and exclude them from Church structure. Female psychologists have written new norms for development based on studies of and interviews with girls and women. The medical community, after suffering the humiliation of discovery of its misogynist practices, is beginning to include women in its research and hierarchy. Women artists, writers, musicians, lawyers are beginning to breathe freely the air of recognition and achievement.

But there is much more to discover. We need to know how to put all the pieces together. We need to fill the empty feeling in our belly with stories of women like us who succeeded. We need to be assured that our lives and our work is holy. We need to recognize and then joyously tread the path that will best lead us to self-knowledge and union with divinity.

Our spirituality must be truly holistic. It must speak to all those parts of us that make us women as well as the parts that make us human. We need a spirituality that guides our emotions and instincts as well as our thinking, and shows us meaning in our everyday lives as well as in the life to come. Women need to find such a spirituality, and probably they must develop one. This task requires courage, of course, and brutal honesty to question what we have been taught to believe, to reinterpret truths on which we have been raised, and to examine our ideas to see if they really 'fit'—if they are indeed leading us to self-enlightenment and full maturity.

It is by sharing our insights with each other and communicating our steps to growth that we express our search for truth. Enlightenment is our birthright, but to have it we must claim it. By sharing and listening to others' insights about life, meaningful rituals, states of ecstasy, and wisdom from altered states of consciousness, we can recognize those experiences in ourselves and validate them as women's ways. We may need to develop a new language so that women's concepts will not be superseded by the traditional male usage of terms.

But whether charting an entirely new spirituality, or reinterpreting the world's great religions, we assist each other by strengthening our confidence in ourselves and acknowledging our own inner light as the sure and right guide.

For many of us, spirituality is a hard word. It conjures up dusty images, ephemeral feelings and old responses from hours spent in the churches of our childhood. It jogs our memory for forgotten saints, bits of memorized prayers, and all that is mysterious. It also seems to carry connotations of the spoilsport: disdain for fun and comfort, wealth, physical beauty. The word is often misused to cover superstitions and dogmas that can be, and often are, antithetical to real spiritual growth. Yet by using the word 'spirituality' we are also put in touch with the experiences of all those who have preceded us on the perennial search for ultimacy. We use the term in the sense of the search for reality, in the discovery of what it means to be fully human.

The women and men in this collection are all unique. They speak of experiences from a variety of cultures, age-groups, religions, lifestyles, and viewpoints. Some have long trodden the mystical path and are honored teachers; others have quietly integrated spiritual concepts into their daily lives. Common to all is a deep personal commitment to enlightenment; each speaks from the flowering of spiritual practice and purposeful striving for real human maturity.

The writers speak in their own voices. When I lived in Nepal and India, I often heard God referred to as "She." When I asked the preferred pronoun in Japan, my co-workers were astounded: "But of course, God is male!" Many of the writers have wrestled with the dilemma of naming God in their essays, but the final decision was left to each of them.

Dogen, one of the patriarchs of Zen Buddhism, counseled, "Do not overlook one drop in the ocean of virtue." Thus we have included in this collection all aspects of a woman's life: self-image, sexuality, health, marriage, motherhood, cooking, her connection of nature, solitude, and community, her relationships with men, her place in society and the corporate world, her creativity, her search for the divine in scripture and in prayer, art, mysticism, prophecy, wisdom. The writers show us new ways to know God and illumine the old ways with fertile, new meaning. They gather our richness as women into a harmony of love, service, and leadership while helping us identify and follow that inner guide urging us on to personal fulfillment.

Going on means going far,
Going far means returning.

TAO TE CHING

What is Spirituality?
The Spiral Path

by

Theresa King

*O*n an early Spring day in Takayama, Japan, under wet, grey clouds, I joined the group climbing up the steep path to the temple at the top of a mountain. The old wooden building, dark with age and the smoke from thousands of votive fires, was barely visible behind the trees. The trees themselves stood like massive, ancient sentinels covered in grey-green moss and crowned with billows of delicate white plum blossoms.

Following the pilgrims up the steps, I wondered what spirituality this temple represented. What form of divinity would the people worship? What ritual would I witness? How would they pray?

At the top I stood under the perfumed branches and watched as the pilgrims smiled and nodded and began to open their baskets of lunch. No one entered the temple at all. None of them bowed or clapped their hands or rang the ancient bell to announce their presence to the divine. Rather confused, I asked an old woman about this strange pilgrimage to the temple.

"Temple?" she answered, "We came for the flowers!"

The story somehow reminds me of the quest of spirituality. Beyond all the structures of spirituality and the various paths devoted to spiritual wisdom bloom the flowers of relationship with divinity. Sometimes we lose sight of the flowers; sometimes we are not sure why we made the climb in the first place. In our enthusiasm for a particular method, we tend to forget what spirituality is all about.

Some months ago I was on the faculty of a university program that trained students for ministry. Among the prominent theologians and psychologists, there were as many definitions of spirituality as there were minds to formulate them. Some held that true spirituality consisted of service to the disadvantaged of society as opposed to contemplation and "navel gazing." Others said that prayer and scripture study was the only real basis of spirituality. Some insisted that the most accurate definition of spirituality is "how I cope with life," while others said it was "reliving the life of Christ." Some thought spirituality was the use of things—stones, candles, beads, cards, dreams, drums, songs—to reach the divine; a few insisted that 'community' was the only genuine way. All implied a firm dichotomy between the spirituality of quiet contemplation and the spirituality of active charity and justice.

Thinking about it afterwards, I realized that everyone had forgotten about the flowers. Why do we pursue a spiritual path and what exactly is spirituality? Whether pursued by those withdrawn from social life in remote monasteries or those firmly in the midst of a complicated and busy life, spirituality is the same. Spirituality is integration. It both incorporates and infuses every aspect of our lives, from our tenuous first steps to our final enlightened union. Spirituality is, after all, development into full human maturity. It is the ultimate integration of our parts—body, mind, emotions, tendencies, actions, values, aspirations, intuition—into a whole. That whole being matches the original idea of the divine creation.

Consciously or unconsciously human beings feel a need to resonate with the thrust of the universe. We seek to manifest the energy of life in our unique, personal way in concert with the entire cosmic manifestation of divinity. Spirituality is none other than the force of that creative energy seeking integration and resonance. Sometimes we feel it pulling us inwards to be healed or inspired or immersed in joy. Sometimes we feel it pushing us out to take a stand for justice, or lead a ritual, or laugh at a party. Who are we to decide how and when God will manifest Itself?

The teachers who say that marching for civil rights is not spirituality but meditating in solitude is, the ministers who tell us our moments of ecstasy are not real but caring for a crying child is, the directors who guide us to pray while ignoring our financial difficulties or health problems are telling us half truths. We are not divided beings; our inner life energizes and inspires our outer life; our external activities are the fruits of, and give impetus to our interior activities.

As the sage, Swami Rama, says, we are citizens of two worlds, an inner world and an outer world. We constantly travel from one to the other, each world claiming us for a time and then relinquishing its hold on us. Some of us prefer the energy from the external world, feel more comfortable there, and spend more time in its activities; some of us feel more at home in the interior world, getting energized and inspired there, spending more time in solitude and quiet. Neither world can hold us all the time, nor would we want it to. We all have periods of needing to be alone as well as in community, of collecting our thoughts and inspiration as well as sharing our exuberance with others. We know the call of the being deep within as well as the delight of divinity in all the events and creatures of the world. Eventually we will mature to that totally integrated being in perfect resonance with all creation, but we seem to reach integration step by step, experience by experience, and not always smoothly.

Spirituality as Growth

One way to examine if our spirituality is genuine is to compare it with other dimensions of human growth. Physical growth is easy to know: the body starts small and grows bigger. Muscles develop, hair lengthens, glands activate, new teeth and tissue appear according to a prearranged plan. Continued growth is dependent upon the body discarding all that is no longer useful: finger nails, baby teeth, old skin, waste products. If the body were forced to remain the same size or keep all the parts it ever produced, it would die.

On the mental level, human beings develop from superficial knowledge to comprehensive understanding. Through the use of almost-constant questioning, the child collects a rich assortment of facts with which to form an ever-clearer image of the world. Eventually the child filters what had seemed absolute truth (Santa Claus and the Easter Bunny) through new knowledge about reality, reforming the image to satisfy the human need for truth. Childish notions that no longer fit the maturing clarity are dropped or subsumed. (The child can now wrap presents from Santa for her little brother.)

Psychological development moves from total identification with another to self-identity. Initial dependence on mother evolves to increasing independence as the child advances through stages of growth, discovering its place in community as a competent individual. Again, human happiness and integration require releasing earlier stages in order to complete the next level of maturation.

The development of these three aspects of human nature furnishes a clue to the fourth. Genuine spiritual development also follows the natural process from small to big, from contraction to expansion, from dependence to independence, from the particular to the universal. Like other growth patterns, beginning stages of spiritual growth are left behind as new phases begin.

Many people attempt to alter this natural process for spiritual growth. Some believers think religious allegiance precludes self-analysis and self-growth. Personal spiritual development seems unnecessary for those who are already saved, secure in their guaranteed place in a promised hereafter. Others find the idea of spirituality unsophisticated and embarrassing. They learned the golden rule along with several 'thou-shalt-nots' in kindergarten and consider them sufficient. Many others adhere to the same notions of goodness and badness, sin and grace, punishment and reward they were taught as children. Their concept of divinity usually matches the one they had at age seven; they are loath to change it. Such believers think the spiritual part of themselves is either always the same or else develops mysteriously, unconnected to their efforts. Few ever consider dropping old beliefs, even though the belief no longer has practical application in their life or meaning in their value system.

For too many people spirituality means being a 'nicer' person and loving a nebulous creator while fearfully retaining all the rules of morality and ideas of God they were ever taught. The accumulation of their old religious concepts often fester into moral guilt or self-righteousness, while effectively sapping strength from any new spiritual inspiration.

Genuine spirituality is a process like other developmental processes. It is dynamic. It investigates that nagging unconscious pressure hinting that there is more to life. It takes counsel from the ancient dictum "Know thyself" by following the inner urge for growth, knowledge, and a relationship with created reality. Far beyond any single belief system or religious authoritarianism, personal spirituality is constantly questioning, reaching out, wanting to experience the meaning of existence. It propels the psyche to find its place in the cosmos. Spirituality changes as one matures, leading the seeker forward to the next step of development. It fights the inertia of religious contentment with the dynamism of ever-new self-knowledge. It balances one's fear of disturbing convention with the insistence that a curious mind may indeed fathom the unknown.

Sacred and Profane

Our inherited patriarchal spirituality made a dichotomy between the sacred and the profane, the spiritual and the physical, the supernatural and the natural. Because women are so strongly connected with nature and earth through the birthing cycle of their bodies, they have often been formally excluded from things spiritual. Spirituality has traditionally been reserved for those who dwell in realms of the mind, or who sacrifice the delights of the body. This has led many women to question whether a spiritual life is compatible with their lives.

The mystics who live in both worlds have, through the ages, told us that the dichotomy is false. They have whispered through spiritual literature that every phase of life is sacred, that all actions can lead us to total integration, and that there is not only one way to know God.

The path of spirituality is intimately connected with every aspect of life. In fact, it is life. To deny our spiritual self is to destroy our psychosomatic unity as human beings. A young woman I spoke with said, "Oh, I'm not at all interested in spirituality," just as if it were merely a topic of discussion along with old movies or the antics of her cat. Spirituality is a part of each of those things; it is the basic stuff of life. We mature as humans from needs for self-preservation, food, sleep, and sex through needs for security and safety, to needs for love and relatedness and esteem, and finally to needs for self-actualization, meaningfulness, perfection, and spiritual goals. We are always drawn to the beautiful, the good, and the true whether it be in the form of old movies or old theological tracts. We cannot really separate spirituality from the rest of our growth. Attempting to do so will make us lopsided individuals, our lives wobbling in the constant efforts of lying to ourselves.

The challenge in our lives is to eliminate the distinction between the sacred and the profane, between our spiritual path and its manifestation in our lives. It means ending the dualities, pulling the poles of life's continuum closer, harmonizing the sets of opposites: birth-death, good-evil, inner-outer. It is a long, adventurous, maturing process, strewn with unpredictability.

Finding God

We all seek the holy in different ways. Sometimes, when we think we have it firmly in hand, we do not want anything around it to change. When I was young, I thought I had holiness all figured out. I would be a saint. So crystal clear was my idea of the spiritual quest that I easily planned my entire life, firm in the conviction that since I had life and truth figured out, nothing would change. I entered a semi-cloistered religious community, and began to contemplate the immutable. After nine years of theology, philosophy, meditation and contemplation, I was forced to a stark realization: God is not this!

So I redefined the immutable and reentered the secular life. I planned to settle down with a professor husband to a quiet life of stability. (I was careful not to choose anyone who would travel for a living). We would live in a charming house with a white picket fence, have 2.4 children, study about spirituality together, and live happily ever after. Soon truth was again tapping me on the shoulder saying, "God is not this!"

The immutable seemed to want to travel, so I moved abroad for more than seven years, living in Holland, Germany, India, Japan, Nepal, and England, studying culture and social mores, learning why we have the beliefs we have, and finding out what people think about the world and its God. Amidst all I saw and heard, I learned: God is not this!

Next I studied many religious traditions in many settings, both academic and practical, cloistered and community—Zen, yoga, Catholicism, New Ageism, Taoism, Buddhism, Shintoism, Anglicanism, psychic phenomena, fundamentalism—living in convents, ashrams, spiritual communities, nuclear families, a rectory, a Buddhist monastery, an attic, a palace. My mind and heart told me again, "God is not this!"

More confused now as I was getting older, and more determined than ever to find divine truth, my life turned upside down once again. The children did not materialize, my husband went on to a different lifestyle, my body changed without my approval, my work made an about-face, and nothing was immutable.

It finally became blindingly clear that change is the law of life; nothing stays the same. Everything changes, and then again, everything returns. And once I realized that thoroughly, and knew it in every corner of my being, truth whispered to me with laughter, "Now you know; God is all this."

That is why I believe the most apt symbol for spiritual growth is the spiral. It is a symbol of change as well as integration in chaos, of unity as well as diversity, of dynamic movement as well as stability. It pulls together all the world's spiritual quests as well as all its daily struggles into a meaningful journey carrying us back to the source of our being.

Spiral as Spiritual Symbol

The spiral is nature's first form. The galaxies were created by the spiraling of interstellar gas; planets turn around their suns in regularly-timed spirals; life unfolds in plants and animals through powerful, spiral energy; air and water move in spiral flow; leaves and flower petals open in spirals; time itself spirals out in circling, returning phases.

The spiral is also one of the most ancient symbols of eternity because it both comes from and returns to its point of origin. Its beginning and end are opposites, yet exactly alike as they rotate around their invisible central axis. As a spiral turns, the rounds of its formation reveal their source; the source can look back, see the movement, and become conscious of itself.

Our whole existence is intricately involved in nature's spirals. We experience in our bodies the rhythms of life and growth and death in a vast spiral dance. We breathe in spiraling columns of air and send it out again to combine with other spirals of air, forming a large, spiraling energy field. Month after month, following the moon, we actualize in our bodies the circle of building up and tearing down, of preparation and cleansing away. Whether or not we physically give birth, we are linked to our mothers and grandmothers and great-grandmothers in the endless cycle of nurturance, the rituals of caring for the sick, the mysteries of the dying. On the continuum of spiraling time we are a child birthing a child, watching our child birth a child.

Day after day we labor in the seemingly endless cycle of work and rest: typing, cooking, cleaning, planting, marketing, driving, writing, processing, comforting, checking, assembling, reading, counting, writing, relating, sleeping. We think we keep doing the same thing over and over again, making the same mistakes, encountering the same relationships, speaking the same lines.

But it is not quite the same. We are not going in circles; we are spiraling. The spiral shows us that each ordinary step in life changes us so that if we look behind us and chart where we have been, we can see that we are not exactly the same person we were, even if the task is the same. And the task itself does not seem so mundane when it is viewed as a catalyst to personal growth and self-realization. Each time we encounter the same situation, it is a new experience. Time has passed. We see the symptoms from a different perspective, approach the situation with more or less strength or insight than the last time. Each time we spiral past the same kind of event, we are given another opportunity to integrate the learning which will move us toward our own personal evolution.

What is the central axis around which we are turning? What is the point from which we begin and to which we will inevitably return? It is our own innate wisdom, our pure self, the mystical hidden treasure which is the living image of divinity. Wisdom is always there, guiding our steps even when they seem to be faltering, leading us forward and returning us again, until older and more confident, we are able to see what we really are.

Attachment as an Obstacle

Many years ago as a newly professed nun, I entered the large community room of my order for the half hour of daily talking, sharing, and sewing known as "recreation." The room was fitted with a very long table, both sides lined with wooden chairs. The original rule ordained that nuns sat at the table (as well as walked into the dining room, knelt in the chapel, received their food, and every other activity) in a strict ordering of seniority, oldest to youngest. That sometimes beloved, sometimes scorned rule had just recently been rescinded and, for the first time, the nuns were free to sit wherever they wished. That evening as I walked into the room, I witnessed a shocking event. Two old nuns, each nearly fifty years in the convent, were engaged in a violent argument. One sat, bent over on a chair, her thin, prominent-veined hands tightly grasping the edge of the table, screaming, "I always wanted this place; I can sit here if I want to!" The other nun had hold of the back of the chair, jerking it and trying to unseat her companion yelling, "This is my place. I sat here for forty-six years. This is mine!"

Years later I asked a sage what he considered the single greatest obstacle for women on the spiritual path. Without hesitation he replied, "Attachment."

There are many obstacles to full maturity and spiritual growth. Attachment is an important one, because it can easily be overlooked, or seen to be something else. The psychological/developmental principle of attachment is absolutely necessary in the human life cycle, as shown in the work of Carol Gilligan and other current researchers. The bonding aspects of love and attachment establish our sense of self in infancy and childhood and continue to inspire feelings of connectedness and empathy throughout life. When we over-emphasize or over-use that bonding principle, however, it changes into the obstacle of attachment. Bonding is life-giving and expansive; attachment is the nun who would not let go. Attachment means addiction to people and things so that one is dependent upon them for one's very identity. Life is full of surprises; openness to life expands the totality of our identity and unfolds myriad possibilities for growth and self-knowledge. Attachment takes away those possibilities. It cuts off our future surprises, mysteries, and potential by restricting the future to copying the past.

Attachment is an inability to distinguish our self from those we serve or nurture, or the objects we possess. It is to forget our connectedness to all creation while grabbing onto a single thing—a person, possession, lifestyle, place, or role—thinking it holds our sole identity. Attachment is a kind of false love. It is total identification with, and absorption in, another being to the exclusion of all else, even one's own needs and self worth.

Attachment to material things is tricky because we need material things in order to survive as well as to be successful in life. But we need remember that material things are never actually our own; they belong to the earth for the use of those that inhabit it for awhile. We are all travelers passing through. A traveler may insist on the best of everything—accommodations, entertainment, food, companions—yet always in the back of her mind is the idea that she will be moving on soon. The things she has at the moment are only that: momentary. She would not think of holding on to the hotel room in Verona, or the restaurant in Kathmandu. She enjoys them while she is there, knowing that tomorrow she will be somewhere else enjoying something new.

Attachment for people is often mistaken for love and concern. A woman may insist that her spouse have no interests or activities without her because they are so much in love they could not be apart; another woman may smother her child with constant attention and ever-present care because she is a loving mother and the child needs her so much. Love, however, always expands and gives freedom while attachment contracts and brings bondage, both to the one who is attached and to the object of devotion. Attachment always brings anxiety along as a companion. One who is attached to another is constantly expecting something; the beloved's attentions are never enough. In contrast, love is given freely, not asking for anything in return. Kahil Gibran says, "Love gives naught but itself and takes naught but from itself. Love possesses not nor would it be possessed; for love is sufficient unto love."[1]

Attachment is a spiritual obstacle because it prevents us from knowing ourselves. By making us grasp onto something so totally and tightly, it limits our ability to have something else. Women's spirituality is always concerned with freedom. There must be freedom to explore our images of ourselves, to establish connections to those aspects of society from which we have been excluded, to develop a new language of spirit through our stories and myths. There must be freedom to make mistakes and try something else. But "if I hold onto my identity of the person I was," says visionary and artist Frederick Franck, "it hangs as a great millstone around my neck."[2]

Changing attachment into love is both a courageous and freeing step on the spiral path. It widens our view, strengthens our relationships and opens the way for new possibilities to emerge in our lives. Letting go of attachment changes our love from something weak into a strong, mature love. Irina Tweedie has a motto which speaks of such love: "Give me freedom to sing without an echo, to fly without a shadow, and love without leaving traces."

Self-Negation as an Obstacle

Another destructive obstacle on the path of spirituality is woman's sense of self-negation. It is our feeling of worthlessness, our passive acceptance of society's definition and limits for us, our self-hatred, our conviction that "there must be something wrong with me."

Children continuously seek approval from their parents, teachers, and other adults in order to identify their self-worth and value to society. In an ideal situation that approval is lovingly given; the child absorbs it and reforms it into a positive self-image and personal strength. All too often, however, children are not given the feedback they need. Sometimes they receive negative input, and horribly, even abuse which assures them that they are not worthy of love and respect nor capable of greatness. Many women have been told in many subtle and violent ways from childhood onward that they are worthless, unimportant, unlovable. Society has much to answer for in failing to protect generations of girls and women and for adding shame to their burden of pain and defeat.

For most of us the experience of self-negation manifests in our failure to fully appreciate and trust ourselves. It is the light mockery we make when someone praises our work or our appearance or compliments our ideas. It is our quickness to point out "flaws" in our work and our bodies, the vague feeling that we live a wasted life. It is the sense of inadequacy we experience before any new undertaking. It shows up in eating disorders, in our put-downs of other women, our discourtesy to shop assistants, our fleeting thoughts of harming ourselves.

How can we realize our true, divine self when we do not appreciate our everyday selves? Is it possible to advance in self-knowledge if we condemn what we learn? How can we travel a spiritual path to cosmic realization and human transformation if we refuse to acknowledge our worthiness to do so? Can we do great things if we deny our intrinsic greatness? How do we get out of this trap of self-hatred?

Somehow we must take another look at ourselves, look sharply, and see clearly. We must awaken to what is really there: our intrinsic power, beauty, and uniqueness. When we realize that society has not spoken truthfully to us, we can reevaluate what was said and come to new definitions about ourselves. When we recognize that the experiences of our lives are steps to maturity, they become of immense value. We can choose to develop in new areas where we formerly did not dare trespass. We can stop the self-defeating comparison of ourselves to others, acknowledging their power while not denying our own. We can reaffirm that which is good in us, in our training, in our relationships, in our service, while maintaining the right to change those things when they are no longer meaningful or helpful to us. We can see ourselves with new eyes.

Seeing more clearly on the spiral path allows us to look back and notice that women's self-negation, when it is a step to new self-worth, is very close to an important stage of the mystical life. Contemporary spiritual writers[3] have noted that women's experiences of nothingness and worthlessness often precede an awakening to new sources of power and spirit. They compare it to the dark night of the soul of mysticism, a time of darkness and emptiness, when ties to conventional sources of value are broken just before new, profound insight is achieved. In this view, our insights from our experiences of self-negation can be the impetus for our spiritual awakening to new realizations about ourselves, leading us to a true sense of our real worth and a genuine love for others.

Fear of Change as an Obstacle

Where there is fear there can be no love. That is why fear is a major obstacle on the spiritual path, fear of change the most insidious of all. We fear change because we believe that externals control our lives. In self-defense, we learn how to live with them, respond to them, be dependent upon them. In order to feel safe, we need all life's externals in place, remaining the same as they were, so we can cope with them. We do this even if we are unhappy with the result. Should we be offered a chance to change our situation to something new or unknown, we often choose to stay exactly where we are. We live the old axiom, "A known devil is better than an unknown angel."

When we are afraid, it is because we feel we have no control over what is happening to us. But when we place our emotional center on anything external, it is inevitable that we will live in fear. Everything external—institutions, people, places—is changeable and cannot be counted on to stay the same indefinitely. It is precisely because of the numerous changes in scriptural interpretation, church structure, family stability, and government leadership that many people today feel betrayed, fearful, and angry. There is a sense that the old rules are gone and the new ones make no sense.

Sometimes we are afraid to learn too much about ourselves; we fear we will not like what we find out. While teaching meditation, I found several people who were incapable of closing their eyes because they feared their own inner darkness and the thoughts that arose within it. They did not know that all the parts of one's being love and protect that being at all costs. Unwilling to trust themselves, they were equally unwilling to learn any tools that might prove them wrong about their fears.

When we become aware that the source of our safety is within us, we will begin to realize that change is a natural part of growth. Change provokes self-revelation. It solicits ever new beginnings together with opportunities to tap into unfamiliar areas for awareness and expansion. Embracing change releases new energy towards our goals. When we become more familiar with the abiding power of our inner being, we recognize that nothing outside of us can ever control our thinking, emotions, beliefs, or actions.

The Goal of Spirituality

Traditional spiritual texts tell us that there are many paths to the mountain top, but anyone familiar with mountain climbing knows that the choice of route is of utmost importance. With so many methods to spiritual growth and so many spiritual traditions available to be explored, the way can become confusing. The only way we can effectively evaluate the many spiritual tools offered to us is to be very clear about our goal. Spiritual goals may not all be the same. Some spiritual methods lead to a moral life; some to the development of psychic abilities; some can assure a happy, contented life; some supply intellectual stimulation; some supply satisfaction for our emotional and communal needs; some lead to self-knowledge and knowledge of reality; some lead to ecstasy; some supply consolation and a sense of safety.

What is your goal? What do you want? Once you are conscious of your spiritual goal, then you must choose the method that will best lead you there. Not all methods can produce what they promise. Ask yourself, Is this tradition capable of bringing me to my goal? Have others in the tradition reached the goal? Did they use the methods of the tradition or something else? Do I admire their journey and want to tread the same path? Once you are convinced of the spiritual tradition you have chosen, then walk its path with confidence.

It is very easy to fool ourselves when we embark on a conscious spiritual path. We so want to believe that we are making progress that we sometimes become gullible. We read a book, attend a workshop, are inspired by a ritual or a sunrise and our hearts feel light, our minds think lofty thoughts, and we surmise that we are especially holy. A few hours later we feel we have fallen off the spiritual pedestal as we catch ourselves yelling at the children or planning little acts of deceit or selfishness. We forget that we do not walk a spiritual path in a vacuum; reality is always our partner, ready to tap us on the shoulder and remind us of life.

Common sense, our characteristics of connectedness to people and nature, our ability to wait, our desire to be of service to others, our ability to surrender to something greater than our everyday selves, our intuition when standing in the face of truth—all are gifts we bring to the spiritual journey and all are essential. The great spiritual teachers were always eminently practical, even in the face of their ecstatic union with divinity. That is why many spiritual traditions speak of the need to be mature through life's experiences, as well as in years, before treading the more advanced paths. Who we are right now is the person that takes the next step toward spirituality.

Spirituality is always about transformation. It is concerned with transforming our narrowness into full awareness, our social struggles into community, our fears and self-loathing into vitality and power. It does not so much make the mundane sacred as it lets us realize that the mundane is sacred and that the sacred is often very familiar. It teaches us that what we are and what we do is holy. It lets us see the many known and unknown parts of ourselves as a hologram, each part necessary to the multidimensional whole, each part reflecting the wholeness hidden in every other. At its core, spirituality is love. It is love of self and love of others, love lived now and love searched for, love as being and as becoming, love as person and as the universe's all-encompassing power.

Our spiritual quest is the basic human search for the ultimate meaning of existence. It is the continuing discovery of our real nature, the wisdom of self-understanding, and the reach for truth beyond our current grasp. It gradually liberates us from the fears of life and death and gives us increasing intimations of immortality. In a mature spiritual life we discover personal sacredness and through it recognize and verify the truths of world scriptures and mythologies. Ultimately spirituality discloses, through experience and direct knowledge, all the mysteries of life. Our spiritual search is complete when all our questions are answered, when our humanity touches divinity, when we understand the unknowable, and when, for us, the transcendent is utterly immanent.

With a B.S. in Education and an M.A. in Human Development and Spirituality, Theresa King has been a teacher in primary and special education, a choir director, and a co-founder and manager of the Himalayan Press. She was a member of a semi-cloistered religious community for eight years, personal assistant to yoga master, Swami Rama, for seven years, and studied for several years in India, Nepal, Japan, Europe, and Mexico. She has been a consultant and organizer for several world conferences on spirituality and health, notably in Kathmandu and Tokyo, as well as in the United States. Theresa lectures and conducts workshops on spirituality internationally and currently lives in St. Paul, Minnesota.

*She is clothed with strength and dignity and
she laughs at the days to come.
She opens her mouth in wisdom and
on her tongue is kindly counsel.*

PROVERBS

Women and Spirituality:
First Steps to the Spiritual Life

by

Swami Shivananda Radha

*M*y spiritual training took place in the foothills of the Himalayas, where I was initiated into *sanyas,* renunciation, by Swami Sivananda in 1956. I was one of only five women to be initiated in the whole of India. I am a very practical person, as was my Guru, who was a medical doctor before taking to the path of renunciation. He realized that many things begin in the mind, and he would not tolerate any display of emotion—tears didn't impress him—they only showed him you were unfit for the high office of *sanyas.* He demanded of me ruthless honesty. This rigorous training is necessary in order to rid oneself of illusions, assumptions, and projections, and to develop awareness.

As a woman comes in contact with her spiritual search, she needs to ask herself many questions, even if the answers are not immediately forthcoming. Your own reflection on each question will bring you one step closer to realizing your goal in life. Just in posing these questions to yourself, it becomes obvious that the demands of spiritual life are very tough.

What is the Purpose of my Life?

In reflecting on your life, ask where you have placed the greatest emphasis. What has been the motivating force that has sustained you through the years? Was it the need to be accepted? There are many things that hold women back from their own development, but the main one, I think, is emotional dependence. A woman may have all the financial security she could want, yet still struggle with dependence. Women's faces often show the tension and anxiety of this struggle, and their eyes beg, "Please accept me." It won't work. You will have to accept yourself first. That is a big job because we have not really looked into ourselves, nor met ourselves on the gut level. Our culture accuses women of being very talkative. Have you ever thought why this is so? It could be that women think no one listens to them, so it doesn't matter what they say. But they have also not listened to themselves. We must be ruthlessly honest with ourselves.

There is an interesting book by Otto Rank, called *Beyond Psychology.* He writes that women are not hysterical, but sometimes they seem to act "peculiarly" because the men do not accept them the way they are. Is that true in your own life? Do you feel that you are accepted as you really are? Look at the tremendous efforts women make to get men's attention—nine billion dollars alone is spent in the cosmetic industry. Is it because you are so eager to live and complete yourselves through somebody else?

What did women do historically, when they found they were not accepted by men nor given any recognition? The man became their Father in heaven. This happened because, at the time the Lord's prayer was introduced, the father was a symbol for great power; the Jewish husband had total power over the family. So simple people understood it this way: if their human father didn't accept them, they could pray to their Father in heaven. But to those who could understand more, the close disciples, Jesus taught that the kingdom of heaven is within, and made no reference to a father.

It would be a tremendous step forward for us to look to the kingdom within our own heart, instead of to a father image. I do not wish to criticize any religion, but only to bring to your attention the fact that changing your image of God can be very important. You will only find a true response to it if you can discover your own divinity within. That divinity does not depend on the kind of religious faith you hold, but it will help you to become a better Catholic, Christian, Jew, Muslim, or whatever. It is we who give the neutral spiritual power a shape and form, based on our own understanding.

The image that many believers have of Jesus is the greatest rival of what Jesus really is—Christ consciousness. Similarly the image that a woman holds of her husband is his greatest rival and prevents her from ever truly knowing him. Couples have to help each other diminish the old images so they don't get caught in outdated roles, but continue to grow together. The image you are putting out is also your greatest rival. If you cannot go beyond that image you will never know who you are. Can you get beyond your own image?

Has the purpose of your life thus far been to find your dream lover? There is a lot of pain and many lost hopes, because we have been trained to indulge in illusions and fairy tales. Of course, advertising and culture reinforce this. Many women pursue the illusion of their fairy-tale prince—the dream lover who one day will come and rescue them. I have met women for whom that dream lover is still alive even when they are in their sixties. They are motivated by the false promise of a dream that cannot be fulfilled. Why do we have such a dream? There is an answer to this question, but no one can give it to you; you will have to dig it out of your own life. Each person has her own way of awakening to the truth and in every life it is quite different.

Many dreams, illusions, and hopes must be abandoned in order for you to become well-grounded, with both feet firmly on the earth. You have to look at who you are and where you are. Most of all you have to look at your strengths. Women really are powerful and it is a pity that they do not always recognize and use the strengths they have.

What Makes my Life Worth Living?

How do I fulfill myself? Do I look to other people to make my life worth living? Look carefully at what you feed your emotions. Consider your emotional needs like the branches of a fruit tree. Fruit trees are trimmed each year so they will produce more fruit, rather than using the sunlight and fertilizer to sustain non-fruitbearing branches. Women must trim the branches of their emotions so they will not take all the available nourishment. Instead, women must find out what truly sustains them and investigate how they can nourish that. Anything that does not further their psychological growth should be trimmed back. That trimming is necessary before any spiritual development can take place.

Emphasize those things that make life worth living. Bring quality into your life so that you feel good about whatever you do. You have a right to be proud of the things that you do well or that reflect your standard of quality. Traditionally, a woman took pride in the accomplishments of the man she was with. She tried to live through him in the hope that some of his glamour would rub off on her. But women today have to find their own way and their own place in life. They cannot be just a nice decoration in a man's lapel; they must live their own life and decide the contribution they can make to society.

Life has become too complex for simplistic gender roles. Women cannot look to men to take care of them. If there is a place for women in today's world, women themselves must decide what that place will be without waiting for someone else to put them there.

To What Degree Do I Accept Responsibility for Myself?

There are many factors in life that reinforce a state of emotional dependence. It starts, of course, in the family, with the roles that are learned there. The mother will say, "Well, father wouldn't like that. Ask your father. Get your dad's permission." This creates a reinforcement of female dependence on males that is difficult to overcome unless the father is a very mature person who knows how to guide a daughter into life. But most of the time he has neither the awareness of the dependence in himself nor the training to overcome it.

Mothers, also, are not trained. Generally women become mothers without knowing that instinct alone is the basis for their actions. In our society, animals are carefully bred, but human beings are still wild. A young woman who wants to get married may be so caught in her emotions and illusions of love and marriage that she doesn't seek any training or education, nor does she find out how healthy she is and what her chances are for having a healthy baby. She rarely thinks of the contribution of the man she wants to marry to the health of a baby.

We still operate from many old cultural traditions. Why was a son more desirable than a daughter in many cultures? A son could fight and defend the food or animals that were needed for survival. In ancient times, the king used his daughter as a bribe so that neighboring kings would not attack. Women became objects of trade. Today women are not used so explicitly as trading objects, but this is the origin of dowries and the idea that women are the property of men. You can meet a woman who has two or three doctorates, but when somebody says, "There is a mouse!" she climbs on the table. This is not because she is afraid that the mouse will bite her, but tucked away in the recesses of human memory there is still the lingering fear of starvation. When there was no means of preservation, grains were the only way for human life to survive the severe winters. The first rat or mouse meant there would be thousands following to eat all the grain. Those old memories create inexplicable responses; it is helpful, therefore, to find out what lingers within your unconscious mind.

We have acquired many customs and traditions from history. There are leftovers that we have to deal with, but we can only do so by learning to recognize them. This means reflecting on why you react a certain way. When you entertain a few women friends along with only one man, watch the faces and the eyes of the women. Prior to the man entering the room, the women will be relaxed and casual. But when he comes in, they all sit up, their eyes bright. He is the focus of their attention because he is a potential conqueror. Every woman must recognize these games and decide when she is going to stop playing them.

The sociobiologist says we are all programmed by our genes. That might be so, but if that were the only way of operating available to us, there could never be any advances to take us beyond our own programming. Consider the great scientists of our time. Are they only working on the basis of the genes? Or is there a way to bypass the gene programming?

In the Eastern tradition there are said to be six stages of human beings. The first stage is called mineral man, and represents a very primitive state in which a person is not likely to learn anything from life. The next stage is vegetable man, which is a little more advanced. But vegetables do not live long and their roots prevent them from moving to new places. The third stage is animal man who lives by instincts. The fourth stage means to be truly human and recognize the need for greater awareness. Then the fifth stage consists of those who are aware; you may call them spiritually developed. The sixth stage of human beings is beyond description.

In my opinion the sociobiologist is referring to the human being in the first three stages of development. But beyond these first three stages there are other realms of possibility that are achieved through awareness. The people who develop beyond the first three stages are sometimes called saints; I refer to them as geniuses in a very specific field. Just as the genius in science goes beyond past scientific programming, so the saint is a genius in the spiritual field. We are all geniuses in the making, and all of us achieve our own level of genius through awareness.

It is important for women to become aware to what extent they are the product of their environment and genetic programming, but also to recognize what is entirely their own, and for which they should take complete responsibility. Although it is often convenient to shift responsibility to the family or to biological makeup, to find her own place each woman must look for a way to reprogram herself to be what she wants. For awhile, one program may be substituted for another, but, I assure you, finally you can go beyond all programming and all game playing. At first you will play each game a little more masterfully, until eventually you can drop all of them and be an aware, spiritually developed, human being.

Where Am I Ruled by Emotional Responses?

Emotions play a very important part in everyone's life so do not condemn yourself for having them. What is necessary is to find a channel where emotions can work for you instead of against you. There is a variety of ways in which you can do this.

First of all, acknowledge your emotions. They are there. Do not deny them—they are the way you feel. Do not judge emotions as "terrible," saying, "I want to be saintly and here I am with these awful emotions." Acknowledge their presence and try to get hold of their power. Watch them carefully and ask yourself, Where do they come from and where do they go?

After some practice, you can watch your emotions arising. For example, you can feel anxiety or anger welling up. When that happens, direct your attention to yourself. If you focus on the subject or what makes you angry, you will miss it. Here is the anger rising up—catch it like a ball right in the middle of the situation. Learn to say without fear, "Oh, never mind. I don't want to finish that sentence. Forget about it." In this way you cut off the compulsory force that the emotions have over you.

The great yogis in the East have always said that pain is self-created. When I first came to India I questioned this statement. What could it mean? Surely I would not create any pain for myself. But it took only three weeks for me to find out. People have the choice whether to be hurt or not if things don't go their way. For example, a friend does not show up for an appointment. Are you hurt or is it your self-importance suffering? You always have the option of admitting that you have just been inconvenienced, not hurt. This choice determines whether one is in control of the emotions or ruled by them. Discrimination makes the difference. We have to learn to be aware and then discriminate. So before you make up your mind about what someone has done to you, find out if the choice you have made is born out of your need for self-importance.

Can You Identify Your Personality Aspects?

One of the biggest obstacles to increased awareness is that everyone has many unacknowledged personality aspects. There is the personality aspect of the wife, the mother, the college teacher, the musician, the painter, etc., and each one has its own ego and its own powerful emotions. Each wants to survive. Shifting from one personality aspect to another does not solve the problem. You have to go down to the gut level and uproot the aspect that you have discovered to be your worst enemy. Learn to free yourself from these enemies.

To gain that freedom you have to be courageous and slaughter those aspects or they will ruin your life. When you reach down into your gut level, do not be afraid. You may think you will find terrible things there; in fact, you will find your greatest treasures buried under all the garbage. As for the garbage, you can easily be rid of it. You have only to decide. Then you can truly have a dialog with yourself and you will not need to talk all day to everybody else in order to avoid facing yourself.

In my workshops I say to people, "If you want to cry because you have so much pent-up emotion, fine, go ahead. But do not cry just because you feel pain. Instead, this is the time to be happy to be getting rid of this garbage. Do not indulge in self-pity." Self-pity is another great obstacle, and it comes from the feeling of being controlled by others.

The problem most people have with authority arises because the ego itself is the most merciless taskmaster. Any woman who can understand that will find authority problems drop away; she will be able to have mercy on herself. Then, as understanding grows, compassion for others will also grow. That will make any woman the most lovable and desirable companion, for other women as well as for men.

Our culture tends to value the rational process over the irrational, logic over instinct. Although women are usually accused of being irrational, men also use the irrational approach. But we do not have to drop irrationality; rather, we must learn to balance the rational and the irrational aspects within ourselves. Business people have admitted in workshops that their best successes come through their hunches, or their irrational mode of thinking. In stockmarkets and investments, people often go by their hunches. They cannot always explain why they invest in certain stocks at a particular time, because it is an irrational process. Women should not feel excluded by their use of the irrational or by the male emphasis on logic. Women are not inferior when they use a different mode of thinking. Self-acceptance will help a woman value and stand up for herself.

As a woman, what makes me worthy to pursue the spiritual path? Where does my sense of self-worth come from? Is it related to my physical appearance? My job? What are my reasons for a spiritual search? Am I just dissatisfied? Do I seek glamour in a different kind of life? Are spiritual women of the past an inspiration to me? Has the life of any saintly woman inspired me to shift my view of life? How did these women reach the steps of their inner temple? Is my wanting to be spiritual coming from a deep desire for change in myself that I sorely need? Up until now I may have spent a lot of time trying to change the world. Maybe I will try changing myself so that I can find my place in the world.

Spiritual Tools Needed for the Path

What tools are required to gain emotional independence?

1. Keep a daily diary. Reflect on what happened during the day and what you could have done better. Do not criticize yourself if you did not make the grade, or if you are not quite clear. Clarity will come. You have to begin somewhere. You might be stumbling around like a baby and fall on your bottom, but you can pick yourself up. Nobody else can. Nobody else will.

Criticism really does not get you anywhere. There is a difference between seeing the facts of a situation, and judging yourself. If you are impatient, recognize the fact that you are impatient but do not sit in judgment of yourself. If you feel your impatience has gotten you into trouble a lot of the time because of its strong nature, then you can decide to deal with it directly. Put all your will behind your decision in the same way you do when you want to control other people to get your own way. If you learn to control your own life and your own emotions first, you are bound to succeed. You can anticipate most of the issues that stir up your emotions. Do not let them become a barrier between you and your friends, loved ones, sons, daughters, husbands.

Every evening, at the end of the day, write the story of your life in a book with empty pages. If you are ruthlessly honest with yourself you will get a very clear picture of your behavior. You may lock the book away; it is not for anybody else to see. It is your book of life and learning. At the end of the week, read your whole story again and take a couple of colored highlighters and mark all the emotional incidents. Those that you feel you have conquered to the degree that they no longer run your life can be marked in a different color. Say thank you to the divinity within yourself for giving you that awareness. Whenever you can say thank you to the divinity within, it will cooperate with you much more intensely than you would ever dream. You will be surprised at all the hidden talents you discover.

2. Workshops. Workshops, in conjunction with your spiritual diary, are a great help in discovering the illusions you still carry. Go to some workshops where you are challenged, where you are really pushed, and see how you survive. That will help you to find out if you are hiding behind your image. Appearances mean nothing.

You need to sit down and find out what your illusions are. Discover which of them have a reasonable possibility of being experienced in life and which, like your dream prince or dream lover, are impossible to achieve. If you are in trouble in a marriage, look for your dream lover image first, and then find out how your husband compares to it. He will, of course, always fall short in that comparison because he is human. Your dream lover is an invention of your mind, mainly created by the little girl in you. This immature aspect has to go.

3. Find a Support Group. If you are determined to become aware of your illusions, join an ongoing study group that deals with such work, or a yoga class. In my yoga classes, you write many papers to clarify what you mean by the words you use, such as love, mind, energy, higher consciousness, meditation, or nirvana. You also investigate the five senses because it is through them that you perceive the world. The papers are read in class and are discussed as a group because the interaction of the group is very helpful. It allows people to discover that they are not alone in their difficulties, and that truth is not the property of any one person. Everyone has valuable input.

In looking for a group to join, find a small organization where it is easier to become part of the activities, to know what is going on and hence to learn to trust. The woman who does not appreciate her own sex would be better off not choosing a spiritual organization headed by a woman. However, she must be careful that her choice of a man as her teacher is not based on a non-spiritual attraction. By choosing such a man, a woman may be trying to protect herself from her own sexuality, and that is not a good basis for choosing a spiritual teacher. However, even disappointment in spiritual leadership has to be seen as a test of whether one is truly committed to spiritual life.

4. Mantra Practice. The root *man* in the word mantra means in Sanskrit "to think." *Tra* comes from *trai* meaning "to protect or free from the bondage of the phenomenal world." Therefore mantra means "the thought that liberates and protects." A mantra is a combination of sacred syllables that forms a nucleus of spiritual energy, serving as a magnet to attract or a lens to focus spiritual vibrations.

Om Namah Sivaya is a mantra. *Om* is the Sanskrit letter for the divine without shape, form, or image. *Namah* means "great name." Siva is one of the three aspects of the Hindu trinity of Brahma, Vishnu, and Siva. Brahma is the creator aspect of the divine; Vishnu is the preserver, and Siva is the destroyer. Destroying, in this context, means destroying everything that is between you and the divine. So this mantra is a call to the divine destroyer. Sometimes blessings come in disguise. An illness may give us time to be holy, time to think and to reflect on the purpose and direction of our life. Destruction on any level means turmoil and this is especially true on the spiritual level. But the old form of the ego needs to be destroyed in order to make room for new insights. It can be very helpful and supportive to join a group that practices mantra regularly, along with other spiritual work.

5. Watch Your Dreams. Pay attention to your dreams. At my ashram we follow the Eastern approach to the analysis of dreams, which helps you to know your own symbolism. The characteristics of the animals, individuals, landscapes, or houses in the dream tell you something about yourself. Many things can be worked out in the seven or eight hours that you sleep, but the dream needs to be recorded very accurately. Watch your emotions when you write the dream down and when you are tempted to change a little here and there. When you do this you are judging yourself. You have to stop all that judgment. Criticism of yourself is unjust most of the time. You will probably also tend to use this same criticism toward others and that stands in the way of a healthy relationship.

Women have a lot of power, and the tools to discover that power. Do you accept this responsibility or would you rather sit in your armchair, watch TV, and dream your impossible dreams? It is a bitter pill to swallow, but it is your choice whether you want to be entertained or help yourself to grow. You can learn to be a different woman, so that eventually it will make no difference if people like you or not. You have to like yourself and hold your position—your rightful place in today's world.

Swami Sivananda Radha was born in Germany and lived there until after World War II when she came to North America. A visionary experience led her to her guru, Swami Sivananda Sarasvati, in Rishikesh, India. There she received an intense training in the philosophy and practices of yoga and the spiritual life. She chose to dedicate her life to the service of others and, in 1956, was initiated into the sacred order of *sanyas,* becoming a swami. At her guru's behest, she returned to bring the teachings of yoga to the West. She founded an ashram and several affiliates in Canada and the United States. She has lectured extensively throughout the world especially on university campuses, for the Institute of Transpersonal Psychology, and at the parapsychological institutes of Europe. She has written many books, among them: *Radha: Diary of a Woman's Search; Kundalini: Yoga for the West; Mantras: Words of Power,* and *Gods Who Walk the Rainbow.*

To men a man is but a man. Who cares
What face he carries or what form he wears?
But a woman's body is the woman.

AMBROSE BIERCE

Self-Image and Spirituality:
Coming Home to Our Bodies

by

Louise M. Paré

s a small child I was knock-kneed and pigeon-toed. My mother cried when I took my first steps—not out of joy over my accomplishment, but because my problem limbs made me fall flat on my face. My older sister received first prize in a baby beauty contest. Very quickly in life I learned that having a beautiful body and being valued as a person were closely linked. In an old photograph my sister and I are standing under the rose arbor in our front yard. I am wearing what I later referred to as "my ugly brown shoes." My arms are defiantly crossed on my chest. My face is set in a scowl that seems to say, "Why do I have to get the ugly shoes, ugly feet, uncurly hair? Why can't I be beautiful like her so I could win a prize?" I was three years old, but I was learning the painful reality that Marcia Hutchinson addresses: "As a woman your body is so intimately linked with your sense of self that your body attitudes readily spill over into self-attitudes. . . . In women, body-esteem and self-esteem appear to be married to each other."[1]

One night, some twenty years later sitting alone in my living room, I had an experience that began to heal the deep pain that was attached to my legs and feet. I had been thinking about "little Louise" and writing my feelings and memories in my journal. The more I wrote, the more the tears poured down my face. I felt within my body all the pain, shame and loneliness of my little girl self. I picked up a small pillow and held it to my chest, rocking back and forth, cradling my small child and saying, "I love you, little Louise, just the way you are. You are beautiful to me. I love you just the way you are." I continued to talk to my little child affirming each part of her body, especially her feet and legs.

Slowly the pain within my chest was transformed into a feeling that was warm and strong. It was a feeling of unconditional love for myself. I felt empowered from within myself. For the first time I was able to say to myself that I had been born with legs and feet that were deformed. Using that word helped me realize that that was how I had experienced my whole self. I had seen myself as a deformed person; I had felt separate, different, and ugly.

My rational mind wanted to objectify my experience: "Oh, it wasn't that bad. At least you didn't have to wear braces. What's the big deal? Quit feeling sorry for yourself." But I knew this wasn't about 'objective' reality. This pain was about my experience growing up in a culture that equated my body with my total identity: since my body was deformed, I was worthless. My pain was part of the pain of all womankind within the system of patriarchy.

Patriarchy in its wider definition means the manifestation and institutionalization of male dominance over women and children, both in the family and in society in general.[2] The patriarchal split carves wholes into halves, ranks the halves, and then devalues one of them. It splits us from ourselves, from each other, and from nature. It splits woman's spirit from her flesh, her mind from her body, her parts from the whole. One side of the split is considered good and valuable; one is bad and worthless.

The Patriarchal Split

God	Devil
Good	Evil
Life	Death
Heaven	Earth (Hell)
Sacred	Secular
Spirit	Matter
Soul	Body
Mind	Body
Intellect	Emotion
Man	Woman
Strong	Weak
Anger	Tears
Hard	Soft
Light	Dark

Patriarchy splits the sacred from the secular and devalues the secular. Patriarchy splits life from death and devalues death (thus denying the cycle of birth, growth, death, and regeneration). Patriarchy splits our cultural archetypes, especially those of women. It splits Eve, the sinful, seductive one, from the Virgin Mary, the holy, pure, nonsexual one. It splits man from woman and everything masculine from everything feminine and then devalues the feminine. It splits so-called masculine independence from so-called feminine dependence and devalues dependence. It splits so-called masculine rationality from so-called feminine intuition and emotionality and devalues intuition, emotionality, and other ways of knowing. It makes men 'hard and strong' and women 'soft and weak.'

Most important of all, patriarchy splits us from our woman-self. It convinces our minds to hate our bodies so that we are constantly trying to control or 'fix' our wayward bodies through diets, diets, and more diets; through douches, feminine hygiene sprays, deodorants; through plastic surgery. Patriarchy convinces our minds that our bodies are an 'other,' an object rather than the flesh and blood through which we live and breathe. It splits our spirituality from our sexuality and devalues our sexuality. It splits our kind, loving, quiet, life-giving selves from our raging, angry, screaming, life-withholding, struggling selves. It makes us lose a part of us that is real, authentic, essential. It names our rage craziness and strips us of the transformative power of our anger.

Patriarchy splits women from women. It sets up a hierarchy of privilege based on class, race, sexual preference, ethnicity, age, and physical/mental ability and coerces women into splitting from other women in order to enjoy the spoils it offers.

Patriarchy splits humans from the earth and the earth's creatures. It splits rational, controlled humans from wild animals and devalues animals and wildness. It splits man from earth and carnal woman from her natural cycles. It splits the earth as exploitable resource from the earth as Sacred Mother.

Patriarchy uses splitting and devaluing to reproduce itself. It breeds a divided world which cries out for healing. It spawns misogyny as its worthy child, manifesting itself through the teachings of honored philosophers and theologians in many cultures.[3]

> Woman is a temple built over a sewer, the gateway to the devil. You have led astray one whom the Devil would not dare attack directly. It is your fault that the Son of God had to die; you should always go in mourning and rags. —Tertullian, 22 A.D.

> One hundred women are not worth a single testicle.— Confucius, 441-479 B.C.

> A woman should be covered with shame at the thought that she is a woman. —Clement of Alexandria, 190 A.D.

> Women are not made to the image of God. —Augustine, c. 354-430 A.D.

> Woman is defective and accidental . . . and misbegotten . . . a male gone awry. . . the result of some weakness in the father's generative power. She is by nature of lower capacity and quality than man.—Thomas Aquinas, 13th century A.D.

> Men are superior to women. —The Koran, c. 650 A.D.

> Woman is slow in understanding and her unstable and naive mind renders her by way of natural weakness to the necessity of a strong hand in her husband. Her use is two-fold: animal sex and motherhood.—Pope Gregory the Great, d. 604 A.D.

This mindset is very powerful. Its basic equation is Woman = Earth = Dirt = Sex = Sin. It teaches that woman's body is sinful and that she is therefore the embodiment of evil. To those who say that these are ideas of ages past, one need only pay attention to advertising in most modern magazines using women's bodies as a way of selling everything from toothpaste to fast cars. Contemporary songs like *Witchy Woman* and *Devil Woman* continue this belief system for the young.

Patriarchal society has not only altered our beliefs about woman's body, it constantly tells women to alter their bodies. It assumes that woman in her natural state is neither beautiful nor acceptable. Pluck it out, shave it off, tuck it in, cut it out, and starve it away are constant messages that society gives women. An article in a Minneapolis newspaper reports:

> Really Plastic Surgery: Breasts That Can Be Adjusted For Whim Or Fashion. Plastic surgeon Patrick Maxwell of the Baptist Medical Center in Nashville, TN, quoted in a recent Cosmopolitan, said "permanently adjustable (breast) implants" will be available in the future, permitting "changing size and shape according to fashion dictates or whim."[4]

A television commercial for Maidenform shows a fast montage of the many different types of acceptable bra images to which women were expected to conform over the centuries. Women's breasts are usually presented as sexual objects whose purpose is male sexual gratification and the selling of products. Gone is the ancient reverence for women's breasts as a source of abundant nurturance.

Patriarchal society devalues women's natural cycles of menstruation, menopause, and aging. Her bleeding is considered a curse, something which makes her mentally and emotionally unstable, and something from which she needs to find release. One brand of sanitary napkin actually calls itself "New Freedom," as if menstruation were a prison sentence.

In ancient times women's bleeding experience was considered a sacred event. Women's ability to bleed and not die was considered awe inspiring. The bleeding time, at the full or new moon, was a time of great power when women gathered together. They received visions to guide the life of the community and were afforded respect and great honor.

Today a menstruating woman is perceived as moody or luny, linked in a negative way to the moon. To some she is even considered dangerous. Aging women are regarded as wrinkled, dried up, and worthless. Ancient menopause rituals celebrated the shifting of women's creative energies from child bearing to birthing wisdom and new achievement for the whole community. An older woman received the respected title Crone—one who reached wisdom in her heart and was called on as mediator in disputes.

What is the effect of the patriarchal split on women's lives? For many women, one effect of the internalization of misogyny is chronic depression. Depression is an experience which is central to many women's lives. Underneath women's depression is an unconscious rage at her oppression. When this rage can find no legitimate outlet, it becomes suppressed, turned inward, and is manifested as depression. Men are generally more able to express anger; male anger is more socially acceptable than women's anger. Angry women are labeled bitches and described as vengeful, spiteful, crazy. Crazy women often end up in mental institutions, while depressed women, not perceived as a threat, are seen as powerless and in need of help.

The Christian tradition presents examples of both an angry and a weeping Jesus, but the images of the Virgin Mary are happy or sad or silent, but never angry. The message is not lost: a good and holy woman is not an angry woman. The virtuous woman works hard and keeps her mouth shut. There is less risk involved for women in turning their anger inward on their own bodies and minds than outward on the system that continues their oppression. Anger in women is unsettling. It demands a hearing; it calls for change.

Internalized body-hatred also finds expression in the astonishing increase in eating disorders among women. Food, our source of physical and emotional nurturance, is refused by self-hating women. "If my body is bad and evil and I'm split off from my own inner spirit, why should I continue to nurture life within myself? If all that is associated with the feminine is denigrated, why should I continue to receive my own feminine energies? If the body of woman is primarily a tool of exploitation for a greedy society and an object of everyday violence from men, then why shouldn't I exercise my own power to limit my growth and stop my life?"

When asked how she felt about the fact that her menstrual periods had stopped due to anorexia, a fourteen-year-old girl responded, "It's OK because it's dangerous to develop." Our internalized negative body image manifests in objective, rather than personal, language to describe our bodily experiences. We often say things like, "It hurts in the legs," as if our physical pain belonged to a store mannequin with plastic parts, rather than claiming the experience: "My pain is in my legs and I hurt."

The most dramatic and terrifying expression of the patriarchal split is violence against women. It is the world's worst and most pervasive violation of human rights. As Jori Heise says, "From the high rape rates of the United States to genital mutilation and dowry death in the Third World, women across the world share a common threat. Fear extends even to nonvictims who must limit themselves physically and psychologically because of the looming presence of violence."[5]

When cultures accept the message that women's bodies have no inherent value, and that women are the property of men, then women's bodies become objects to be exploited in pornography, to be beaten, raped, and mutilated at will by others.

Women's spirituality seeks to heal the patriarchal split by transforming the disconnections into connections. It is about reclaiming what has been split off, taking back our women's bodies, women's minds, and women's spirits while valuing all the parts. Women's spirituality is about taking the self-hatred and self-negation out of our own eyes.

The scriptures tell us to love our neighbor as ourselves, but perhaps the hardest exercise to practice is that of conscious self-love. Miriam Greenspan tells us that "self-love was not simply something that I found, like buried treasure in the back yard. It was something that we won by acting together as women."[6] When we begin to practice conscious self-love we begin to experience the powerful, life-giving presence of the Divine within our women's bodies, minds, and spirits. That experience changes everything . We embody the song that says, "She changes everything She touches and everything She touches can change." Learning to love one's body as it is is often difficult work for women. It involves a struggle, a fight with the deeply internalized messages of patriarchy. It involves a choice to either remain blind to the truth of our own power and beauty or to face the mirror and see clearly the embodiment of our own flesh and blood as sacred. Facing the mirror is an act of truth telling about the lie of patriarchy. It is a way of coming home to our bodies. It is claiming our own strength to move, to dance, to feel, to go within, to know and experience the sacredness of woman that is our true self.

Women's inner work involves hearing the lessons of my life through the muscles of my body. Coming into my body is a transforming and revolutionary act. It is a way of stepping outside patriarchy's boundaries. It crosses the line and heals the split.

> The White Fathers told us: I think, therefore I am.
> The Black Mother within each of us—the poet—whispers in our dreams:
> I feel, therefore I can be free.[7]

Emotion is energy in motion in my body: embodied energy. This energy can become blocked or trapped in muscles gone tight from old-held patterns of unexpressed anger, fear, anxiety, rage, and deep grief. Our bodies manifest the energy patterns of our minds and hearts. When we begin to move through our bodies, giving physical expression to these held physical patterns, the blocks are broken apart and new energy is released. The old patterns are transformed into new ways of thinking, feeling, moving, and expressing.

When women begin the transformational process of conscious self-love and coming home to their bodies, fear often arises. Some fears come from the outside. In the past when women stepped outside patriarchy's boundaries, they were met with burnings, beatings, ridicule, and imprisonment in asylums. The revolutionary act of coming into our women's bodies is risky. Patriarchy hates women.

There are also fears that come from inside. There are voices inside our heads saying, "You're not good enough." "Don't be too beautiful, too powerful, too successful because they won't like you any more." "Don't change your ways because you'll be left all alone." Other voices add "You can't help the way you are; you're just a weak, helpless woman." "Don't rock the boat." They can sabotage our desire for growth. But because these voices are expressions of facets of our inner selves, we must not destroy or repress them, but rather find a way to transform their message.

In our bodies is our aliveness. Aliveness has to do with an area of consciousness called sentiment. We usually associate this word with feelings, sentimentality, nostalgia, the remembering of good times gone by. But sentiment is much more than things past. Real sentiment has to do with consciously connecting with the powerful, intense energy of the universe that flows through our bodies, minds, and spirits. It is about being fully present with this energy now. Sentiment comes from the Latin word *sentire* which means "to sense." Where are our senses? In our bodies.

Sentiment as consciousness has different levels. The first level is the powerful, intense life force which is present in the universe. This force or energy is experienced as our basic aliveness. This level gives rise to what can be called our felt sense of reality. One woman, commenting on the abusive language of her spouse said, "It doesn't sound good in my body!" That was her way of expressing how the words she heard were connected to a felt sense of herself.

Where is this felt sense? It is in the muscles of our bodies, in the flow of our blood, in the beating of our hearts, and in the flow of our breath. This energy gives rise to feeling or emotion. Sentiment is an energy which bubbles up in us. It's been called 'enthusiasm' because it comes from the Latin words for "divine energy within." Calling sentiment an area of consciousness means that it is a way of knowing. Not only do our minds and hearts know reality, but our bodies also have a way of knowing that is vital to our experience of being fully human. When we are split off from our bodies we are disconnected from this way of knowing who we are, and our experience of full aliveness is severely diminished.

Many of us don't feel alive in our bodies. How can we connect with our basic aliveness? How can we transform energies of dullness, blockage, and deadness into the energies of new life? How can we experience the divine energies of our women's spirits, the energies many women refer to as the goddess?

I dance! I awaken my aliveness by free-form dancing to music of many different rhythms; I move without music as I give physical expression to my emotions; I sing and chant as I play my drum, rattles, or violin; I dance as I sing and sing as I dance. Then I feel myself coming alive, waking up, becoming consciously connected with the fullness and beauty of my own unique self. I become aware of how wonderful and mysterious it is to be the woman that I am. I become aware of how good it is to be a woman. I become aware of how good it is to be in my woman's body. I experience a new connectedness with all women, with all people, with the earth that grounds and supports my movements and with the air and sky that carry my singing and chanting. I become more conscious of the need to choose foods that will nurture and energize my body. As my body moves and stretches I experience new levels of my own consciousness revealing my connectedness with all life across all periods of time. Every day brings new movement and new experiences of the multidimensional person that I am.

Each time I begin to move into my transformational life-dance work I experience again my fear of the unknown, the unknown of who I am, the unknown of what may come forth in me. I experience my fear of being foolish, of not being enough, my fear that it does not really make any difference that I am here because it's all been done before perfectly by someone else. My inner voices can get very loud. Doing my life-dance is my commitment to physicalize my fear instead of letting it freeze my creativity and block my growth. It is a way of experiencing these fears as part of my aliveness.

Giving physical expression to my fears teaches me that that energy is connected to other emotions that are also waiting for me to reconnect them. I need to give physical expression to my emotional self, not just talk about my feelings. As I flow in movement from one piece of my story to another I begin to experience the contractions and expansions of my own birthing process. I remember the words of a poster that says, "I am a woman giving birth to myself." I experience through my body the sacredness of my own life. I find myself pushing through dark inner tunnels of shame, perfectionism, and insecurity. It is messy work giving birth to new life whether it is the life of another human person or new expressions of one's own life. As I move through those dark tunnels, I begin to discover light coming forth within me. At times it is experienced as deep forgiveness and nurturance that makes my body feel crystal clear.

At other times I have experienced myself as a beautiful eagle soaring high and grounded in her flight. With each breakthrough I encounter and recognize the mystery of the Goddess within my own being. The words of Arisika Razak echo through me, ". . . remember the beauty and sacredness of your womanbody. And remember that no matter how your personal body is shaped, whether it is abundant or slight, somewhere in the world a goddess is venerated who looks just like you."[8]

The essence of the Divine is mystery. The encounter with mystery is found for me in entering the movement of life. Since the movement is in my body, body-movement work is my spiritual path. On this path the mystery is hidden not in a golden tabernacle or behind a veiled cloth. It is hidden in my muscles, my blood, my breath. Body-movement work brings new meaning to the words "This is my body. This is my blood given for the life of all."

Walking this path involves choosing to love my woman's body, my woman's mind, my woman's spirit in all their parts. Walking this path involves being healing for myself, for others, and for our Mother Earth. Walking this path is transformative work. It involves experiencing that I am a Women of the Universe being born anew each moment.

Louise M. Paré, a native Oregonian, is founder and director of the Life in Harmony Center in Bismark, North Dakota. She holds an M.A. in Religious Studies from Mundelein College, Chicago with a specialization in Holistic Spirituality and has extensive training in Enneagram work and transformational movement. Louise is a violinist, singer and ritualist, combining these skills in her work with women's spirituality circles and personal direction. Besides her consulting work for organizations and individuals in body work and spirituality, she also teaches at the SUMORE summer program at Seattle University and at the University of Mary in Bismark.

Perfection of the body consists of beauty, radiant complexion, grace, strength, and virtual indestructibility.

YOGA SUTRAS

Women's Health and Spirituality:
An Interview with

Chandra Patel, M.D.

ou are known for your pioneering research in spirituality and health and particularly the practical use of spiritual tools for physical wellness. Will you speak of spirituality and the body?

Yes. Spirituality is basically our relationship with reality. It is understanding the meaning of life, all of life. Saints and sages from the East and West show this quite clearly. Buddha's enlightenment began by seeing an old man, a sick man, and a dead man—physical aspects that happen to the body. Most of us have seen these things; they are not extraordinary in any way. But they were the instrument to Buddha's enlightenment because in trying to understand what these bodily experiences meant, his quest for the meaning of life was sparked. Other saints had similar experiences that set them on a course to spirituality: for Ignatius of Loyola it was a severe wound in battle; for Augustine it was the death of his mother; for Francis it was guilt and disgust over his extravagant life; for Ghandi it was the agony of injustice for his people in South Africa; for Mother Teresa it was death and suffering in the squalid areas of Calcutta. So spirituality is coming to terms with reality—the value of life and its meaning—through the everyday experiences of our lives.

The traditional concept of spirituality is quite different, of course. There we are told that the only way to reach spiritual maturity is by living an ascetic life within a religious community. The spiritual being was one who lived a celibate life in a monastery, wearing special robes, practicing mortification and fasting in order to escape from the temptations of the flesh. The common lives of ordinary people like us, lives of domestic love, work, and social life, were considered temptations of the world and unworthy of spirituality. The world itself was viewed negatively as material, sexual, and a potential trap for a would-be seeker of God. In traditional scriptures, women are considered temptations, not human beings. Their bodies are considered evil, real obstacles to a true spiritual life. To achieve enlightenment one was supposed to view life not for living and enjoying, but as a vale of tears, only as a means to a goal beyond itself.

By denying real spirituality outside this traditional definition, we deny the majority of humanity the spiritual value of their lives. By denying the worth of the body and sexuality, we deny the maturing growth of our everyday experiences. Similarly, the exclusion of women and women's unique experiences as expressions of spirituality is likely to be detrimental not only to women but also to the spiritual life of all people.

What do you see as the unique contribution of women to the spiritual growth of the community?

Women are in a position to reveal the nature of reality and shed light on the questions of the meaning and value of life through insights into the experiences of life which are unique to them—like childbirth and mothering—in addition to insights which can be gained through experiences common to all human beings: love, joy, fear, loss, trust, despair, ecstasy, birth, and death. What is required is a consciousness that will reflect on these experiences and that will not let go until their meaning has been understood.

Women have the primary responsibility for the survival of the human race. Man may feel proud of his dazzling technical achievements and his control over the environment, but no man can reproduce another human being. To ensure that every woman devotes herself unceasingly to this vital task, nature has infused her with sexual energy unsurpassed in the animal kingdom. After the union of sperm and egg, the entire process of reproduction depends on the woman. Using the raw material of her own body, a unique, new human being is produced. Then, in our culture, the principal nurturer of the child, and usually the teacher of the child, is also a woman.

When we speak of the body, we must bring medicine into the conversation. How does modern medicine fit into this broad idea of spirituality?

The dominant theory of human function in medicine has been that of Cartesian dualism. In fact, modern medicine still views humans as a fundamental split between the mind, the spirit, and the body. As a rule there is no interaction between them. The body works on a mechanical principle; the non-material mind or spirit cannot, even in principle, affect the mechanistic, material body. Since disease is viewed as a mechanical breakdown or a material process, it is confined to the body, and the spirit can neither cause it nor heal it. But the body is not a machine; we in the medical field must be concerned with the entire person.

In your books you speak of the need for people to take a very active role in maintaining their own health rather than relying solely on the physician. Will you elaborate on that?

A few decades ago medicine was focused on the great infections like typhoid, cholera, pneumonia, tuberculosis; earlier it focused on small pox, various fevers, and so on. Once these diseases were conquered through better nutrition and hygiene, as well as immune therapy and immunizations, disease emerged in new patterns. Now we have coronary heart disease, hypertension, and cancer.

People's own behavior is a major contributor to this type of disease as well. Doctors cannot actually take away any disease; people themselves must change their behavior to prevent or cure it. We are now realizing that people respond better medically and also learn more when they take control over their health and behavior rather than when they remain passive. Sometimes we feel that our illness is bad luck, or we think some germ has made us ill, and so we must go to a doctor to have it taken away. But if you realize that somehow you have contributed to your own illness, you can learn something. You can ask yourself, What was it that I did that might have contributed to this illness? or What can I do now that will help me get well? This new medical thinking is a way for both doctor and patient to become more mature health-wise.

Are you saying we can learn from the illness itself?

Absolutely, but only if we take part in the treatment. Healing does not happen mechanically. To treat someone in a mechanistic way is to threaten the relationship with that person. Freud stated in his late writings that he was concerned not with scientific knowledge but with empathetic understanding, not unlike the mother's knowledge of her infant. In psychoanalysis, he says, the rational account of etiological factors brought to the surface from the depth of suppressed material in the subconscious may be correct but not therapeutic. This may explain why patients frequently do not get better. Those who do improve do not do so because of the knowledge of the facts; more important is the relationship which develops between the patient and the therapist during the course of analysis. Their relationship of trust, respect, understanding, and empathy is the therapeutic agent.

Before modern scientific research methods were established, medical practitioners used substances which were of dubious value, if not positively harmful, by today's standards. Yet patients often got better because the patients, as well as the doctors, believed in the treatment and both were able to establish a positive, trusting relationship. Even now there are practitioners using animal, vegetable, and mineral products whose value is doubtful. But because of the positive and trusting relationships between patients and practitioners, the medicine remains popular. How often have we heard of a recovery when doctors have stepped back and said, "We've done all we can" and contrary to all expectations, the patient musters up inner strength to pull out of a seemingly hopeless illness?

When Dr. Herbert Benson had an audience with His Holiness the Dalai Lama to request his permission to study mind-body feats of Tibetan monks in the Himalayas, the Dalai Lama requested that Dr. Benson also take a look at Tibetan medicine. In particular, he said, "pay attention to the three main components of Tibetan medicine: the belief of the doctor, the belief of the patient, and the karma (the spiritual force generated by interaction) between the two."

If both the patient and the doctor start with a belief in a common spiritual or non-physical curative power, remarkable things begin to happen. The vast majority of patients—about 76%—are helped merely because they visit their doctor, believe in the doctor, and get assurance. The trust between doctor and patient can actually alter a patient's physiology and effect the cure of bodily diseases.

So the role of the patient must be an active one. Is that correct?

Yes, definitely. In a study of women with breast cancer, 75% of all women who showed a "fighting spirit," who decided they would be well, actually triumphed over their disease and had a favorable medical outcome five years later. Of those women who responded with stoic acceptance of the disease or a hopeless outlook, 88% were dead within the next five years. In general, those who were least successful in fighting cancer were described as despairing, helpless, or poor copers. Developing coping skills which foster a sense of belief and control has been an important factor in the longer survival of cancer patients.

Patients give up when they feel they have no power, when they think they cannot do anything for themselves in order to get better. Another study showed that long-term survivors of metastatic breast cancer asked their physicians a lot of questions and expressed their emotions freely. Because of this they were often considered difficult or uncooperative patients. In fact, they asked questions because they wanted to understand their illness and wanted to participate fully in their treatment. Sandra Levy, at the National Cancer Institute of America also showed that patients with breast cancer who expressed their emotions freely survived longer than those who were passive and apparently showed little distress. Those 'bad' patients who found meaning in their lives fought their disease well and had more killer T cells (the kind of white blood cells that destroy cancer cells) than those docile, 'good' patients.

It sounds as if the patient needs to have a strong self-image in order to actively assist in her healing.

Indeed. Love of one's self, including love of one's body, seems to be the single most important element in good health. A woman's self-image is the catalyst that triggers her happiness or despair, as well as her illness or healing. Strange as it may seem, religious nuns who consider their bodies unimportant and not worth loving, even though they live dedicated lives, have a greater incidence of breast cancer than ordinary women who love themselves and are loved. Dr. Segal also reports that housewives who feel unfulfilled or trapped in an unenjoyable role are more likely to get cancer. He quotes a study that showed housewives got 54% more cancer than the general population, and 157% more cancer than women who work outside the home and feel more fulfilled. The breast of a woman is meant for nurturing others, but those women who only nurture others and never themselves seem to develop diseases of the breast.

Our mind and body are completely connected. It is all inter-related: self-esteem, taking care of yourself, illness. The mind controls the body. Those who give up, those who believe they cannot do anything for themselves, those who feel sorry for themselves, those who are low in self-esteem really do less well physically.

When people learn that they are responsible for their illness, do they experience guilt? Wouldn't that be another problem in the healing process?

Yes, it can be, but a patient's reaction depends upon how the doctor actually handles the whole situation. If a doctor tells a person that she is totally responsible for the illness, then the patient will feel guilty. But this does not happen if you explain it in the context of changing behavior. I have dealt with thousands of people and have yet to find one that felt guilty because of what I have said to them. I believe if their disease is explained to them properly, there is no need to feel guilt.

People already accept that they may have contributed to their own stress, their own anxiety. Many people go through similar situations in life but not all of them get the same physical problems. There may be a constitutional element in their inheritance, a susceptibility over which they have no control. Under stress, some will get a migraine while others will get high blood pressure. Some people with healthy genes and all the stress in the world might never get ill. We can mitigate some of the inheritance and direct the tendency by changing our behavior. All disease is a result of an interaction between that inheritance and the environment, both internal and external. By internal environment we mean our beliefs and attitudes, hopes and fears, aspirations and worries. We can't do much about our inheritance, but we can do something about our environment. This knowledge can help to alleviate guilt and use the energy for changing that which can be changed.

What are some of the behaviors that people might have to change or take a good look at?

One of the chief contributors to disease that we need to look at is emotion. Anger, hostility, resentment, aggression—these are emotions that people need to examine. Why are they angry or why are they bottling up their emotions? What is the real problem? Sometimes when people are bottling things up they are afraid to say things that might upset others. So they swallow the emotion rather than say what they feel. It then creates turmoil inside them, causing all kinds of ills.

Research on high blood pressures goes back to the 1930's when it was shown that people who have high blood pressure struggle with their emotions. They cannot express themselves; high blood pressure is the result.

Hostility is a huge factor in coronary heart disease. People have resentment and hate towards others who have done something wrong to them. Perhaps a spouse has been unfaithful, or those you thought were friends have talked about you behind your back. It hurts you and if you don't do anything about it, it becomes a chronic hate. That can be disastrous for health. These emotions act like a boomerang; they will come back to you. You get angry because you want to hurt those that have hurt you in the first place, but you end up hurting yourself with poor health.

Another harmful behavior is the constant striving to get as many things accomplished in as short a time as possible: materialism in its most naked form. People who do this have no time to reflect on life and the meaning of life. They really do not know why they are striving to work so much, or to acquire so many things. Once they have achieved the goal, it has lost its meaning and they strive for something else. But they never get that sense of accomplishment necessary to feel good about what they have done.

Women today are catching up with the same stress illness once thought the domain of men. They have made so many sacrifices, and work so hard that it takes a toll on their bodies.

Yes, and not only on the body. Women are under siege these days. Women are actually working at two jobs. Because men have structured the workplace over decades, women must compete in a man's world in jobs, career, and politics. Then they go home in the evening they still have their domestic and family responsibilities. Women feel guilty when they kiss their babies good-bye in the morning or when they have to send their child to boarding school or their aged parent to a nursing home, because it has been socially engraved in our minds that this is our responsibility, that we ought to be taking care of them. Because many women experience conflict between career and this domestic responsibility, there is a continual feeling of guilt and conflict in their lives. They are pushing themselves under this workload and guilt load and it is making them ill. Research has proven that when men come home from work their blood pressure goes down, but when women come home their blood pressure stays up because they come home and start another job. They also have to take more active roles in caring for the elderly or for dying relatives.

In one way, these multiple roles make them more flexible and resilient mentally, but they are doing too much. The emotional strain in addition to the work load is harming them. I don't think women's bodies are meant to take all that.

You think women are more resilient than men?

Yes, I do believe women are much more resilient. They usually visit the doctors more, but they live longer. The problem is that because women are competing in careers with men, society expects them to be better than men to get the same job. They work harder to keep the job, while continuing to be good mothers and wives and the principal caretakers at home. This is why they have symptoms of stress and fatigue. Then when they do notice symptoms, they are afraid to fall back in their performance, afraid that men might use the situation to say women are unfit for the work, so they suppress their symptoms with smoking or coffee or tranquilizers. Eventually they have to pay the price of poor health.

For these stress problems you use the tools of breathing and meditation don't you?

Yes, absolutely. I think there are certain things that we can have control over to help ourselves. Suppose, for example, that you are mistreated at work. You may be able to assert yourself and demand your rights. But there are other things, like layoffs, bereavement, children growing up and leaving your nest, parents' poor health, traffic jams, and so on, over which we have no control. In those situations the best thing is to use simple skills like breathing and meditation to counteract those areas of stress. You can then take control of your body and do something about it. The tools are quite powerful even though they seem quite simple. I have shown this in a number of research studies I have carried out. In one study of 192 high risk subjects, I taught relaxation and meditation and other stress management techniques to half the subjects while the other half served as controls. During four years of follow-up, there were six new cases of heart attacks in the control group compared with one in the group taught meditation and other simple techniques.

You use them in your medical practice?

I certainly do. I have been using them for nearly twenty years now and I see a tremendous difference in the health of my patients.

How did you begin to use spiritual tools with patients?

I had first studied Ayurvedic medicine in India. When I married and moved to Kenya, I was not allowed to practice medicine under the British rule. Because I wanted to continue to practice medicine, I then went to London and took the entire course of Western medicine. When I finally went into practice I was well equipped with all the modern medical knowledge, but I was not equipped to deal with people's everyday problems. Most of our medical education is for crisis medicine. We know what to do when someone is dying, but we don't know what to do when somebody has a headache due to conflict in the family, or because children are not behaving well, or because someone is overwhelmed by debt. We really don't know how to deal with these stress causes of illness.

　　　One man I remember well came to me when his wife had gone away with another man for a weekend. She was bored and frustrated being home alone and so she left, returning on Monday morning. The couple had two children under five. The husband was devastated, wondering what to do. He came to me absolutely in tears, saying "I can't get over this." I asked him what he really wanted to do, if he wanted the marriage to end. He told me he needed to stay together with his wife for the sake of the little children. When I told him to forget the episode and put the incident behind him he said, "Doctor, teach me how to forget it."

　　　You can't keep giving prescriptions to people for this type of emotional problem. As more people came with symptoms related to problems of life and living, I realized that I had to do something other than what I had been trained to do. I also realized that I was under stress too, not able to sleep because I could not do my job properly! I could only write prescriptions for pain relievers or sleeping pills and I felt inadequate as that was not right.

I had learned breathing, yoga exercise, and meditation techniques as a child but like most of us who take up good things like aerobics, I was enthusiastic for two or three months and then stopped. But now I started the old practices in earnest. I found that I felt so much better! So I thought, "Why not teach this to other people?" At first I bought lots of little yoga books and started giving them to my patients, telling them that if they regularly practiced what was in the book it would help them feel better. But most people took the book and put it away on a shelf because they needed to be taught by a person and not by a book. Then I thought, "Well maybe I can't teach hatha yoga postures in my office, but at least I could teach them to breathe and meditate." And I did.

The next time someone came in asking for valium so they could take a driving test, I refused to prescribe it. Instead, I had them lie down and do breathing and relaxation exercises for ten or fifteen minutes of consultation time. I told them to practice it twice that day and also the next day before they went for the test. Immediately people liked doing the exercises. I could see people were grateful because they felt better. I also know the look on patients' faces if, under pressure, I quickly wrote them a prescription and they felt I was fobbing them off. When I took fifteen minutes to teach them the exercise, I could see how glad they were that I took time with them and to know that they could control their own anxiety. It was so amazingly simple and they were so pleased to have that power.

That is how it all started. I began to use breathing and meditation for high blood pressure particularly because this was something I could measure. You see, anxiety and such things are not so easy to measure, at least not for people who were scientifically trained and taught to believe only what could be measured. So I began doing research in high blood pressure. It was not a planned research to start with, but undertaken because of the needs of those who came to me for help.

After doing breathing and meditation techniques for health, have any of your patients made the next step of connecting the practices with an interior life?

Oh, definitely they do. They make it in a very practical way. Initially I started using meditation because I feel that it actually stills the mind. So many times our anxieties come because our mind is so busy, thinking so many things. Very, very early in my work I realized the deeper benefits.

There was one man who had just been promoted to bank manager, or what Americans call bank president, at the age of thirty-nine. He felt very anxious; his blood pressure was very high. Because he was so young and because his blood pressure had gone from normal to very high in only three years, he was sent to a specialist in the hospital. In the hospital, he was kept waiting for three hours to see the consultant. In that time his pressure jumped even higher to 220/130. He was immediately admitted and put under observation. Nothing was found except the high blood pressure and a strained heart, but no cause for either. So the doctors put him on drugs. One drug did not suit him so they gave him another; after six months he developed a neurology problem so they gave him another drug. The drugs did not mix well in his body so they had to give him another drug. Finally he was taking three drugs, first three tablets, then six tablets, then nine tablets a day. He became like a zombie.

One day he decided he just could not take this any more. He wanted to resign from his job. In order to do this, he needed a medical certificate for the bank and came to my office since his doctor was on vacation. When he told me his plan, I asked if that was what he really wanted to do. He answered, "No, of course not. My wife and I are not pleased because we will have to sell our big house; and our children will have to change from private to public schools. But I feel so dreadful. I cannot cope any more."

I had an opening in my study of high blood pressure and told him he could enter the study if he wished and we would see what we could do to help. He agreed, coming twice a week to learn breathing, relaxation, and meditation. A few days later we reduced his medication to six tablets; three weeks later he went down to three tablets; after about three months he stopped all medication. He is still a bank manager eighteen years later, still not taking any medication. Three months into the study I asked him if he still wanted to resign.

"No!" he answered. "It was your meditation that helped me. Before I used to come to the office and get very apprehensive because I had so many things to do, but through meditation I have learned that all I have to do is concentrate on one thing at a time. As a result I am not so apprehensive and I can handle everything."

This is what meditation in action is all about. It is not about a ritual, but about training the mind so that whatever you are doing, you do it as if that is the most important thing in the world.

That is what yogis call a one-pointed mind isn't it?

Yes, and it is very powerful, very powerful. Actually I was surprised by what my patient said to me. At that time I was still a beginner and had no idea what meditation would do for these people. I only knew how meditation was done but had no real idea of its effects because I had so little experience. I myself had good concentration but I did not know that it had to do with meditation.

Did you learn meditation in India as a child?

Well, it's rather a funny story. I grew up in India, the eldest daughter in the family. My grandmother was half blind, and it was my duty to look after her. Early each morning I had to get up and read her the scripture because she could not do it herself. I also had to meditate with her. The way of our meditation was simple: I read to her from the scripture and then we meditated on a mantra using a rosary timed by the hourglass. I had to sit there until all the sand fell through the glass. Initially I hated it so much that I would shake the hourglass to make the sand run faster. Every day I had to go through this same procedure, reading, sitting quietly, and fighting with the hourglass. You know, one can only fight so much, and finally I just started to meditate out of boredom. The meditation made me very concentrated; I always had much better concentration than anyone else. My own family members were surprised that I could sit for sixteen hours and work. They would sometimes put food down next to me, but I would just continue my work without stirring. So I got a wonderful benefit of meditation without realizing it.

I often find that women are reluctant to practice breathing and meditation because they must set aside a block of personal time to do so. They feel they are being selfish. Their training to take care of everyone else sometimes prevents them from taking care of themselves.

I believe that unless you take care of yourself you cannot take care of anybody else. Taking care of yourself is the most important thing, it is actually your duty to take care of your health, both physical and mental. After all, why are we doing things, what are we working so hard for if not to care for the body in which the soul resides? Spirituality is, after all, trying to understanding something called life. That life resides in the body. I believe that when the body is no longer a suitable place for the soul, it will leave. So it is our duty to make sure that the body is suitable and in good condition for our soul to reside in. Then we can go on serving others, nurturing others, and discovering the meaning of life. Taking care of self is not at all selfish; it is absolutely necessary.

This goes back to the idea of self-esteem, doesn't it?

Absolutely. It has been shown over and over again that people who have poor self-esteem, who are constantly telling themselves that they are no good, not deserving, or that they are failures, will actually make those statements come true. Those who think well of themselves will take care of themselves. They have a positive self-image and are physically healthier. Research also shows that Type A people, those more susceptible to heart disease, are usually very low in self-esteem. If their self-esteem rises for any reason, the Type A symptoms decrease.

I am familiar with the effects of physical exercise on self-esteem. Women who take up running or do aerobics or some sport usually find that they feel much better about themselves.

That is definitely true. Taking care of yourself raises your self-esteem because you are in control and doing something good about yourself. Feeling good about yourself is good for your health.

You work very much in the area of hypertension and heart disease. It appears that hypertension is becoming more of a health issue for women. It that true?

It is commonly thought that women need not worry about heart disease. But hypertension is one of the major risk factors for heart disease and heart disease is the number one killer for women as well as men. It just so happens that women develop heart disease a little later than men. This why in the younger age group, more men than women die of heart disease. Unfortunately this creates so much misunderstanding. Eventually women catch up; menopausal women have the same risk as men and after a certain age it goes even higher. In fact, if we survive long enough, one of two women will die of a heart attack while only one in ten will get breast cancer, even though it is reported that breast cancer is the number one cause of death in younger women. Actually, number wise, while one women in ten will get breast cancer, one in two will have a heart attack. And for some reason the fatality rate among women is higher than for men; when women have heart attacks they are more likely to die from them.

Because of this misunderstanding about women and heart disease; not enough preventive action has been taken. Men are very conscious of heart disease; doctors also give much more advice about it to men who smoke, are overweight, do not exercise, have high cholesterol. But doctors do not pay enough attention to the women until it is too late.

Hasn't it been the norm to exclude women from all health research?

Yes. Most research has been conducted on men only, for all disease. Women were not included in studies because the researchers felt that the results might be unpredictable due to women's menstrual cycle. Particularly in studies where measurements were taken over a period of years, it was felt that the cycle would confuse the data. It was a very wrong decision because now so little is known about women's health or women's reactions to drugs, and so forth. In all the studies in which I am involved, I have always studied men and women both.

What have you found?

Chiefly I have found that both men and women benefit from relaxation and meditation based programs. High blood pressure positively can be significantly reduced or the amount of medication necessary to control high blood pressure is significantly reduced. There are strong indications that coronary heart disease can be prevented as well.

Do you accept that women are more immune to heart disease?

The idea of women being immune to heart disease is a misconception. Even younger women are developing heart disease these days. Women in the child-bearing years, previously thought to be immune from heart disease, have emulated men to become emancipated and have taken on the same health risks. Women on the pill who work, and are thus more inclined to smoke, increase their risk forty times. Women have been taking contraceptive pills for decades and so the data is very clear. Women need to take better care of themselves to reverse this trend.

The large tobacco companies are focusing their advertising on women in their teens and twenties because it is the next best market.

That is very dangerous for women. Those who are on contraceptives and who smoke, or are overweight, or working outside the home, or under stress are much more liable than home workers to have heart attacks. Women who have no control over their environment, particularly women who are doing a job with no control over what they do, like working on an assembly line, are at high risk. Also, stress is very high among women who have a boss who is not very positive or supportive. These women particularly need to look at their lifestyles and do something to counteract the stress or they will definitely suffer.

Dr. Christiane Northrup, past president of the American Holistic Medical Association, says that simply being female in our culture is cause of medical stress. She writes, "in a culture that devalues the feminine and glorifies masculine values, how could we fail to be affected? I believe this helps to explain why 40% of women have fibroids, 50% of women between the ages of 35 and 55 have had or will have hysterectomies, 40-60% suffer from PMS and one in ten of us will get breast cancer." She believes that the symptoms in the body are often the only way that the soul can get our attention.

Absolutely correct. Women's health care is in a terrible state. There is now talk of requiring a gynecologist to get a second opinion before performing a hysterectomy because of widespread abuse. It is now the most commonly performed surgery in the United States. When women referred their cases to another specialist, it was found that 98% of the planned hysterectomies were not necessary. I have met gynecologists who have said that in a few year's time there will be hardly any mature woman left with a womb!

It is true that all the values in our culture have been decided by men; it is also true that women try to conform to those values. This causes untold stress and health problems. For example, a job outside the home is considered more respectable, but who makes it more respected? Women are trying to emulate men's positions and conform to men's values and are hurting their health. We need to make sure that we make mothering and nurturing families more respectable. The most important work of nurturing and teaching the children is given the lowest priorities, the lowest pay. This is not right.

So women will have better health if they listen to their innate value system? In other words, spiritual life, one's spiritual values, are important to health?

Yes. Those who have a spiritual life will do better physically. Those who have spiritual priorities will feel more meaning in what they do and feel more love for themselves and for others. This definitely means they will do much better physically than those who are not so sure whether they are supposed to love or wait for others to model love for them, or those who are not guided from inside. Those who hold back like that often fall into medical symptoms.

The hostility component has been shown as a basic cause of stress and illness. Hostility is eventually very damaging. I think hostility is present if one is suspicious of other people's motives, if one stands back waiting to see how she is treated before speaking kindly to someone else. I believe that the spiritual values of love, openness, caring, nurturing are much more healthy.

If all the readers were sitting with you now, what would you want to say to them?

Love is the one message I would like to leave with them. Be a little more giving. You will not dry out from giving too much love; you always have more love coming back to you. This may be an unusual message from a physician, but I have found that we needlessly hurt ourselves by holding back. Keep in mind that you need to take care of yourself first; that is most important. But then love others. You will not run out of love. The more you give, the more you will have. I think that we need to do this ourselves, model it, and then perhaps everyone else will do the same thing.

Chandra Patel, M.D., F.R.C.G. P., is an internationally acclaimed expert on the prevention and control of hypertension and heart disease. She was awarded the British Heart Foundation Award in 1980, the James Mackenzie Award for research in cardiovascular medicine in 1981 and several other awards for her research and work with patients.

She is a past board member of the Royal College of General Practitioners, a Fellow of the Royal Society of Medicine, an Honorary Fellow of the Society of Behavioral Medicine (USA), founder member of the British Holistic Medical Association, a member of the Advisory Council of the Yoga Biomedical Trust Cambridge, and adviser to the World Health Organization.

Currently Hon. Senior Clinical Lecturer in the Department of Community Medicine, University College London and Middlesex Hospital Medical School, Dr. Patel is also author of *Fighting Heart Disease* and *The Complete Guide to Stress Management*.

Everything harmonizes with me, which is harmonious to thee, O universe. Nothing for me is too early nor too late, which is in due time for thee. Everything is fruit to me which thy seasons bring, O nature: from thee are all things, in thee are all things, to thee all things return.

MARCUS AURELIUS

Nature and Spirituality:
Time of the New Dawning

by

Brooke Medicine Eagle

other, you gave us our very cells, you who are the deep, deep nest of all your children that ever have been, are now, and will be. You nurture and renew us. Our true mother, Mother Earth, we thank you for our life.

Father, you share with us the spark of aliveness, you who are the light that shines within us and all our relations from the beginning to the end. Father Sky, we thank you for our life.

It is well that I have been asked to talk with you about woman and nature, and the potential for deepening our spirituality through nature. Spirit is father, sky, light, creation, the spark that ignites and lives within us all. Nature is mother, earth, womb of all possibility, nurturing and renewing place where we receive our bodies. These are our true parents.

When light reached into the dark, ever-present womb and pulled forth two-leggeds, not just dust was made real, but starlight as well. We humans are earth and sky. We can be represented as a cross, a blending: Mother seen as looking across the horizon, Father as looking up. They cross at our heart.

Thus Spirit lives within Mother and within each of us. Father Spirit is not angry and vengeful as some of the old books would tell us, and certainly has not given up and left, as some modern thinkers propound. To stand quiet in Mother's beauty is to immediately recognize the aliveness that abounds. Spirit is incredibly alive, moving and dancing and singing in Mother's beauty.

Before we can say we have finished what is begun here, you must take yourself to a quiet place of Mother's beauty and see the life around you. Sit upon Mother. Balance and quiet yourself and consciously join yourself with the circle of all that is alive. If you find this difficult in the beginning, look at every tiny thing you see around you as you sit there, and picture it dead, as though its life is gone: no movement, no sound, no breeze. Every blade of grass, every tree lifeless, every four-legged, all the crawlers, the waters stagnant and putrid, the wingeds fallen and still. Then bring yourself into contrasting reality, and really see the life dancing around you. Breathe in the aliveness and find it in yourself. Feel and listen to your heart beat. Stop doing anything about breathing, and let yourself be breathed. Remember, then, the words "Father is alive within Mother Earth, within me and all things" and give thanks for life. When you have experienced this, then the remainder of what I say can be real within you rather than merely words.

Our present challenge is to awaken and embody Spirit within us, rather than to leave earth or our bodies to find Spirit. We are entering the time of the nine-pointed star, the star of making real upon earth the golden dream of peace that lives within us. We understand that finding heaven is not going somewhere else, but co-creating it here upon this beautiful earth. We are completing the cycle of the eight-pointed star, Venus, star of the heart, where the lesson has been about ourselves as the cross between sky and earth, and about letting the light and love of Father and Mother join at our hearts and shine forth unrestricted. Having understood and taken within us this knowing of Spirit, we can then use that light and love to manifest a peaceful, abundant, harmonious world around us.

In doing this we have a strong ally in our elder sister, White Buffalo Woman, mysterious holy woman who appeared long, long ago to the Lakota people bringing the sacred pipe and seven sacred rites. Her message, as was Creator's message in the beginning, is of oneness: Spirit lives within everything and thus we are related to all things through Spirit. Spirit is the vibration, the hum, the movement of everything from the tiny atom of a rock to the spiral growth of the tallest tree and the playful fun of children. Mother has her own special hum, as do all things. Her vibration, eight cycles per second, is healing and renewing to us when we experience it. In this modern world we have cut ourselves off from this song of Mother's body, alienating ourselves from her spirit, by producing noise and vibration to surround ourselves: electricity, motors, radio waves, interference of all kinds. Thus we feel the necessity to go into Mother's vastness to reconnect ourselves with the renewing and nurturing of her spirit.

Inipi—Purification Lodge

One of the sacred rites Buffalo Woman gave is *Inipi* or Purification Lodge, more commonly known as the sweat lodge. A lodge is built of willow and covered with hides or blankets until it is pitch black inside. Earth is taken out of a center hole, where hot rocks are placed to create steam from the water poured upon them. When one enters the small opening, one must crawl upon hands and knees, thus humbling oneself. (Humble does not mean abject or pitiful; it comes from the same root as humus, and means "of the earth"). Thus we are coming close again to Mother Earth as we come within her dark womb, sit upon her, and feel her spirit song. The heat from the rocks causes us to relax and surrender, to let go and open, to release what we hold. This is a very powerful form of healing since it allows us to release all that which separates us from Mother and from Spirit, makes us safe within the womb to open to the new and amazing possibilities that lie within us. Norma Cordell, who carries a Nez Perce lineage, reminds us that the first sweat lodge is our mother's womb from which we emerged new into our physical world.

Our challenge in this time on earth is not to create some new invention, but to heal ourselves, become whole, by surrendering to the larger life, the source of all life, within and around us. My friend, Nancy Swanson, gave me a new perspective on Darwin's theory of survival of the fittest. Rather than the masculine interpretation that the fittest was the one who could fight the best, the deeper and more useful feminine interpretation is of fitness as the one who fits with, and thus is in harmony with, all around—the one who surrenders to the larger life of all relations. When we emerge from the purification lodge, clean and clear of body, emotion, mind, and spirit, we emerge reborn and new into the world. We come again with the eyes and heart of a child, as the great masters have said we must do to recognize the life of Spirit within us and all things. In entering and leaving the lodge, and often in the ceremony within, the phrase "all my relations" is used to remind us of our deep and real connection with all things.

Hanblechi—Crying for Vision

Buffalo Woman also gave the rite of *Hanblechi* or Crying for Vision, through which one retreats from daily life to Mother's quiet, leaving behind clothing, food, and often even water, to clear oneself and call vision to oneself for the people. Messages come from Mother's children around as well as from Spirit within. One of my elders often tells stories of guiding 'city folks' on a vision quest. Occasionally a person would come down from extended time in a sunlit, grassy, forest meadow and report that nothing happened. "Nothing happened?" My elder would then point out all the things that had likely brought the lessons that came from each and every thing around. "Did you notice the soft grasses, how they sway in harmony with the lightest breeze, yet how soon they spring back upward when the heaviest of footsteps move away? Did you know they even break up concrete with their gentle strength? And did you notice how the trees are deep rooted in Mother Earth to stand the high winds? Those who are not are toppled and gray. Did you learn from the rocks near whom you sat, who are the teachers of patience? Did you hear the sweet song of the aspen leaves above you? Did you feel Father Sun describing the cycles of the larger life in his continuous movement across the sky? Did you notice the ant people: how cooperative they are, how each one does his job with vigor? Did you see especially that ants do not kill each other on the freeways of their life?" And so he chided them and made them laugh at themselves for their foolishness and blindness.

I smile, remembering my beginning vision quest when I learned amazing lessons from the winged ones. I was sitting high above Arrow Creek, my back toward what we call the Castle Rocks where Absarokee (Crow) people have been vision questing for centuries. I sat upon a rock outcropping, flat and somewhat grown over with soft grasses. Beside me a small pine tree at finger tip's reach shaded me. From there I could look far down to see the miniature purification lodge by the creek and my helpers small as ants around our camp. Above me the grassy hill sloped up to another lone rock about four feet high, standing alone. I had heard the tales of animal, bird, and spirit helpers coming to my elders, and in my beginning excitement I kept looking around for something to happen right away. I sat and waited, not even remembering to call to the spirits for help. The long, hot day wore into thirsty afternoon; I relaxed and softened. Just then a magpie flew into the tree near me. I snapped to attention and watched every move, waiting for his message. But he simply sat and sometimes hopped in a very regular magpie way, and said nothing. The only unusual thing was that he was nearly within arm's reach and paid absolutely no attention to me. Soon he flew off. Quiet again. Then in the blue skies stretching out away from me, I saw two dark dots—big birds flying strongly toward me. As they drew closer and glided down into the cliffs below me, I identified them as a pair of golden eagles, majestic and beautiful. I found myself wishing they had come closer, so I stilled myself again. Before long, into the pine tree flew three chickadees, small twittering birds who are at home sitting upon or hanging from the branches. They did their chickadee thing without noticing me, again hopping remarkably close.

Now I could see that an interesting sequence was developing, and I studied the 'medicines' (meanings or powers) associated with these three birds. The magpie for me represents the buffalo with whom he is symbiotic, Magpie sits on Buffalo's back, getting fed by the grubs there, and at the same time acting as an alarm for short-sighted Buffalo when the bird sees something far off and flies squawking away. So Magpie made sense to me since my blessing for this quest had come in a sacred Buffalo Lodge, dedicated to the nurturing power of the feminine. I acknowledged and gave thanks for all these things in my life.

My thoughts then turned to Eagle, who flies highest and sees farthest, representing Spirit Above. He also reminded me of my name and the accompanying assignment to touch Spirit Light and carry it across the sky, sharing it. Thus Father Spirit spoke to me again through his high-flying wingeds, an obvious message and reminder. The chickadees, too, made sense. Upon this very mountain our last braid chief (an old-time chief with traditional braided hair), Plenty Coups, had vision quested as a young man, and the power he received was that of the chickadee, whose smallness and gentleness allows her to be anywhere without disturbing whatever is happening, hearing everything, knowing much. Plenty Coups died just before I was born, yet I have always felt close connection with his fatherly energy. I gave thanks and honor to Chickadee.

The most fascinating thought now was, Who will come next? Four is a very significant number among Indian peoples so I was anxious and impatient again. It didn't take long for the next wingeds to come in. I heard a whir of wings above my head and up the hill. Turning around to my left, I was disgusted to see five pigeons fluttering and landing upon the big rock, about fifteen feet from me. Pigeons remind me of big cities and the noise and confusion I hoped to escape upon this quiet hillside! Then too, there was the time in El Paso when I walked under the cornices of a downtown building in a new white outfit and a pigeon dropped a very unwelcome message to me! So I turned my back on them, wondering why the magic number four had been left out and why pigeons, of all things? Aggravated by their clucking, I looked around again to see one of the five sitting upon the very nearest edge of the rock. Then he dropped off the rock into gliding flight directly toward me, and disappeared into thin air. I looked everywhere, unable to accept his midair disappearance, but could find no other explanation. Glancing back at the rock I saw my four 'magic' birds. Pigeon had spoken again! Of course, I felt chagrined and chastised for my impatience, for my judgment, for holding onto the past instead of opening to the present with joy. In that moment I forgave the El Paso pigeon and gave thanks for the humor and gentleness of the lessons: a gift of the mysterious unknown through Mother's winged children.

The Sacred Pipe: Oneness with All-My-Relations

When the mysterious holy one, White Buffalo Woman, came to the Lakota people and gave them the sacred pipe, she spoke to them, and now to all of us, in this way:

> With this pipe you will send your voices to Wakan Tanka, the Great Spirit, who is your father and grandfather. With this sacred pipe you will walk upon the earth; for the earth is your grandmother and mother, and she is sacred. Every step that is taken upon her should be as a prayer. All the things of the universe are joined to you who smoke this pipe. When you pray with this pipe, you pray for and with everything. Every dawn is a holy event, and every day is holy, for the light comes from your father, Wakan Tanka. You must always remember that the two-leggeds and all other people who stand upon this earth are sacred and should be treated as such. This will take you to the end.[1]

I spoke earlier of approaching the world with the eyes and heart of a child. That leads to other stories and thoughts about Mother Earth's many peoples.

Teachings from the Four-Leggeds:

A student once told me a very touching story of her encounter with a bear. Elaine was about three years old, out with her father cutting trees in a mountainous area. Her dad had pointed out the caves upon the mountainside nearby, warning her that there might be bears there. Soon she wandered while playing and found herself at the mouth of one of the caves, which she entered. There was a bear in the cave, lying in the sun near the entrance. The hungry little girl recognized her as a mother bear; the nursing mother invited her to suckle. She was happily walking forward when the blast of a gun sounded behind her. The bear spouted blood and died. Elaine's father ran to her, so thankful for having saved his child from the bear that was about to eat her. She was broken-hearted and shocked because she knew Mother Bear was peaceful and nurturing and loving. Father and daughter's stories differ to this day because Elaine experienced the truth of the bear's gentleness and love.

This same childlike knowing and loving relationship was instilled in Lakota children when the old ways were practiced. When a woman found herself pregnant, she began to spend more and more time upon the land, harmonizing herself with all her relations. After the birth, she then spent many more months taking the child into nature and teaching the brotherhood of all creatures—otter, frog, water bird, deer and coyote and squirrel—learning the lessons and powers that each had to give, and most importantly, calling them 'little brother' and 'little sister.' Our elders understood that we are not fully human unless we stay close to Mother and in good relationships with all her children. Yet so often now in the wider culture children are laughed at for their wise understanding that trees and wind and kittens and clouds all talk!

For me personally, cats are amazing models. They have a deep understanding of the physical world and of the efficient use of energy, which is the warrior's central challenge. Their strong sense of self, their total relaxation when at rest, their magical purring, their lithe ease of movement and incredible leaps all speak strongly to me. I would like to share with you a teaching I received from two kittens that lived with me several years ago.

My look-alike cats Heeta (Loving Child) and Nochita (little Night Girl) have come in to curl up with me as I dry myself by the fire. They have been with me steadily since their birth, and long before they were born they had come to me in a waking dream. They have made their magic known to me, as I have watched for it since Eldest Grandmother told me how the feline people understand and make profound use of the rhythms of life, of the vibrations which underlie all things on earth below. She said, "They know how to travel on the humming, leaving their bodies behind." Although I had no idea exactly what she meant, and though others sometimes scoffed at her, I knew she had planted a seed that would bear fruit in time.

Coming home after a drenching walk on a cold evening, I sincerely wished to learn of traveling an easier way, so I said to the big kittens as they crawl up on me, "Show me this medicine of yours." They didn't acknowledge hearing me, and yet they did a very unusual thing. Heeta lay on my upper chest over my heart, stretching herself across me in a most uncatlike position, with her chest glued to mine, front legs down over my left side and hind legs over my right. With her head on the opposite side, Nochita then did the same over my solar plexus. Then they simply began their contented purring, or so it seemed until I noticed that their humming became gradually and enormously full without growing louder; the whole room and my own body began to vibrate and pulse with the rhythm of it: wa waa waa waaaa. I have experienced this only once before when my elder chanted with me in special tones: "The Great Spirit and I are one, the Great Spirit and I are one . . ." on and on until this same kind of 'warping' happened, and I traveled through many marvelous places, exquisite beyond words.

And then I was free on their purring, far outside the house, moving rapidly and in the direction of my thoughts. I went far across the great water to a wise old one who is growing blind, and I worked on her eyes. With my right hand I lay fine fish gut on her cataracts, winding and circling it from the center, left and outward until it covered the surface of her eyeball. I blew my breath on it in steady, even, deep breaths until it just begins to dry. Then, with infinite care I lift the thread off her eye, unwinding inward with my left hand until her eye was clear, the cataract coming with the lifting.

It is complete. I kissed both her eyelids goodbye and I moved like a blur through space/time. I opened my eyes in bed to pat and thank Heeta and Nochita. They rose, stretched, and went into the kitchen for a drink.

When the next trading vessel came, there was joyful news of the wise one's renewed sight, and a package for me that no one else understood: an iridescent abalone shell filled with dried fish for Heeta and Nochita.[2]

In his wonderful little book,[3] J. Allen Boone tells stories of his experiences with the incredibly intelligent and communicative dog, Strong Heart, and of lessons given to him by many other endearing creatures. I also highly recommend the thrilling and moving experiences of a Yukon Indian who is befriended by a huge, silver, female wolf pack leader.[4] There is a saying among this particular tribe of Indians that when you have a special, close, and long-lasting friend, you 'stand in the shadow of a rainbow' with them.

Many of our animal friends, including domestic animals, have so much to teach us. We all know stories of 'man's best friend,' the dog: his faithfulness, courage, intelligence, bravery. My Chow dog, Empress Silky Bear, is a wonderful and loving being. I was busy working with a large group of people at the time she was near the end of her first pregnancy. I had massaged and worked with her, relieving her back of the burden of all those puppies within, and was looking forward eagerly to their birth. Silky came to me in the middle of my work and took my hand; she grasped it gently, her canine teeth holding my palm. I patted her and then tried to go back to work, but found that her gentle clasp was very powerful. It hurt my hand to try to pull away. She gently but firmly took me down the trail and across the meadow to her bed under the house where she immediately proceeded to birth the litter. Of course, I had wanted to be there!

Another sweet and wonderful little animal taught me a very important lesson of Spirit a few years ago. It was Autumn in the high country and I lay down to rest with my blanket on a bare spot at the foot of a huge aspen. The sun was shining down and I felt more peaceful than I had in months. Hearing a slight rustle next to me, I turned my head to see a fat little ground squirrel happily making her way toward me. I realized that the bare spot and little hole I was lying on was the entrance to her home. She continued toward me, even though I moved to better watch her approach, and I felt sure she would hop upon me and explore around trying to find her door. Just then I remembered a message I had been given often as a child when rabies and other animal diseases were epidemic, "Don't let them near you; they might bite you and give an awful disease." Suddenly fearful thoughts occupied my mind and at that exact moment the little ground squirrel screamed in terror, herself feeling fear and danger, and ran in panic to hide. I cried when I realized that my fear had instantly communicated to her, that I had destroyed a potentially beautiful encounter by recalling my old programs of fear. I shall not forget that lesson from Spirit through the little animal; I'm sure that same instant wordless communication is consciously or unconsciously felt by all other creatures, including the two-leggeds.

Dhyani Ywahoo recounts times with her gentle Cherokee grandmother when mountain lions would come and rub on her legs like great kittens. When I was a child I told my mother that heaven is just like our home in the wonderful Montana wilderness, except that in heaven the animals are not afraid of us. I still believe this to be true, and am working to release all fearful thoughts from my mind and replace them with peaceful and loving ones. As we all replace fear with love within ourselves we do our part toward recreating the Garden of Eden on earth, making heaven real right here and now by embodying Spirit within ourselves.

Big Medicine from Tiny Fliers

So often we two-leggeds deny that wisdom can be gained from any of Mother's creatures. We hold ourselves higher, better, more intelligent, more important than them, and refuse to look upon them with open eyes. Reptiles and insects are two very specific examples. Yet the reptilian part of our brain is the source of the mechanism of feeling which keys our memory for recall; my elders say it is the 'tape recorder' Mother Earth gave us to use and that we are denying our own incredible powers of memory by using mechanical devices outside ourselves. Lizards remember how to regenerate their limbs, and I believe this ability as well lies in the reptilian, or old brain, of humans.

In the past few years, I have opened myself to the world of insects and been given profound lessons there. When I lived in Oklahoma in an open studio, insect people took that opportunity to show me their beauty and diversity. Each night for the whole summer a new beetle or moth would show itself to me, lighting under my desk lamp to give me excellent viewing. There were simple brownish moths whose elegantly patterned backs gave me designs for rug weavings; shiny black beetles with cardinal red wings; delicate iridescent yellow-gold fliers, and tiny green shimmering bees. They reminded me that there are more insects upon Mother Earth than all other kinds of beings put together, and that they have been here for much, much longer than two-leggeds; they know how to live well upon our Mother. The most stunning insect to show herself to me was a moth shaped like a simple miller with a tiny head and an exquisite furry collar, below which descended a collar that looked as if someone had poured cranberry juice over it, which had then spilled down upon her snowy cape, fading into lighter and lighter pink until the very hem of her garment was again radiant white. She was beautiful beyond words. It was clear to me as she regally showed herself that she was a princess, a tiny improbable princess, but one nonetheless.

The lineage of southern seers that has come to me has strong connections with the insect world, and often insects come as messengers or omens from that shamanic family. The women of that family communicate with me through insects that are so shiny black they have a coppergold iridescence and often gossamer wings.

One day in a telephone conversation with someone close to me about a dream I hold dear, I felt my dream had been crushed by his negative attitude, and crying said, "I feel like the egg of my dream has been stepped upon." Finishing the conversation I went outside to talk with my friend, Caer, who was hanging wet clothes to dry in the New Mexico sun. Behind her I noticed a lovely tiny turquoise egg lying on the rocks and sand of the driveway. I assumed that she had found it and laid it there to take in when she returned to the house. But when she almost stepped on it, I asked her about it. "What egg?" was her reply, and I knew that it was the egg of my dreams being returned, beautiful and whole, to me. When I picked it up and took it to my car, there on the window was an exquisite insect I had never seen before. She was like a huge flying ant, shiny black with copper-gold iridescence and clear wings with veins of copper. To me it was the women of my seer's family come to return my dreams.

The men of that same lineage signal me through blue-green insects; some are an inch tall with long, bent legs, and some are like beautiful scarab beetles. Last year I journeyed to the Tulum ruin on the turquoise Caribbean coast of Quintanaroo, Mexico. In the center of the ancient plaza is a temple dedicated to Itsa Ma, the Descending God, the one Father Spirit sent to be with us on earth. At the top is an image of Father God, Kulkulkan, as a king. Under him is a man, head down as though being birthed, with his right hand reaching to Father God and his left hand reaching down to us on Mother Earth. He is the one our people call Elder Brother and Dawn Star, the one who journeyed all across the Americas two thousand years ago teaching the way of love and uniting the peoples under the light of Father Spirit.[5] His names remind us that he came before us to show the possibilities of a whole new time to come, just as the dawn star presages a new day. He was the beginning of our shaman's line of seers, bringing spiritual light to those in darkness.

As I stood near the temple of Itsa Ma, listening to the waves and waiting for the old Maya man I was to contact, I noticed beside me a tiny, radiant light. Looking down at its source, I saw an exquisitely beautiful beetle, about the size of my little fingernail. Its iridescent colors echoed the beauty of the turquoise sea beside us; its light shone warmer and brighter than I had ever felt or seen. It was unmistakably the Dawn Star's energy. With it came a message to remind my people in the North of the truth of their stories about Elder Brother from long ago, and the urgent need to bring ourselves together again in the spiral of love and light under Father Spirit that will bring our people to health and abundance once again. Then he flew away toward the sea, leaving me awed and filled with light.

Hummingbirds have some of the most powerful medicine of the wingeds. As all good flight scientists know, hummingbirds cannot fly; they defy aerodynamic principles! But tiny and delicate as they are, hummingbirds are able at any moment to fly in any direction, reminding us to be flexible and 'on our toes.' They live, trusting, on the very edge of life. A good friend of mine who has an aviary of these tiny birds from around the world told me something quite astounding: if you go into the aviary and startle a hummingbird into flight, then do not feed him a droplet of nectar when he settles down again, he will be dead of starvation by morning. He lives that close to the edge. Hummingbird's beauty, quickness, courage, as well as his defiance of what we think we know to be true are profound lessons for all of us.

Dragonfly, too, is seen as powerful medicine since she has that same ability to instantly move in any direction, and demonstrates even more flexibility and adaptability by living in all the mediums of earth—water as a larva, land and air as an adult.

Wisdom of the Deep

Our water creatures, fish, dolphins, and others, have much to teach us. My friend, Lalo, recounts a true adventure he had while swimming off northern California. He swam and played at the joining of a river and the ocean, enjoying the mixing of the waters. Being an excellent swimmer, he paid little heed to warnings about the currents until he found himself very far out and having a difficult time making it back to shore through the undertows. Difficulty turned into panic as he fought against the currents until he was exhausted and pulled under. Desperate and confused, he was swirling around under the water when several seals came to him. Between them they nosed him up and helped him forward until he was through the rip tides and into safe waters.

Dolphins have demonstrated something we are finally beginning to use in the form of underwater birthing; creating relaxed, alert, playful, highly intelligent children who dive and swim, totally at home in water. Dolphins also share a profound lesson with us two-leggeds, who through our manipulation of the world have caused grave damage and pollution. They do not have an opposable thumb and so cannot manipulate, yet they live a beautiful, free, harmonious, and mutually supportive life, having developed the additional brain lobe that we humans have. The great whales, too, have these same lessons and more for us.

Will we learn the lessons of harmonious living from them, or will we insist on killing our brothers and sisters for the products they provide? We must listen with open minds and hearts to the words of Chief Seattle:

> If all the beasts were gone, men would die from great
> loneliness of spirit, for whatever happens to the beast
> also happens to man. All things are connected. Whatever
> befalls the earth befalls the sons of the earth.[6]

From Out of the Earth

One of my spiritual benefactors, Younger Brother, is a plant shaman. As children, both he and I experienced much craziness among the two-leggeds around us; while I turned to animals for love and learning, he turned to plants. A very special understanding he gave me is that plants love us.[7] I had never thought of it in this way, yet every day I see them giving themselves for our nourishment, our healing, our spiritual awakening, the warmth of our homes and fire. He reminds me that the flowers and grasses and trees came before us, creating a cycle of oxygen and clear air without which we cannot exist. He calls Tree People the teachers of Mother's law; where we destroy them we very quickly destroy the very breath of our lives. The master Jesus, our Elder Brother, used parables of grape vines and fruit-bearing trees often as he gave the great lessons. He spoke lovingly of earth as Mother, the creatures as brother and sister, and Father God's caring for the least sparrow that falls.

In our modern world, the community of Findhorn has shown us the enormous abundance of huge, magnificent plants that come as we acknowledge and work with the spirits, or devas, of the plants. We learn in many ways that we must honor and use well the green ones Mother gives us. An enormous number of people use refined plants such as cocaine and alcohol to damage their lives and those around them. On the other hand, peyote cactus, used in a sacred way in the Native American Church, is opening the way of Spirit and healthful living to a unified pan-Indian group of people across Turtle Island, creating the most unification we have seen among native peoples since the Dawn Star's spiral of light centuries ago. Many people abuse tobacco, forgetting that its medicine is the uniting of all things, and thus they die from cancer and lung disease. Tobacco's spiritual use is in Buffalo Woman's sacred pipe, each pinch added with a prayer which includes two-leggeds, wingeds, those with fins, the green growing ones, the stone people, those who burrow and crawl within the earth, the ancestors and the children to come, and all things in the great circle of life. We must awaken and learn the clear lesson Father Spirit and Buffalo Woman are asking of us: that we mature and step into the great circle of harmony with all our relations.

I must also speak briefly of the stones, gems, and crystal people. We are now finding more and more beneficial uses for these beings, from gem elixirs for treating diseases to the powerful energy of crystals that can be programmed for specific uses. Once I was spending time with Dhyani Ywahoo, a loving and gifted healer using the energy of crystals for healing, for ancient information, for protection, and many other things. She said, "We set our especially big clusters for peace, except in the winter when we set them for warmth." What a wonderful practice, and how efficient a use of energy: warming ourselves with crystals rather that killing our trees to provide our warmth!

My own experience is that crystals act as transformers. We are told that a new tone, a new vibration, is being set on earth to lead us into a golden new time. Since crystals are used as transformers in everything from radios and wristwatches to computers, I feel they are also acting to transform this high new energy into an immediately usable form for us, possibly helping with the transmutation of our very cells into a new kind of harmonious, loving being.

From these stories and lessons I hope you hear again and again the call for a conscious surrender into the greater circle of life, to listen to the full and healing voices, touching Spirit through Mother.

Hunkapi—Making of Relatives

Another of Buffalo Woman's sacred rites is the rite of *Hunkapi,* the Making of Relatives. Through this rite one takes someone who is not a blood relative to be a part of the family. The first and most obvious *hunkapi* is marriage. However, when the Lakota people made the vision real, they enacted a larger level of the rite. They took a neighboring people, the Rees, to be their family. *Hunkapi* reminds us of the larger understanding of all two-leggeds as family with each other. The rite's deepest symbolism is the remembrance of Father Spirit within each other and all things, the oneness which brings true peace. The Lakota holy man, Black Elk, has this to say to us:

> Through these rites a three-fold peace was established.
> The first peace, which is the most important, is that
> which comes within the souls of men when they realize
> their relationship, their oneness, with the universe and all
> its powers, and when they realize that at the center of
> the universe dwells Wakan Tanka, and that this center is
> really everywhere, it is within each of us. This is the
> real peace, and the others are but reflections of this.
> The second peace is that which is made between two
> individuals, and the third is that which is made between
> two nations. But above all you should understand that
> there can never be peace between nations until there is
> first known that true peace which, as I have often said,
> is within the souls of men.[8]

I perform many ceremonies to make relatives, creating the opportunity for people to recognize their oneness with each other. Among my native people, it is customary to adopt as family those who are special to us, and that beautiful rite is being extended to people of all cultures. I truly believe that we two-leggeds are now being asked to do a great *hunkapi,* one in which we consciously adopt all Mother and Father's children as our family. This year I have conducted a ceremony to pray for the trees that are being destroyed so wantonly and dangerously, and for the creatures and plants that we are making extinct by the hundreds. Part of those ceremonies is always a form of hunkapi, consciously remembering our oneness with all things. This is what my spiritual benefactor calls 'the third attention'—holiness. It is keeping one part of our attention upon this kind of oneness.

Another aspect of Buffalo Woman's message is this: we are one with all things, and thus what we do to any one of Mother Earth's creatures we do to ourselves. The pipe she brought represents that oneness, with its red bowl symbolizing the fire of life (or the blood) through Mother, and its stem representing the open channel to Father within and around us.

Thus our elder sister's call to us is one of creating good relationship, through recognizing and honoring spirit and aliveness in all things. It is a call to the feminine within us, that part which carries this relationship aspect. And as we chose female bodies, we accepted the charge to model and teach and require good relationship among earth's children: two-legged, four-legged, winged, those who crawl and swim, green growing ones, and rock people, all peoples. Buffalo

Woman is calling in her accounts with each of us: are we living the oneness in our daily lives, and are we bringing the message of spirit and oneness that she modeled for us as women?

There are two practices here that bring up the balance on our side of the account. The first is to understand that Mother lives within us. Mother's mind lives in our belly, in our center. This may seem strange as you read it, since we have been told to numb ourselves to the feelings that occur there, to lock our stomachs in tightness to prevent them sagging. And we have done as was modeled and told us, cutting ourselves off from Mother's life within us. We must reconnect. To do this takes time and practice, so let us begin.

First, loosen your clothing and reach down, finding your navel, and then an inch or so below it, finding your center. In order to be more accurate, use this image, given me by my mentor, Moshe Feldenkrais. If you were to stick a huge pin through yourself and want to spin evenly around it, you would put it through your center. I am speaking of your actual physical, weight-distribution center, and it lies there beneath your navel. Stand in front of a mirror if you want to see, but primarily you must 'feel' that place which is your center. Pull and release your belly with your muscles and keep feeling until you find what seems to be your center. This is where Mother lives within you, the place of the invisible umbilical cord which connects you with her, and thus joins you with all her children as well. It is here that we will learn to truly live the law of oneness.

Let me give you an example that came to me. I was given vision to create a ceremony to block the cutting of trees in the Amazon and other such acts which threaten the life and breath of the children of earth. In meditating on the trees, part of our family and so necessary in the cycle that brings us the breath of life, I realized that for many of us saving the trees is a logical or mental thing, something we think about and decide. I realized that Tree people are usually seen as something outside us, not truly felt as related. If we can actually begin to feel our relationship to them through the cord that connects us to Mother and all her children, then we will have the same experience of the trees that we have of our children who come from our bellies and with whom we have that invisible cord of love as well. If someone were to suggest killing a group of our children, it would not be an intellectual question, one for us to think about and judge and decide. It would be an obvious "No! Unthinkable! For no reason!" And as we feel our same deep connection and relationship with trees through our belly, we will respond deeply and differently to the question of their decimation. It is through this center of ourselves that true relationship will be experienced and lived, not through our minds where we seem to be stuck at present.

So reach down and find your center often. Do it frequently enough so you can begin to feel it internally, rather than having to find it from outside. Pull the muscles inward often so you begin to feel your belly and tone it. My spiritual benefactor asks me to "press my belly against the world." In doing this I think of my belly as the head of a drum upon which everything vibrates. If the head of the drum is loose it doesn't resonate, and if it is too tight it cannot resonate. It must be toned, and your attention must be there to pick up the resonance, the song within you created as your surroundings vibrate there, giving you another kind of knowing.

The other practice concerns our use of the moon cycle, the cycle of our menses. We are presently reaching toward a whole new time on earth, a flowering of the tree of life. The dawn star has long since faded into the pale morning light, and golden day is close at hand—yet much still lies within the womb of mystery, in the womb of Buffalo Woman. We are being called to bring forth into reality what is waiting there for us, to awaken ourselves in the dream. And finding the dream is the function of the moon cycle, especially for the daughters of the earth, whose blood expresses itself with the tides of moon's pull.

It is now that I speak to the feminine, the nurturing and renewing power within all, and especially I call to those who chose a female body, for we express Grandmother's pull most eloquently. Your moon cycle determines the thinness of the veil between you and the great mystery. As the new moon comes toward you, the veil thins, becomes gossamer and transparent. You feel the openness and sensitivity that begins to increase. You pay closer attention to where you allow yourself to be, the energy in which you are immersed, for you imprint very deeply in this receptive time. What you wish to receive, create, and magnify, you choose to surround yourself in now. You turn toward beauty, peacefulness, song, and thus call vision for a radiant, harmonious life for your children and the children of seven generations. You define what you give your attention to until the blood comes and then you retreat into the peaceful beauty and quiet of the Moon Lodge, leaving behind for a few days the everyday world: going within to center, paying attention to the womb, to Mother's mind within you, and on then into the great mystery waiting there. In the moon lodge you remember your vow to use this transparent veil in calling vision for your people, praying, "Not for myself alone, Great Spirit, do I ask this vision, but that all the peoples may live."

This information received as the menses begin is the clearest human picture from within the womb of the great mystery, from the unknown of our future. Among our dreaming peoples, the most prophetic dreams and visions (of the coming of the white peoples and other such almost incomprehensible changes) were brought to the people through the moon lodge. In other words, the most useful information comes from each of us women who use our moon time well. Conversely, for each of us who do not honor this time, much is lost, including the respect of others for our bleeding.

My call to you is to begin now to honor your moon time, to come together in small hoops (of perhaps eight women) and create a moon lodge, a communal women's retreat and meditation room for the beauty, for the quiet, for the transparent veil. Dedicate yourself to the quest for vision that will guide us and our families at the time. Within this lodge keep a large and lovely book for recording your visions, dreams, imaginings, and intuitive flashes. Make possible also a simple art expression for another kind of cord. These expressions will unify the information and make it available to all who come there; the dream will begin to unveil itself through strands woven from many women's dreams. The weaving created through the gatherings of shared vision on the new moon and the gatherings to actualize those visions during the full moons will create a fuller tapestry, more easily understood and made real in the ordinary affairs of life. For this is the ultimate action—making the dream of peace real in the 'everydayness' of our lives.

Grandmother's cycle and Mother's mind within us assist us then with the task of coming again fully present into the world, when at the full moon we are at our most powerfully attentive and aware and present for action in the world. During the days following the first flood of clearing blood whose potential for life we gift back to Mother, the flow gentles, wanes, slows, and completes itself; we integrate the vision within ourselves and ready ourselves to come forth. From the womb of Buffalo Woman we carry new creations to join with the light, and birth takes place. The dream is made real in the beauty of earth.

This call, then, is for honoring the deep function of Mother's gift of life blood within us, to bring forth vision and make it real for our families at a time when vision is so important for us and for the healing of Mother. The honoring cycle within us will then be more than empty form and words; it will be giving new life for men and women alike. And wonderfully, we will notice healthier, more comfortable menstrual cycles and birthing.

These simple, ancient ways are powerfully useful when put into practice. Your feeling may be one of not knowing what to do; the line of feminine teachings may have been lost to you. Yet Mother's truth is always within us. Be willing to discover it within yourself. Reach back across the gap. Be willing to not know, to reach into the unknown, the great mystery. Then you and we are following the model Buffalo Woman gifted to us—we are carrying the water of Spirit to all the people through our own bodies. We are nurturing and renewing at the most profound level.

Her-Alone-They-Sing-Over: Puberty Rite

Another aspect of woman was given when Buffalo Woman sent one of her rites in vision to a man named Slow Buffalo, who saw and made real the rite called Her-Alone-We-Sing-Over, given as a young girl comes into womanhood through her first blood. This powerfully beautiful puberty rite reminds the young girl that she is now like Mother Earth and can bring forth children, can renew the people through herself. She is highly honored at this time by all the people, who also wish to touch her and receive some of the power she is now manifesting.[9] We who have perhaps never been given such a rite, must remember to honor ourselves and the gift of this power of Spirit within us. We must as well find ways to bring this kind of honoring and understanding to our young women, and thus to all the people.

And so we understand that Mother's and Grandmother's cycles within us are part of the process of deepening our spirituality and of bringing spiritual gifts to ourselves and to the people. We can be clear and glad as Buffalo Woman turns her eyes upon us. We can sing this song, given to me especially for women in their moon lodge and meaningful always: "We are the daughters of the moon and earth, who live within us and give us birth. We are the turning of the tide; we are the love that lives inside."

As women we have easier access to the life of Spirit and creation if we refuse to buy into the old stories of Spirit being angry or absent. Creation lives within our wombs; the life of our people is renewed there. It has been shown through recent research that what is necessary for creation of life is first the egg produced by the mother and then something to disturb the integrity of that egg. Sperm from the male was designed to do this second job remarkably well, yet sperm are not the only possible things to break that boundary. When the egg is broken by anything, life begins to unfold! This gives us clues as to the old one's honoring of the feminine as the beginning of all things, and the womb as the most powerful aspect of Spirit within us. Male shamans say that they 'fly off the woman's belly' when journeying to other realms, seeming to mean that the source of power rests there.

Within the native mind there is a remembering of our relationship with all beings from the beginning of earthly time. In the purification lodge we acknowledge the hot rocks in the center as our eldest grandparents—the first things upon the earth. Thus all things from one-celled beings to fishes, grasses, reptiles, birds, and mammals come down from them. It is through our bellies, through Mother's mind within us, that we will remember and honor this family tree, past and present.

As we see, there are many ways to think about Spirit within nature. My examples are brief, yet my hope is that from them you will gain a perspective that gives you the openness and interest to seek the profound lessons so constantly and freely available from Father Spirit within Mother Earth and all our relations.

In black there are all colors.
Where darkness always the light.
Iridescent the raven's wing in sunlight.

Brooke Medicine Eagle was raised on the Crow Indian Reservation in Montana. She is a native earthkeeper, a visionary, a teacher, a healer, poet, singer, and celebration leader. She is also a licensed counselor, a practitioner of Neurolinguistic Programming, a certified Feldenkrais instructor, a ropes course facilitator, and an ardent outdoor adventurer.

Brooke's visions have been documented in *Shamanic Voices, East West Journal, Whole Life Times, Shaman's Drum,* and in her book, *Buffalo Woman Comes Singing.*

Brooke travels extensively, offering teaching, ceremony, celebration, and outdoor excursions, carrying to all the ancient light of this land.

What do women want?

A person's a person, no matter how small.

Psychology and Spirituality:
God the Father and Freud

by

Jean Young, Ph.D.

hat does Sigmund Freud have to do with God the Father? How does the familiar male image of God influence our relationship with divinity? How do both figures affect women?

Most of us who have grown up Christian or Jewish may be so inured to the phrase and image of God the Father that we don't even hear the gender connotation anymore. Indeed, for many years past childhood, my image of God was the Sunday School vision of the old, white man with a white beard. In school I also learned that Sigmund Freud was the Father of Psychology, psychology being the study of the mind, the investigation of consciousness and behavior. Like God, Freud was also a white male and had a white beard. [1]

Some years ago when I first heard an argument that God was genderless and that gender language describing God was sexist, I was upset and horrified. If I didn't have my Sunday School picture in mind to think about God, I couldn't imagine how to think about God at all! Besides, I liked the idea of a loving and benevolent parent. I enjoyed the image of myself being cuddled up to a Father-God who would take care of me and protect me from harm.

It followed that if 'father' meant a loving and benevolent parent, then I could expect father-Freud and his colleagues in psychotherapy to protect me from harm as well. But I, and thousands of other women, have received something quite different from the patriarchal structures of psychology. The male image of God has undergirded those very structures and theories of psychology and human development by which women have been judged, diagnosed, and abused, and by which we have come to judge ourselves.

Those traditional theories are patriarchal, or male-centered, and form the criteria by which all psychological processes and behavior have been assessed. This means that all women's experience and behavior has been judged by males and through the criterion of male experience. A current and dramatic example of this bias was brought to light by Katharina Dalton, M.D., who, with other health professionals, campaigned to have premenstrual syndrome accepted as a valid medical condition. She found that some women, judged criminal or psychotic and incarcerated in institutions for years, responded to hormone therapy and became normal within a very short time. These particular women had indeed committed gross behavior, but because the hormonal chaos faced by every woman of child-bearing age every month had not been recognized as a legitimate situation, their behavior was judged apart from their physical differences from men. Many women speak of themselves during that premenstrual time as feeling 'crazy' and 'out of control.' I myself have been told it was 'all in my head' by more than one doctor and am sure my experience is not unique.

Although this physical difference is often touted by patriarchy as a reason not to promote women to positions of power, most women cope very well with their hormonal shifts. However, the hormonal shift in the bodies of some women causes extreme psychological disorder and needs to be considered in their overall case. I cite PMS (pre-menstrual syndrome) as an example of women's experience being ignored because, until the late 1970's, this particular women's experience was declared by the patriarchal medical and psychological world as invalid. On the basis of this 'invalidity,' some women spent years in mental institutions or prisons, while countless others suffered through monthly physical and emotional symptoms precisely because their experience and complaints were not taken seriously.

Our experiences as women in the world are what inform our internal experiences of ourselves. As a white, middle-class American woman, I know that my own experience is not universal and that women of other cultures, ethnic groups, and social classes will have experiences different from mine and unique to their own culture or group. As a student of feminist spirituality, I struggle with all the male images I've encountered in a lifetime of Christianity and realize how those images have affected me, for better and worse. As a psychotherapist, I join an increasing rank of feminist thinkers who have identified the naming of male socialization and experience as normative to be a major problem for women. As the wife of a Methodist minister, I struggle to find a balance between the role the congregation likes to put me in and my search for a way to relate to God as myself.

In spite of twelve years as a licensed psychotherapist in private practice and eight years of concentrated study in feminist spirituality and theology, when asked to write this essay I felt an old combination of feelings surface: "I don't have anything to say that hasn't been better said by others." I reviewed past papers I'd written and found some version of this self-assassination in almost every one. This makes me ask how this lack of confidence can persist.

I think about the women I see in my consulting room who have generously shared their most private thoughts, feelings and fears with me. I regularly hear bright, articulate women from all walks of life and a wide variety of career choices, including wife and mother, voicing similar doubts. "What do I have to offer? How could I possibly attempt that?" Or a different, yet equally painful position, "If only this one aspect of my life were in order (love life, children, career promotion, body size, etc.) then I would have it made!" We all share a deeply ingrained feeling that something is amiss. We also share a feeling that this deficit belongs to each of us in isolation—that everyone else is okay, or is at least coping better. Why?

When attempting to unravel a dilemma, it is often helpful to go back to the beginning. My own early childhood training seems to intersect generally, if not specifically, with that of many other women. As an only daughter with one younger brother, I learned the responsibility shared by most of us who are first-born girls: I was to be a small extension of my mother. It was not a punishing role, but it was unrelenting. When I was little, my mother trained me to tattle; I was her best spy. Of course, this also meant I had to be vigilant and watchful. My brother had a very different childhood experience. In me he had a guardian of sorts, but he also had to contend with the spy-factor. He learned to be careful of what he revealed while going about his life. To this day, I am known in the family as the 'nosey' one and he is 'the strong, silent one.'

This little snippet of my childhood is generalized and theorized by psychotherapists and sociologists, bringing us closer to the core of the matter. By socialization, little girls learn what femaleness is from their mothers or primary care-givers (who are usually female in Western-European culture). By separating from that female care-giver, little boys learn that being a male is different from being a female. If there is a male close by, the little boy looks to him for clues about maleness. Since the adult male also learned about maleness by separating from his female care-giver, the little boy learns that to be male is to be separate. Conversely, the little girl sees the primary care-giver taking care of those around her. In order to copy that female behavior, she must often learn to anticipate the needs of others, while her own needs wait or go unmet. She watches her mother give up everything from a hot supper to time for herself. The definition of femaleness is thus internalized by the little girl to the point where she often begins her own version of the scanning, even of the mother who is herself scanning the atmosphere to attend to the needs of others. What evolves is female radar tuned to the emotional climate and needs of the family.

It follows, then, that I would interpret my spying on my brother as a natural extension of my femaleness, of 'taking care' of him and helping my mother. He would, in turn, experience his quest for privacy not only as escape from a nosey older sister, but emulating his father in having a separate life. He and Dad would later do 'man things' like hunting and fishing and working on cars—separate but parallel activities. Mom and I would do 'woman things' like planning family gatherings, cooking together and talking—more relational activities.

In short, women learn to relate and attach emotionally by looking after the needs of others, while their own needs frequently go unmet and unacknowledged, even to themselves. When a woman's emotional needs go unacknowledged, she herself begins to judge them as shameful and bad, so she tries to hide them. The more deprived she becomes emotionally, the more she may be frightened of the very feelings which cry out for attention. The more frightened she is that this great need might creep out, be discovered, and overwhelm a potential need-satisfier, the more underground the needy feelings are likely to go. One vital aspect of herself starves while she tries desperately to get for herself by giving to others.

If she must hide her needs, then she is likely to feel that she must try to get them met in indirect ways. For instance, if she is needing reassurance and affection, she might go shopping. The fantasy is that she will feel the needed reassurance and affection when others admire her new acquisition. The tragedy of this way of coping is that it never works for long. The new purchase does not love her; others grow accustomed to it and stop admiring. Our consumer economy plays precisely on this fantasy, encouraging her to get the 'new, improved model.' So, again she hits the mall, shopping for reassurance and affection.

A current and dramatic example of getting needs met indirectly is the proliferation of eating disorders among women and girls. No matter what the feeling, and for very little money, a woman can eat or refuse to eat. Both activities serve to dull the ache of the unmet need temporarily and can be done entirely by the woman herself. No one can disappoint her here. As with all indirect methods, food or its refusal are doomed to disappoint. All the cookies in the world cannot give the woman what she really wants. Yet as ineffective as she may feel in her life, she can always put something in, or withhold something from, her mouth. Eating disorders are deviously effective precisely because food may be the only arena in her life she can control herself.

Patriarchal psychology and medicine have labelled eating disorders as self-destructive. Exactly the opposite is true. To eat or withhold food often represents a woman's only defense against powerlessness. It is a move toward survival, no matter how ill-placed and painful. Asking straight out for what she needs feels too risky; too much may be revealed and rejection feels intolerable.

Another way the woman may be able to express need is in stereotypical male arenas, such as mechanics, mathematics, or finances, where she allows some of her need to come out in disguise. In these arenas, it is socially acceptable and considered normal for a woman to be dependent, even stupid. When I was growing up, my mother handled all the finances and checkbooks and was definitely not stupid. Yet she insisted she could not read a map. She also claimed to be a mechanical dunce, exactly the area where my father excelled. This meant that whenever Mother had to go somewhere, Dad had to drive her or give her detailed instructions complete with landmarks and mileage, and whenever something mechanical needed fixing, she asked him to do it for her. For that time she was taken care of by him in a personal way. While interdependence is accepted generally as a healthy state of relationship, a woman may feel free to depend upon her partner only in those few time-honored arenas allowed by culture. Because these needs are more visible than the true emotional pain buried within her, she is often perceived as less strong and more dependent than her male counterpart.

A closer look reveals a different reality. What is often mistaken as a dependent aspect in a woman is really her wish to have her own legitimate needs for connection and intimacy met—precisely because she has not been allowed to depend emotionally on anyone else. She has been busy anticipating and undergirding the needs of others. This wish continues, not because it is inherent in femaleness, but because it goes unmet. As discussed earlier, men learn to separate from others and seem to stand alone emotionally. To be sure, they have the same basic emotional needs for affection, understanding, and holding as women do. The difference is that women are usually there to give them that support. Men appear to stand alone because women are there with the emotional safety net. Women seem to need support because they do not feel the presence of such a net.

In my work as a psychotherapist, I've come to believe that regardless of an individual's religious orientation or perceived lack of it, we are all influenced by the patriarchal structure of Jewish, Christian and Moslem tradition. Indeed, this structure informed the thinkers in the field of psychology, including Freud himself. The connection between the image (and theology) of God as male and the psychology based on male experience as normative is one which must be acknowledged to fully understand women's experience in the world outside and inside herself.

At the beginning of the century, when Freud first observed what he called mental illness in his patients, he noticed that the distress was felt mostly by his women patients. Since he himself did not experience the distress, nor did his fellow colleagues (male), he theorized that the distress must be aberrant and abnormal. He did not take into account the strictly controlled social atmosphere of the time nor the oppressive conditions of women's lives which may have made their emotional responses to their lives very understandable.

What Freud said, in effect, was "I am a normal man. I function in the world. I am respected in my profession. Therefore, if I don't experience the difficulties these women experience, then the women must be abnormal." Why would a brilliant physician make such a grandiose assumption? Why would the medical profession as a whole accept what became a theory of normative development based on only one-half of the population? Of all the social and political analyses of patriarchal structures, the one which makes most sense to me takes as its basis the idea: God is male, therefore male is superior and normative. Anyone or anything non-male is inferior.

Although there is very little evidence of Freud having had a personal theology, what is known is that he was born in Austria in 1855 of Jewish parents and for the first two years of his life was tended by a Roman Catholic nanny. As the eldest son of seven surviving children, he was the undisputed favorite of his mother. He was perplexed by religious themes and worked hard to discredit religion and spirituality as mere psychological processes. Still, he was fascinated by religious beliefs, their origins, and the psychological processes involved in them.

One of Freud's most important contributions to our understanding of psychological process—the unconscious—was very much at work here. The unconscious is defined as that aspect of the psyche not available to the rational conscious mind, yet which influences impulses, drives, feelings, and premises. The social context of Freud's life, the time, place, and religions of his household, cannot be extracted from his theory. His social context was decidedly patriarchal. A case can be made that Freud was acting out of his own unconscious belief that since God is male—the God of the Hebrews and Roman Catholics portrayed as male—then male must be better than female. Everything was to be judged by that criteria. That same unconscious premise was operating in the culture as a whole, in what Carl Jung later called the 'collective unconscious.' Freud was part of his culture.

Like Freud, I, too, am a product of my culture. Growing up as a mainline

Protestant, it never occurred to me to question that I had experienced only male pastors. I had become so accustomed to all the images and symbols of patriarchal religious structure that I couldn't even see what they were. I had only seen men at the altar in plain black robes. I had heard of women evangelists, but they had nothing to do with the 'real' church. Even later, when women would assist in a service, the male pastor did all the important things like preaching, presiding over the sacraments, and organizing the service. When feminists spoke of the problem, I protested immediately that gender made no difference in the character of God and deliberately proceeded to avoid the issue.

The Bible was used to discourage my questions. After all, God is constantly referred to there in all male titles: Father, King, Lord, Master. Somehow I got the impression that God personally wrote the Bible. I didn't stop to analyze how this would come about (perhaps fiery finger on stone tablets or magic typewriter with red ink for Jesus' quotes?) but the 'word of God' became the 'dictation of God' in my mind.

Most upsetting of all to me was when I began to question the patriarchal character of the Bible translations. I do not doubt that the Bible is a vehicle through which God reveals the divine to us, but I have come to accept, after much study, that the book itself is a work of human beings set in the social and political climates of the times in which the sections were written. Before I began to question, I had no concept of how disparate a collection it is, what enormous spans of time it covers, and for what political ends those writings were originally intended.

Once, for instance, I was very troubled by the dichotomy between the Household Codes of behavior listed in Ephesians 5:21 through 6:9[2] and the single verse of Galations 3:28. In brief, the Ephesians passage says:

> wives, obey your husbands
> children obey your parents
> slaves, obey your masters
> husbands, fathers, and masters, be nice.

By contrast, Galations 3:28 says:

> There is neither Jew nor Greek,
> slave nor free, male nor female;
>   for you are all one in Christ Jesus.[3]

They seem to be in direct conflict with one another. Ephesians exhorts a hierarchy of obedience while Galations says plainly that there is no hierarchy. For the believer who sees the Bible as the literal word of God, to be obeyed without question, the dilemma poses a problem. It certainly did for me. I was taught that to question any part was to question the whole. It either is or is not the word of God.

Enter the feminist Bible scholars and theologians. Their recent scholarship, going back to the original languages and related materials not included in the Bible we have today, gives us a drastically different view of the texts. While traditional biblical scholars acknowledge the historical contexts and humanity of the texts, feminist theologians and scholars have identified the gender bias, part of which was present in the culture of the time, and part of which was added in later translations. It is this gender bias, this naming of God as male and all things male as superior, which has fortified the current patriarchal structure under which women struggle today.[4]

What I had never considered was that the Bible I was reading was itself someone's translation. Coming back to the problem with the passages in Ephesians and Galatians, and using my own experience as one element in making meaning, I find that I can question the severity of Ephesians by remembering the historical context: Paul was writing to an early church where structure was desired. In his letter to the Galatians, he was addressing a bickering church where feuding and competition were rife. Here, he quells the argument with a simple statement of equality: "you are all one in Christ Jesus." I find there is much to be said for this last imperative statement. It seems that in Galations 3:28, the Bible itself questions and corrects its own patriarchal hierarchy. If we are all one in Christ Jesus, then the patriarchal hierarchy is null and void. Gender and class become irrelevant as criteria for who or what will be considered superior. There are those who criticize extracting a passage as 'picking and choosing' to prove a point. But all preaching is based on choosing a passage, and whole denominations and sects have been organized around just such a particular point of view.

Passages such as those quoted in Ephesians are central to the way several fundamentalist churches understand and enforce family structure. For them, ultimate power and authority reside in the male. I once watched as a fundamentalist Christian father seized the arm of his almost three-year-old child and said to her in a stern, loud voice, "I'm not playing now. I am instructing you in order to correct your depraved nature!" The little girl hadn't seen much of her father all day, and wanted him to look at her. So she started giggling and touching him, trying to get his attention. When he yelled at her, she looked stricken and embarrassed. We may understand his loss of patience, but his course of action was based on the fundamentalist Christian premise that all children are born with a depraved nature which must be controlled and squelched in order for them to become obedient.

More horrid yet was the fact that the child's mother did not protect or soothe her. Under the fundamentalist authoritarian system, it would be unthinkable for the mother to intervene. To do so would be to question the father's authority and would be contrary to the Household Codes. What was a normal assertion on the part of the child was considered selfish and manipulative by the parents. The little girl looked to her mother, who turned away; she looked back to her father, who still looked angry; finally, she just lowered her head in humiliation. Indeed, the behavior stopped temporarily. This little girl probably learned to stifle her spontaneous bursts of affection for her father. She probably judged as bad her desire for his attention because she will have been reminded over and over again that she was born with a depraved nature. She probably submerged her natural self and became a 'good girl.' But at what price?

In extreme cases, the Household Codes have been invoked to justify spousal and child abuse. Because the authority of the father must be unquestioned, a spanking can turn into a beating. Because the authority of the husband must be unquestioned, physical force is not only tolerated by the wife but may in fact be used on her by her husband, either to 'keep her in line' or to claim his 'marital privileges' in sex.

In our patriarchal society, much of our legislation reflects the influence of the Codes. The way rape is handled in our judicial system is a prime example. It is a well-known fact that a woman who is raped is not taken seriously if she bears no signs of a violent struggle (cuts, bruises, internal injuries). Without outward signs of brutal force, she may well find herself being accused of provocation. What was she wearing? Was she walking alone at night? Were her bedroom windows unlocked? Seekers of justice call this attitude 'blaming the victim.' A rape conviction is very difficult to get and if it seems that the woman 'was asking for it,' the male is declared innocent.

An equally insidious and even more difficult situation for women is 'date rape' or 'mate rape.' This occurs when a woman is forced by her companion or spouse to have sex against her will. Prosecution in such cases is very difficult because the underlying assumption is that her presence with the man in the first place connotes tacit agreement on her part. He may say, "She really wanted it; she gets turned on when I force her; she likes to play hard-to-get." The arrogance of these statements reflects the ultimate authority of the male in the Household Codes: he knows better than she what she wants. That such statements are upheld in our courts of law reflect the pervasive influence of the Codes in our society.

Under the Household Codes, children must submit without question to the male in authority. In too many households, this submission involves incest. If our patriarchal society supports male domination, then how does a child justify, even to herself, protesting a touch that 'feels bad' or a request to touch him? The increased cases of reported incest do not reflect more incest now than before; the increase reflects a greater incidence of reporting due to a shift in contemporary thinking since the feminist movement.

In this area, Freud has much to answer for. Early in his practice of psychotherapy, Freud noted that a majority of his female clients reported incidents of incest. So striking was the prevalence of these accounts that he drew a correlation between the sexual abuse and the current neurosis of the patient. This was a new theory, so he wrote about it in a paper he planned to present at a prestigious medical conference. On the advice of a colleague, Freud left the findings out of his paper and later recanted his incest theory. Instead he named the dynamic the 'sexual fantasies' of women. Freud's patients were prominent women from socially powerful families. To have maintained his original observation would have implied that the men in these families were sex abusers. It was far easier and more politically astute to blame the female victims. The theory of women's 'sexual fantasies and wishes' is still with us today. Occasionally a woman's problem may indeed be a fantasy or wish, but this theory calls into question all the victim's memories with sexual connotations and undermines her own confidence in her experience.[5]

Less dramatic and more subtle in homes invoking the Household Codes is the disappearance of the woman as an equal partner to her husband and, often, as a person to herself. She becomes a reflection of him, as she is exhorted to be, and can only assert herself in very subtle or devious ways. In the fundamentalist scheme, this is called 'femininity'—having some influence without anyone noticing. She would probably not contradict her husband in public or administer discipline directly to the children for major infractions. The famous line, "Just wait till your father gets home!" is a signal that the woman has authority only until the man returns to the scene. If she is a truly 'good Christian wife' she will come to this submission on her own without his force. She will give up her self voluntarily because it is 'God's will.'

I recently met a woman who told me about suffering a major depression many years ago. She and her young family had just moved to a new city, her husband's job was in question, and she was utterly alone. She went to her minister for counsel. In essence he told her to pull herself together for the sake of the family and that in so doing, God would bless her. She ended up in a mental hospital undergoing shock treatments and heavy medication. Later she said, "What I really needed was someone to talk it out with." How might her life have been different if that minister had just listened to her? Where was the benevolent and protective father-image she was seeking?

Benevolence and protection have also been profoundly absent from the lives of slaves, the last subservient group mentioned in the Codes. The phrase "slaves, obey your masters" was often invoked to support slavery in the United States before the Civil War and is used to defend abuse of underpaid laborers today. The Codes regarding slaves listed in I Peter 2:18-21 are particularly destructive. They tell slaves that it is noble to suffer, that God is pleased with it, and that this is their lot in life. "What credit is there in fortitude when you have done wrong and are beaten for it? But when you have behaved well and suffer for it, your fortitude is a fine thing in the sight of God. To that you were called, because Christ suffered on your behalf, and thereby left you an example, it is for you to follow in his steps."[6] While I do not believe that a literal interpretation is correct here, I know that this sentiment has been used to assuage the consciences of slumlords, cruel prison guards, and legislators who refuse to confront the greed that deprives some of enough so that others may have abundance.

Most cruel of all is the interpretation of the words, "to that you were called" which takes away hope for the victim. Street drugs to anesthetize the pain make sense in this context of hopelessness. If these 'less-than' groups (women, children, and slaves) are to be submissive, and if this submission is the will of God, how could they complain? What about the man who is 'head' of his house? Not only does he have enormous power, he has been given enormous responsibility to carry without the support of a real mate and equal partner. The patriarchal model is a trap for everyone.

It is my growing conviction that the patriarchy which I see present in the roots of modern psychology is the same patriarchy which automatically grows out of our biblical heritage. Without the undergirding of religious patriarchy, psychology might have taken a different course. Theologian Rosemary Radford Ruether provides a succinct and potent summary when she says, "religion has been not only a contributing factor, it is undoubtedly the single most important shaper and enforcer of the image and role of women in culture and society."[7]

By questioning any premise which undercuts the humanity of any group of people or, conversely, exalts any group at the expense of others, we may all begin to claim the dignity and legitimacy of our whole selves. This means women and men might then be free to express the full spectrum of emotions and feelings without judging or being judged.

This freedom would also apply to God, who would then be free to grieve with us at tragedy and rejoice with us in our growth and maturity. Released from the patriarchal model of an untouchable and removed power, this would be a God who would be in relationship with us, touched by us, as indeed we are touched. It would look and feel more like the God revealed by Jesus as he openly laughed, wept, lashed out, and loved everyone equally.

Questioning the very roots of our religious and social heritage is not easy. It takes courage and requires support. None of us has done it alone. It is important to find like-minded people, groups, or writers who share this perspective. We must claim our right to support. If psychotherapy fits, we must be sure we feel understood and respected by the therapist. If this dynamic is missing in a therapeutic relationship, we should leave it and find another.

There is a price for this questioning. Some people will be angry with us and we, in turn, may find ourselves disappointed with individuals and institutions which didn't bother us before. But the payoff is feeling valid and empowered as a woman and a human being. The challenge is to persevere, for the sake of ourselves, our daughters, and all the daughters who follow, that we all might experience an equal, compassionate and more whole world.

Jean Young has been a licensed psychotherapist in private practice in Los Angeles, Ca., for over fifteen years. She did her graduate work at Antioch College specializing in psychology and child development. Her special interests are women's issues and eating disorders in women. She has taught and consulted at hospitals, corporations and institutions, including UCLA, for many years. Jean enjoys leading retreats for lay women and clergywomen. She has been married to a Methodist minister for sixteen years and has earned a Master's degree in Feminist Spirituality from Immaculate Heart College, Los Angeles. She is intimately aware of balancing roles while maintaining herself as a woman.

You shall love the nothing
Flee the self
Stand alone
Seek help from no one
Let your being be quiet
Be free of the bondage of all things.

MECHTILD OF MAGDEBURG

Freedom and Spirituality: Archetypes and Biology

by

Sarah Eagger, M.D.

*T*he issues within freedom for women are changing. They are moving from the external, political ones to involve internal aspects of consciousness. We are becoming aware of the spiritual, psychological, and behavioral areas within woman herself. The socio-cultural doubts of whether women could perform as well as men have largely been dispelled, while other, more subtle, influences obstructing a woman's path to freedom are being revealed.

Archetypes and Models

The role of archetypes in the psychological development of women is being revived as a key to wholeness. Myth and symbol are very relevant to the development of a positive psychology for women. Within both the Greek and Indian traditions the goddesses are seen as those with wealth. This wealth is not physical (although it may be symbolically represented as such), but spiritual. It is a sign of her completeness, the richness of her femininity, her power to sustain life: the earth mother. It would appear that women have become impoverished due to their lack of self-awareness and their sense of self as an object. This has meant that we see ourselves as objects rather than as those with the wealth to sustain the world. Time is encouraging us to move away from this object consciousness and take personal responsibility for the fact that we, through our own ignorance, have sold ourselves short.

Certainly the more powerful psychological theories of our time have contributed to this sense of impoverishment. Freud tended to describe women in terms of what they lacked anatomically. This perspective maimed women and made them inferior. In his view they suffered penis envy, were masochistic, narcissistic, and had inferior consciences. If competent, self assured, and accomplished, they were exhibiting a "masculinity complex." Jung, on the other hand, describes women as "feminine-conscious personality" with a masculine component called animus in their unconscious and men as a "masculine-conscious personality" with a feminine anima in their unconscious. These terms have had popular currency but there are further developments of his theory that are inherently oppressive. He sees the feminine personality as characterized by receptivity, passivity, nurturing, and subjectivity whereas the masculine personality is characterized by rationality, spirituality, and a capacity to act decisively and impersonally. Jung believed that a woman's capacity to think was inferior, and if she was competent in the world it was only because she had a well developed masculine animus, which was, by definition, less conscious and inferior to man's. The functions of the animus that Jung emphasized were those of being hostile, driven by power, and irrationally opinionated. He didn't see women as inherently less creative, but as less able to be objective or take action. Generally he saw women as they served and related to men rather than as having independent needs of their own. He discouraged women's striving to achieve and felt that taking up what he called a masculine profession was doing something not wholly in accord with her feminine nature.

Those things which have been "taken away" from women either through society, men, or psychological interpretations have up to now been the main issues addressed by political action. As we move into the spiritual realm the question, What have I done to sell myself short? becomes implicit. When addressing things of the spirit we have to acknowledge that we are more than the bodies we live in. The area of "psyche" applies to both male and female, and on many different levels the man within woman and the woman within man is becoming evident.

Biological Evidence

Neuro-biologically, what was once thought to be instinctive is now recognized as learned behavior. The belief that the social behavior of men and women is a natural extension of some predetermined biological set is being challenged. Most significant are the split-brain studies, (principally by psychologist Dr. Robert Ornstein at the Langley Porter Institute in San Francisco), that have identified that certain skills of conceptual and intellectual abilities are associated with specific anatomic locales of the brain.[1]

Left Brain	Right Brain
Day	Night
Intellect	Intuition
Time	Timelessness
Active	Receptive
Explicit	Tacit
Analytic	Synthesizing
Propositional	Aesthetic
Lineal	Non-lineal
Sequential	Simultaneous
Focal	Diffuse
Verbal	Spatial
Causal	Inductive
Argumentative	Sensory
Masculine	Feminine

The implications of this discovery are profound. It means that each male with a functioning right hemisphere has available to him the abilities which are culturally considered to be female. Similarly, the qualities of masculinity are available to each female through her left hemisphere. Our culture creates prototypes of maleness and femaleness by subtly and continually rewarding different behavior in boys than girls.

Beyond the Brain

It is to the inner part of the human being, to the "psyche" which these brain hemispheres subserve, that we now need to turn our attention. One could postulate that as this innermost part is spirit and able to survive death or even to exist in other lifetimes, the experience of being either a woman or a man has been available to each of us. We are neither male nor female but something more. As this awareness increases, the concept of androgen becomes tangible. Some archetypes within Hindu mythology show four-armed figures which depict the perfect balance of masculine and feminine qualities. Within that culture, folklore about the time when earth was paradise describes the differences between men and women as slight. Harmony is seen within the self and externally in nature. This can be contrasted with the extreme polarization of masculinity and femininity today and the external discord and destructiveness of the human race. Changing the current socio-political climate of our world is profoundly linked to balancing the masculine and feminine aspects of the self. We need to move from polarization towards maturity.

Barriers to Harmony

What is it that prevents us from regaining equilibrium? Strong identification with either body type places limits on us to being either male or female. A lack of balance implies overemphasis to either superiority or inferiority. If we are neither of these, then we are free. Clearly the identification and resolution of those things which place us in bondage is not a simple task, yet we also know that misuse, manipulation and artifice is not really what we want. To be true to ourselves means knowing, on an inward level, who we are and allowing that to come out of the eclipse of conditioning, both societal and educational. Psychoanalyst Clara Thompson wrote in the 1940's that, "Even when a woman has become consciously convinced of her value she still has to contend with the unconscious effects of training, discrimination against her, and traumatic experiences which keep alive the attitude of inferiority."[2]

Becoming aware of the cultural bias is realizing that in some way we are metapsychological beings packaged in a culture. Our spirit cannot be seen, but our bodies are the cultural vehicle for it. It's a bit like selling fresh air in cans. We have to understand this distinction without denial of, nor disassociation from, our bodies. However innocently, we have still used the female body to gain things. This eventually leads to abuse. The blatant use of the female body to sell products is an example of our culture's condonation and insidious encouragement. Strong feelings of indignation or even rage have been aroused in many women as a reaction to the conditioning that our only value lies in how attractive we are to men.

Knowledge is Strength

How do we develop a sense of self which encompasses the true feminine qualities of being a sustainer of life? Again, within Hindu mythology the shaktis are powerful women goddesses remembered for destroying evil and ignorance. Saraswati, for example, is known as the goddess of knowledge. To comprehend spiritual information at the deepest level and articulate it, that is this goddess within. The possessor of that knowledge comprehends it often when no one else can. This kind of self-revelation—where one has the experience of "original thought"—is so very rare in our society of processed thinking that one can feel lonely, 'out on a limb,' or even crazy when stepping the path of self-exploration. As one becomes more connected, the clarity of what makes sense and what doesn't becomes evident.

Spiritual education is the key to liberation for women. Traditionally women have been discouraged from being educated because educated women were seen as a threat, not corresponding to the idea that they should be an object for men. However, men who are developing spiritually are also moving toward ideals of the feminine. So we women must address those things in ourselves that have led to the sellout. We have settled for less due to our conditioning. Our acceptance has bought with it insecurity. Our conscience feels uneasy because we are holding on to an idea that is dissonant with our true selves. This spiritual inaccuracy causes loss to that true self. The fact that we are taught to consider ourselves as weak has obvious harmful effects, but the same self-depreciation may also be present in men. We have to look deeper. By drawing on the powerful female archetypes we can respond in a truthful manner that will have a subtle but profound role in making society function in harmony.

Dependency

The main issue revealed as thwarting women's path to freedom is her own dependency. Dependent behavior can be defined as the normal infant's way of relating to people. Later, in children and in adults, it seems to be a way of dealing with stress, a reaction to frustration, or a protection against future frustration. There can be affectionate, coping, or aggressive types of dependent behavior: Affectionate—grasping or forcing affectionate or protective behavior from someone else. Coping—getting help to solve a problem that you can't solve on your own. Aggressive—grabbing attention or affection for yourself to prevent others from receiving it. In all cases dependence is leaning on someone else to supply support.[3] It should be recognized that dependent people also show aggression by criticizing. It is a common response in those with low self-esteem and anxiety. Women's anger towards men has also been described as a 'character defense,' a way of fending off dangerous feelings of dependency.[4]

Karen Horney, a renowned psychoanalyst and contemporary of Freud, in a paper called "The Overvaluation of Love" commented that many women in a patriarchal society have a desire to love a man and be loved that is compulsive and driven in its extremeness. They are not able to have good and lasting relations with men; they are inhibited in their work, impoverished in their interests, and often end up feeling anxious, inadequate, and even ugly. In some cases they develop compulsive drives for achievement which, instead of following up themselves, they project onto male partners. Horney draws the distinction between a healthy and spontaneous need for love and one that is compulsive, self-serving, and neurotic.[5]

Clara Thompson also states that "woman lives in a culture which provides no security for her except a permanent so-called love relationship. It is known that the neurotic need of love is a mechanism for establishing security in a cultural situation producing dependency. Being 'loved' not only is part of a woman's natural life in the same way as it is part of a man's, but it also becomes, of necessity, her profession."[6] Elizabeth Douvan[7] suggests that girls deliberately strive for a lack of definition, a colorlessness, because they need to remain fluid and malleable in personal identity in order to adapt to the needs of the men they marry. This reflects forces that are felt more or less by most girls in our culture. There have also been studies between recognition for achievement and attempts to get love and affection than in boys. Girls are involved in achieving as a way of securing love and approval whereas boys achieve more for its own sake.

By defining personal development holistically and dynamically we see the individual and society, internal and external forces, present and past influences are all mutually interacting and effecting the personality, its defenses and symptoms, in a multifactorial way. This shifts the interpretation of women's inferiority from such irreconcilable concepts as "penis envy" to take into account current life situations and destructive attitudes. The conflicting desires of a woman's need to be loved and her equally strong wish to reject that need are one of the major forces that keep her bound. We wish to be both free and safe. Statistics may corroborate this conflict; they show that the mental health of married women is worse than that of single women, or of single or married men. If we both cause and maintain neurosis within ourselves, then there also lies within us the ways, means, and strengths to change it. Hopelessness in external circumstances will not really do the trick. The paradigm of personal responsibility has more optimism. To become one's own person, to take responsibility for one's own existence is to create one's own life. This shift from other to self makes more energy available to nourish our inner dependency. Freedom and independence cannot be wrested from others, from society at large, or from men; they can only be developed painstakingly from within. To achieve it means giving up dependencies.

The Way Out

Unfortunately, women have tried to break free by imitating the apparently stronger male traits. This has led to high materialistic expectations for success and achievement. In this way our freedom is eroded and eventually backfires because somewhere along the way we give up our spiritual power. In this situation men and women are equal. We are, as a race, having to face our need to develop spiritually. This has to be done consciously, of our own free will, and not by the force of circumstance. It requires inner work (What are our values? What is success?) and matching our inner and outer worlds. This means exploring androgyny where we are not limited by externals. It means transcending the extremes of materialism, knowing that at the point of extremity a thing becomes its opposite. It means addressing what we have done and what we have allowed to be done to us; taking responsibility for being both manipulated and the manipulator and breaking out of these cycles. Identifying the contradictions within and beginning to work through them is a process. As dependency is a mechanism for defending against insecurity, we must begin to identify what our deeper insecurities are.

Melanie Kleine, a well known post-Freudian child analyst, speaks of our fear of annihilation as stemming from our infant's ignorance that mother will return and feed us. This fear can be re-enacted in later relationships through a process known as 'fusion.' Fusion, psychoanalytically speaking, is the attempt to recapture a state of primitive empathy (such as that an infant has with its mother when there is no perception of individuality), and avoid separateness. To do this means to forgo intuitive and mature empathy. Perhaps the sexual act itself can be interpreted as an attempt to experience fusion, that is, not boundaries between self and other.

We can trace the fear of annihilation still further. On a spiritual level it stems from our ignorance of what the self really is. We do not "know," in an experiential sense, what will happen to us if our bodies are destroyed. We fear that if we are separated from our bodies we will no longer exist. As our bodies are external and obvious we tend to identify with them. The identification overemphasizes the sexuality of that body in order to try and stabilize our identity. This type of identification then extends into other obvious external material things around which we build our sense of self, for example, status, possessions, roles, achievements. The inherent paradox in this type of behavior is that it is the nature of matter to change and transmute, yet we look to it for our sense of stability and security.

The Root of the Problem

Intrapsychic conflict arising in the instinctual realm was Freud's analysis of the human predicament. This force for life, 'eros,' with its libidinal energy works in opposition to the death instinct, 'thanatos.' He did, however, also describe the 'nirvana principle' as the tendency of the psychical apparatus to reduce the quantity of excitation in itself, whether of internal or external origin, to zero, or as low a level as possible. Drawn from Buddhism, the term 'nirvana' connotes the extinction of human desire, a state of quietude and bliss. This radical tendency to reduce excitation to zero point is something more than his principle of constancy or of homeostasis. According of that principle, 'constancy' is achieved on one hand through discharge of energy already present, and on the other hand avoidance of whatever might increase the quantity of excitation, and defense against any such increase that does occur. The word 'nirvana' evokes a profound link between pleasure and returning to zero—a link that always remained problematic for Freud.[8]

If we understand, however, that the intrinsic nature of the self is to be distinct, individual, and free, then this resonates with our true reality and is experienced as a lack of psychic conflict (in the deepest sense), and profound pleasure or bliss. This tendency to zero is in fact the underlying motivation for much of our behavior. The pleasure principle is achieved through release from the ego. We seek to emulate this by temporarily escaping from our egos by a variety of physical means. The root of addictive behavior can be seen as the soul's desire to experience this true state of self. To be 'out of your mind' on drugs or to experience 'the little death' through sexual climax are examples.

Addictive, dependent behavior in relationships is, in fact, an attempt to reconcile the need to experience constant love and security with the illusion that it is obtained through something or someone else. To be able to experience consciously that I am more than my body, more than my masculinity or femininity, or right and left cerebral hemispheres, or cultural conditioning, is in fact to be bodiless, silent, 'zero,' but still intact and whole. To experience this bodilessness is wholly satisfying and is the essence of spirituality. This kind of knowing about my real identity has to be experienced to be of any real use to me. It is something that cannot be just theoretical information. It is the process of spiritual development and requires discipline, and often a lot of pain, to relinquish all the previously held beliefs about what I am. But ultimately it is the only thing that will teach me about my own eternal integrity and freedom.

Filling the Defects

Superseding the Freudian models that say the cause of psychic conflicts is due to opposing instincts and objects, Self Psychology, pioneered by Kuhn, sees these conflicts as the 'result' of defects in the self rather than the primary 'causes.' These primary inner conflicts are seen to arise as a result of structural deficiencies, distortions, and weaknesses in the self. The self struggles to maintain its coherence in the face of continual threats to its integrity. The self is seen as a 'particular structure' where goals and values are experienced as a cohesive harmonious unit in time and space, connected to the past and pointing meaningfully into the creative-productive future.

Jung also spoke of the process of 'individualization' where one is becoming aware that one is separate to and different from others, and able to recognize oneself as a whole indivisible person. Within ontology, a branch of metaphysics dealing with the nature of being, 'self-consciousness' has been described as the awareness of oneself, as a being with a center, who affirms and participates with other beings. The primary security derived from this awareness arises from a centrally firm sense of one's own and others' reality. Therefore it appears we have a structure of the self as an indivisible unit whose conflicts arise due to certain deficiencies.

To begin to replenish those deficiencies is to understand that I have lost my spiritual wealth—my own purity, peace, love, and power. It requires a resolute search for the source of these qualities both within myself and universally. These are the qualities that enable me as a whole, mature being to sustain both myself and others. They are not qualities that I need from others, rather my own fundamental properties that I share with others. In the same way that the body draws into itself those things of which it is made, that is, water, oxygen, organic compounds, and minerals, the spirit, my 'self,' also draws to itself those things which are primary to it. Our attraction to and need for love, peace, contentment, will, happiness, freedom—for pure self essence, in fact—reflects that this is what I am. Manifested in life, these fundamental qualities blossom into a variety of skills and attributes. They can develop into virtues or power and enhance and enliven any situation with truth.

Let us take, for example, the quality of purity. Jean Shinoda Bolen has developed this theme after the work of Esther Harding in her description of the archetype of the 'virgin goddesses,' likening virginity or purity to that quality of being one-in-herself:

A woman who is one-in-herself does what she does not because of any desire to please; not to be liked or to be approved, even by herself; not because of any desires to gain power over another, to catch his interest or love but because what she does is true. Her actions may indeed be unconventional. She may have to say no when it would be easier, as well as more adapted, conventionally speaking, to say yes. She is not influenced by the considerations that would make another trim her sails and adapt to expediency. If a woman is one-in-herself, she will be motivated by a need to follow her own inner values, to do what has meaning or fulfills herself—apart from what other people think.

Psychologically, the virgin goddess is that part of a woman that has not been worked on, either by the collective (masculine-determined) social and cultural expectations of what a woman should be, or by an individual males' judgment of her. The virgin goddess aspect is a pure essence of who the woman is and of what she values. It remains untarnished and uncontaminated because she does not reveal it; because she keeps it sacred and inviolate, or because she expresses it without modification to meet male standards.[9]

We begin to see that the things that distress us, our defects, are just that—deficiencies in the primary properties of our true essence. Anger is an example. Rather than a 'thing in itself' or a primary instinctual force, anger is present due to the lack of the experience of eternal, self-existent peace. Hatred is seen as a lack of love, arrogance the ignorance of the true nature of things, greed the inability to be nurtured spiritually. Misdirecting my sense of identity towards my body, until it is derived only from my body, has led to my desire for external validation and reassurance in all that I do.

Freedom from Freedom

It is real freedom to be liberated from these desires and tendencies. It means we lose our fear, both of ourselves and others. It implies a 'wholeheartedness' that Karen Horney describes as the ability to be without pretense, emotionally sincere, and to be able to put the whole of oneself into one's feelings, one's work, and one's beliefs. This gives an emotional mobility to be able to move towards things that are satisfying and away from those things that are not; to be free to succeed and free to love others because of loving oneself. It is being able to let go of the destructive or damaging experiences of the past by realizing the lessons they have taught and transforming them into a potent, motivating force for change. This true, refreshing, spontaneous independence means that we are more emotionally available to respond to any situation or person. Not because of our own needs in a situation but because we have tapped, within ourselves, the resources that enable us to do so. These are the resources of the spirit, that begin before masculinity or femininity but can seek expression beautifully through whichever prism they choose. Knowing that they come from me, and that in some sense they are me, means owning them rather than relegating them to some opposite-sexed part of myself. This rise above duality and polarity is the journey back to one-centeredness, one-pointedness, that leaves behind limitations and gently soars towards the ocean of all possibilities. Freedom is being able to fly.

Sarah Eagger, MBBS, MRCPsych specializes in psychiatry in London, England. Her various appointments have included the Tavistock Clinic and the Royal Free Hospital and the Institute of Neurology and the National Hospital, Queen Square.

Dr. Eagger is an active member of the Brahma Kumaris World Spiritual University based in Mt. Abu, India.

Dr. Eagger is on the councils of the Scientific and Medical Network, the British Holistic Medical Association, and S.I.G.M.A. An assistant editor of the British Holistic Medical Journal, she also travels and lectures on meditation in many countries including Australia, India, Europe, the United States, and the British Isles.

If people were told: what makes carnal desire imperious in you is not its pure carnal element. It is the fact that you put into it the essential part of yourself—the need for Unity, the need for God—they wouldn't believe it.

<small>SIMONE WEIL</small>

Sex and Spirituality:
Sexuality as Holiness

by

Joan Timmerman, Ph.D.

omen's experience of God is an important topic of discussion in theology as well as a concern for personal spirituality. Those who have identified themselves as feminists and engaged in a spiritual journey have felt that the burden of proof has been upon them to identify that process—to discern what in it is distinguishable from men's experience of God and from traditional religion, and to find words to formulate that which begins and ends as wordless, self-validating experience. The outcome has been fortuitous. Thinking and talking about women's experience of God has empowered women, both those who spoke and those who listened. It has liberated the theology of God from ways of thinking about the divine that are exclusively masculine in imagery and language. God has thus been rediscovered by countless women and men as Mystery, as the Nameless One who answers to many names, as Mother, Friend, Lover, Holy Wisdom, even Wife (Helpmate, as is translated in the Psalms).

Yet this great advance toward a spirituality in which the God who calls speaks with a woman's voice and can be known as the Image in which women are is only one-half the task. It reclaims the transcendent reality of God from being imprisoned in finite forms that have forgotten their finitude. The other half of the task is to reclaim the sacred reality of female sexuality that has forgotten its transcendence.

That process is also underway in the unexpressed certainty of many centered individuals and in the searching anguish of the many who feel torn apart by the rival claims of their sexual desires. The majority have just never put together their sexual expectations with the awareness of a desire for God. They may not be consciously disturbed by that dichotomy, or the absence of a felt connection, but in fact they are settling for an experience of human life which delivers less than can be promised. Our birthright as sexual beings is the potential for sexual experience that is a vehicle for and sign of divine love.

In this exploration, I will begin with some assumptions and definitions of terms, then move to an analysis of some cycles through which one can expect to move in the integration of her sexual and spiritual impulses, and finally propose some practical steps that may help in finding the way to a sexual maturity that resonates with spiritual growth.

Assumptions and Definitions

While our relationships to God and others are grounded in preverbal experience, rational formulations of truth can either enhance or obstruct and caricature those relationships. In a word, theological insight can be the source of spiritual awareness. Even so, unexamined, uncorrected, outdated theological (or biological, historical or political) doctrine can prevent integration of the whole person. I list some definitions and statements of relation in the interests of challenging such half truths, as well as being clear about what positions I find persuasive. Since they have been developed elsewhere, they will not be argued, only indicated here.[1]

1. Nobody lives well who is not spiritually well. Humans need to be connected with the cosmic, the sacred, the mysterious, the transcendent. One could characterize the spiritual life as the conversation—sometimes interrupted, sometimes lively, but always ongoing—with that unknown with which one is connected.

2. Sex is good. The impression that has been so widespread and so destructive in the Western world, that there is an ancient enmity between the sexual impulse and the "higher" faculties of the person, can be explained and refuted through the analysis of philosophical, historical, political, and socioeconomic ideas which depended upon the subordination of the physical to the rational, and wrongheadedly reduced sexuality to a function of the physical body.

3. "Sexuality," as used in this essay and increasingly in educational materials, refers to the entire range of feelings and behaviors which human beings have and use as embodied persons in the world, and by which their relationship to themselves and others is expressed, through grace, touch, word, and action. While sexual vitality is a matter of hormones and physical states revealed in the movement of particular organs and their physiological response to stimuli, it is not reducible to the material or hormonal. It is required to express the mind and imagination, knowledge and memory, of the person, and might be said to be in relation to the body somewhat as the mind is to the brain. My sexuality is not a faculty of my body but of my person, as is my intelligence, my will, and my spirituality.

4. Human sexuality has a history. It does not exist in God's mind, but in finite human persons. It is "made, not born"; among humans it belongs to culture, not nature. Although its dysfunctions are not well understood because not often studied, they can be caused and cured. Sexuality is valued and feared and buried under an unwritten rule of silence. To challenge that silence, even in our own minds, is a fearful thing. Therefore the 'history' of human sexuality, either as a formal account of human becoming or as informal stories of personal pain and fulfillment, remains unwritten. So long as this is the case, individuals feel isolated and alone, each feeling odd and inadequate for a different set of reasons, while the ideal of human sexuality remains unattainable, functioning more effectively as a paralyzing source of guilt than as energy for fulfillment and maturity.

5. Thoughts and actions arising from human sexual potential are morally significant although neither more nor less so than other actions that call upon the whole of an adult. In fact, one might be able to ascertain the progress of an individual person toward "agency," that is, the ability to function as a decisive

adult, from the level of responsibility they take as subject of their own sexual acts. The person who is used as sexual object is abused, but the person who never can function as sexual subject is morally undeveloped. It has been anomalous within the Christian moral tradition that single actions of a sexual nature were presumed, without consideration for knowledge, consent, or circumstances, to represent a moral "option,"[2] that is, to carry the seriousness of a habit of mind and heart. Thus any acts of deliberately induced sexual arousal would have been judged either to be blameless (as within legal, heterosexual marriage) or mortally sinful (as in any other circumstances).

The presupposition of sexual acts having greater moral weight than other kinds of actions and of being more likely to lead to sin follows from a number of intellectual errors, two of which will be examined here. One mistake was to define coitus, or more precisely the impregnation of the female, as the explicit goal and intentionality of all sexual feelings and actions, and the only justifying purpose of sexual pleasure. The second was to affirm that in terms of the material act (not considering motive or circumstances or consequences) there is no lesser or greater moral significance between particular acts. In other words, there are no "single acts" in sexual life. The effect on individuals, especially women who internalized this perception, was that there could be no mistakes in the arena of sexual relation that were not sins of the worst kind. Contrary to biblical teaching, the popular mind considered one who had 'fallen' sexually to be guilty of the "unforgivable sin." In the consciousness of some women this produced a permanent state of guilt, since most women neither were nor could be in total personal control of their sexual reproductive lives. Few clearly chose their sexual life; most acquiesced to what family, society, or partners chose for them. As the most dangerous moral area, the sexual sphere was also the one least one's own to control. No wonder the questions of sexual morality, when not irrelevant textbook exercises, looked more like taboos than proactive principles to guide a holy and happy life. No wonder they were enforced with sanctions (often by women against women), maintained with fear and ignorance, and surrounded with religious legitimation rather than examined, evaluated and appropriated through education.

6. Sexual identity and gender role refer to aspects of the human being's development to normal adulthood. The term sexual identity refers to the fact that identity as a male or female is assigned to an individual according to their genital organs. When persons speak of crises in the development of "sexual identity," however, they are often referring to confusion, not about being male or female, but about being sexually attracted to the same or opposite sex. Strictly speaking, one's sexual identity is not in terms of being heterosexual or homosexual. Those terms are of very recent usage. One's sexual identity is in terms of being male or female. In contrast to the anatomical determination of sexual identity, gender role as masculine or feminine is much more ambiguous, being the product of cultural conditioning, family patterns, and religious sacralization of particular characteristics or values. While it is obvious that a functioning adult needs a clear sense of gender role (What is it for me to be a valued and effective woman in this

social and political world?) it is equally obvious in our time that an overly restrictive separation of roles between males and females and a too-complete identification of the person with her role can stand in the way of personal, social, professional, and spiritual development.

7. Human potentialities are given to be developed. As this is true with regard to physical grace and strength as well as intellectual and artistic power, so it is with sexual potential. Sexuality is a gift given by the Creator to the human race and to each individual human. As the relational and reproductive impulse, sexual potential is a coin to be cherished and invested, with its dividends distributed widely. The norm and expectation, therefore, must be toward sexual activity. The form and frequency of that activity stands under the same sort of guidelines that limit and enable all other human development within an interpersonal context of freedom and justice. Sexual self-expression will be virtuous insofar as it expresses and causes love and justice, peace and growth, joy and beauty, life that is centered and productive.

There is a lingering perception that the norm is, or ought to be, complete sexual continence, at least, abstinence from coitus, and that those who cannot achieve such a lofty ideal should be allowed sexual activity only within limits strictly controlled by an external norm, (for procreation, without "lust," within marriage). Such limits, at certain times, for certain people, within certain situations are appropriate, but to insist that the normative human life is to be without sexual expression, development, or responsibility is a concept that was bootlegged into the Christian tradition from Montanism in the third century, and remains deeply rooted long after it was declared heretical and pernicious.[3] The idea that one has to choose between a serious spiritual and an active sexual life remains one of the implicit and unexamined assumptions of religion. For most women for most of history, that choice meant acquiescence to their sexual destiny and the internalization of the notion that they belonged more to the flesh than the spirit, more to the husband who needed her services than to the Holy God who called her by name. While the history of women who chose the spiritual way by making the choice against sexual expression of their womanhood is glorious, it stands as a reminder of the dualism inherited with the tradition.

All of this is simply to assert that there are good reasons for thinking that one's sexuality is neither inimical nor irrelevant to one's spiritual growth. In fact, a pattern can be discerned by which the realities of sexual awakening and spiritual development may be recognized as proceeding in tandem.

Recognizable Cycles toward Spiritual-Sexual Wholeness

Why is it so much easier to call to mind examples of persons whose sexuality is a problem or whose spirituality marks them as otherworldly than of those who have attained integration of both? One reason, of course, is the lack of data. The problematic and eccentric become data for the daily journalistic record. The integrated and the centered, the wise ones, have not had their stories told in sufficient depth and detail to serve as signs of hope through the everyday morass of small decisions, necessary functions and unfulfilled longings. Positive models are not rare, but their narratives are, as are the formulations of critical turning points at which they made right choices, or perhaps more accurately, made choices rightly. To imagine the goal—a life characterized by interacting sexual vitality and spiritual maturity—is not a luxury for persons who have already had to take the entrance onto the freeway of their life. Like it or not, every adult human being is on a sexual journey. If a pattern can be discerned by which a fulfilled sexual life is lived in spiritual awareness, it would be important to lay it out so that it could be recognized, critiqued, paralleled or even followed. In the interest of discovering what such a well-integrated spiritual sexual life looks like, I have identified various stages, a spiral of cycles, that appear to be common to successful human development. The person who has learned to walk in two worlds has made them one in her own awareness; she might remember, however, that it was an ungainly posture that made the first steps possible. I do not claim that all individuals go through these and only these stages. The pattern is simply described and will be valuable insofar as it is reflected in one's own experience.

Sexual Awakening and Personal Agency

Awareness of oneself as a sexual subject breaks upon a person through a series of events, some tumultuous, some almost imperceptible, by which physiology, culture and personal history intervene to awaken her to her sexual self. This is a process that recurs in a new form whenever life changes drastically or when the person passes a cultural, physical or spiritual milestone. When anything in a system changes, everything must be rearranged and reintegrated for continued harmonious functioning. One may awaken easily to knowledge of one's attractiveness and longing for the company of the other in adolescent awakening, but the same person may struggle with adult sexual decisions in which this hope and longing must be channeled into a particular relationship. Or one may agonize with the fears and tensions of work or parenting, wondering where the sexual ecstasy and playfulness have gone. Not to let the particularity of a finite life with its disappointments, failures, and mistakes confine oneself within a grieving and narrowing world in the older years demands a spirituality that has integrated the narcissistic child, the responsible adult, and the wise elder. The sexual person does not act out the same script over and over. It is more like exploring new roles in a complex and fascinating drama until the richness of self expression makes her more complete as a person and reveals others' potential to them. She finds she has discovered in her freedom to give and receive pleasure the generosity of God, and in the intimacy of her relationship, the divine intensity and depth.

    In the language of theology, the movement from one mode of life to a new transformed life is characterized by three intelligible moments. There is a moment of separation from the previous form of life, an experience in ritual or symbol of death, which in fact produces a psychological letting-go. One then enters a liminal period, in which everything is possible but nothing is fixed. Finally, newness of life is characterized by symbols and rituals of reincorporation, where the individual not only is unified within a new experience of self but is named anew within a community which recognizes and names her as complete. This conversion experience is a pattern articulated in men's spiritual autobiography as well as male patterns of initiation. Women's writing has revealed that her pattern of spiritual growth is less likely to be marked by crisis events in which the whole of a past mode of being is renounced in favor of a new mode. Women's stories of spiritual growth exhibit a greater sense of continuity, aptly expressed in the image of the spiral path, in which there is growth without discontinuity.[4] A woman can, of course, become aware of a stage already passed, and can in that recognition know that she is not odd or unusual, not ahead of or short of the 'norm,' but that she is alive sexually and spiritually, and therefore changing.

The activity most characteristic of the stage of awakening to the power of sexuality and one's call to live it could be called the "shedding of taboos," those prohibitions and superstitions that surround any culture's regulation of sexual interaction. These prohibitions protect a society from unwanted and potentially disruptive sexual expression along with the potential for conflict, uncontrolled reproduction, and emotional satiety. The very worst punishment a society can inflect on its members is exclusion. In primitive societies, if a deviant member is excluded from the group and subjected to rituals of exclusion, the member usually dies. In our civilized society we do not punish nonconformists in such a drastic way. We simply isolate them, refuse them understanding, and declare for them a "death of the soul" rather than physical death. Taboos functioned effectively in past ages and still do for children. They produce a stable order, but not individual moral persons with well developed consciences. The system of taboos is meant to give way to moral reasoning and to the adult ability to see rules in the context of the values they are meant to serve. Shedding these taboos is a sign that a person is taking possession of her own sexuality and making progress toward integrating all aspects of herself into a unified autonomous personality.

Sexual awakening is thus an invitation to take a new step on a spiritual journey. Among the developmental needs of adults with regard to their sexuality are the following:

1. To be able to identify questions concerning sexuality and search out answers from appropriate sources;
2. to recognize sexual dysfunction and seek competent counseling when necessary;
3. to integrate their sexuality into their whole person and into relationships with others;
4. to fulfill the roles of spouse, friend, parent where appropriate;
5. to exhibit values through responsible sexual behavior;
6. to act knowledgeably and positively when involved in sexuality-related cultural and societal conflicts, for example, gay rights, women's liberation, concern for the disabled and elderly, or the debate over the issues involved in legalized abortion;

7. to remain open to new learning through formal and informal educational opportunities and through experience.[5]

It is obvious that each of these needs requires letting go of the particularly rigid silence and external control surrounding every aspect of sexuality other than conventional marriage. In many societies the ritual of the wedding marked the point at which the taboos no longer applied to the couple, and marriage today is still widely thought of as a kind of public permission to be sexual. The list of the sexual needs of the typical adult also implies a taking hold of one's questions, relationships, roles, values, dysfunctions, attitudes toward conflict, and requirement for lifelong education and nurturance.

It requires spiritual discipline to let go and take hold; it is spirituality which gives a person the insight and power to know when to do which. Letting go of a taboo can be an unsettling experience, especially if social order and one's own place in it has appeared to be upheld by those taboos. By "shedding" or "letting go" I mean something quite different from "breaking" the taboo. He who breaks a taboo is still held by it; it can be reinforced as a social power by the sanction imposed. The breaker of taboos is not free, but reverberates between excitement and guilt. Ultimately taboos fail to protect a rational social order, for they are more exciting in their breaking than in their keeping, and even the guilt that they produce makes it more likely that the taboo will be broken again. As psychologists affirm, guilt provides the energy for the continued repetition of unacceptable acts. Moreover, the breaker of the taboo is shamed, loses status and self-esteem, whereas the person who posits an action that is understood to be wrong stands above and judges the action. One's being is diminished by the taboo; one's actions are judged to be wrong because they fall short of expressing the dignity and value one knows to be one's being. It may be a subtle nuance in its conceptual formulation, but the difference is obvious in a lived situation.

As a stage, the shedding of taboos creates new space for an individual to redefine boundaries and commitments. It is not accomplished once and for all but recurs with greater depth toward personal moral freedom. It is a process begun typically in the imagination, not in the intellect. Daydreaming, erotic lyrics in musical compositions, romance or adventure literature, the love imagery of the mystics directed toward the humanity of Jesus, the physical care of oneself through long baths, massage, even applying cosmetics—all are effective ways of recreating one's self image. Shedding taboos about physical touching, psychological intimacy, and sexual arousal prepares one for the two realities of mature sexuality: knowing oneself as receiver and giver of love and reaching out to others. Not surprisingly, these are also the two realities of adult spirituality. One comes into personal power through sexual awakening when one takes hold of one's bodiliness (no longer alienated from oneself because owned by taboos) and one's spiritual destiny (no longer seen as beyond the here and now of one's bodily experience).

The realization of power is one of the signs of growth in the spiritual life. This meaning of power is of course different from that denoting the use of force to overcome the weak. The power that signals growth in spirituality is that shown in gentleness, freedom, compassion, being able to enter into the heart of another. It is more powerful than force because its fruits are efficacy and duration. This kind of power is the ability to love effectively. It produces without fail what it means—a loving person—and it lasts.

Liminality

Another intelligible moment in the process of sexual-spiritual integration is marked by experimentation, if only in the attempt to embody symbolically and culturally the new mode of being one is entering. Philosophers of religion, drawing upon the image of the limen or threshold, refer to the second stage of initiation ritual as liminality. The stage of liminality is characterized by ambiguity, by a sense of being between worlds. As individuals attempt to articulate their self-understanding beyond the taboos and polarizations of prepubertal life, they enter into the difficult task of accepting ambiguity as the adult's way of life. The larger truth of adult lives requires that "shades of gray" are given their due and that the inevitable ambiguity of human life is honored and embraced.

One of the qualities surfaced by Abraham Maslow as characteristic of self-actualizing people is that their talk about sex is considerably more free, casual and unconventional than the average. The 'average' seek simplistic scenarios, whether about good and evil, male and female, or secular and spiritual; the 'advanced' recognize that anything that is really important is ambiguous. Gender roles, for example are important, yet self-actualizing people make no sharp differentiation between the roles and personalities of the two genders. According to Maslow, they are so certain of their maleness or femaleness that it is no threat to them to take on some cultural aspects of the opposite sex role.

Because culture conditions women to carry on the ideals of the community with regard to family, relationship, religion, and virtue, it may be more difficult for them to accept ambiguity. The ideal of mother's absolute and unconditional self-sacrificing love and the cultural myth of the 'good girl' as obedient and responsive have been internalized by many women. In their internalized ideal, there is little room for a hearty, self-starting sexuality. They have been taught that sexuality is acceptable when it is merely responsive to a man's needs, or fulfills the duties of the woman's place.

But the notion that a clear and distinct ideal should be exemplified in an individual woman's life without modification can become an impossible burden, and can leave one looking back sadly on a life which appears to be little more than another instance of the stereotype. Life and creativity break out of the molds, whether those are rules, ideals, or stereotypes. The Spirit is not static but blows where It wills, calling sometimes to self-denial, sometimes to self-fulfillment, but always to risk and to ambiguity. The acceptance of ambiguity is a spiritual as well as a psychological task.

The everyday practice of sexuality brings a person repeatedly into the agonizing realization that adult lives are spent in the shadowy space between the great truths. They want love and intimacy, yet they must rest content with only the smallest glimpses of what this could be. The everyday practice of spirituality takes place in the same arena. Ever-widening circles of relationship call for love and justice, yet in the global context of late twentieth century life, there is no longer the possibility of the illusion that one person alone can create a new world. The need to balance the personal and the social, the spiritual and the secular, the absence and the nearness of God, the inward and the outward of life is the call to accept ambiguity.

Some people seek spiritual growth to avoid the conflicts of life, to withdraw and perhaps protect themselves from the moral struggle that in itself can compromise one's ideals. But such a motive is ultimately useless. The spiritual life itself takes one back into life. A temporary retreat can strengthen one and equip one for meeting conflict. The sexual and spiritual in fact suit each other because the sexual is for women a primary arena of the experience of conflict, risk and danger. A balanced spirituality can provide the courage of a new perspective and the patience of a larger vision.

To be fully oneself before God is to accept imperfection, to know that human beings always show weakness, make mistakes, and deliberately sin. To know and accept this shows a positive sense of self. Of course, not all people have this positive sense of self. Some have an inordinate need to seem perfect. They can admit no wrongdoing in themselves nor accept another's having equalled or surpassed them. They have, in fact, mistaken themselves for God. But perfectionism is just one form a negative sense of self can take. There are also those who believe themselves to be of no worth, and are always found inadequate when they measure themselves against others. For them the fruit of the acceptance of ambiguity is inner forgiveness by which they can experience God's gifts of peace and freedom in the spiritual life.

An area of great importance for spiritual growth through the acceptance of ambiguity is that of body image. Body hate would not be too strong a term for the relationship between many women and their physical appearance. Polly Young-Eisendrath says: "I have yet to encounter an adult woman who did not evaluate herself in some highly convincing way as uniquely deficient or inadequate."[6] Current research shows that normal women now suffer from the same body image problems that bulimics do. Women who have no weight problem, who have objectively fine, healthy bodies, look in the mirror and perceive their bodies to be fat and revolting, and the more inaccurate they are, the worse they feel. Steven Levenkron, a Manhattan specialist, says this is not a visual problem, not a distortion of body image, but rather an anti-female ethic about body image. We know we look like women; we just hate the idea. "Looking like an undeveloped adolescent girl is out. What's very much the rage is looking like a well-developed adolescent boy."[7]

Self image affects spiritual experiences. If there is conflict between the body developed for functioning in the world and one's deeply felt yearning for a spiritual reality, albeit a caricature, the casualty is likely to be one's sense of unity.

Self awareness is articulated as a good sense of the self—neither claiming perfection nor enslaved by a sense of unworthiness. This level of self-awareness builds on psychological insights, but has theological connotations because it defines people in relation to God. Trusting God involves the risk of one's life. One symbolically acts out that trust with each human encounter. One might say that when facing a new task, letting go an old equilibrium, the person is more open to the relationship with God, at least open in a new way, than she would have been continuing in the routine circumstances. An aspect of the ambiguity to be accepted here is that sexuality and spirituality are not rungs on a ladder of achievements, as if one could take care of needs in sexual development and then turn one's whole attention to the spiritual task. Our sexual-spiritual growth is not climbed like a ladder, but is expanded by proportional growth like the fingers of a hand.

Re-Naming, Re-Incorporation, Celebration

Bringing the whole life into relationship with God is the mark of a maturing spirituality. At each turning point in a person's life, the new meaning needs to be consolidated. Acts of incorporating one's newly articulated sexual self around a new name or symbol or ritual are among the most significant acts of a full life. To see one's life as a vocation is a spiritual experience that usually happens, when it does at all, during late adolescence. It is related to the ten categories of change that go with sexual unfolding.[8] During that period one needs to adapt to the bodily changes of puberty, overcome the guilt, shame, fear, and childhood inhibitions about sex, shift primary emotional attachment from parents to peers, be able to answer questions about one's sexual orientation, learn and communicate what is liked and disliked, cope with sexual abuse, dysfunction or compulsion, understand the place and value of sex in a human life, become responsible about one's own capacity for sexual expression, learn to combine love and sex in intimacy, and prepare for first intercourse. Our interpersonal lives are expressed in the public and social forum, so those new beginnings are often celebrated as rituals in which the spiritual community proclaims as blessed the sexual events in the lives of its members.

Since no inner experience is complete for a human being until the event has been reflected upon and connected to other events in one's own life and to similar events in the lives of others, it is appropriate that we help each other name the nearness of the holy to our sexual lives and the nearness of healing to our mistakes and tragedies. For most people that spiritual community is a church, though for some it is a gathering of like-minded people—fellow feminists or activists or senior citizens or support groups. It could also be less formal and less public, for example, an entry in a personal journal, a heart carved into a tree in a wayside, a special dinner with a special person. Marriage has long been the normative celebration of sexual fulfillment seen as a vocation in spiritual terms; yet marriage is far from adequate as an expression of the complex series of spirals by which one's sexual spiritual reality needs to be named and renamed.

As it is commonplace to say that to live is to change and to live well is to have changed often, so it is likely that a rich, full life is reincorporated often. Even if there is no change of partner nor change in outward circumstances, a new inner naming of oneself in relation to others and to God is warranted. When the unthinkable happens and a happily married woman becomes a widow, she is challenged toward a mature spirituality, as well as toward development of aspects of her sexuality that may have been invisible to her in her previous equilibrium. A test of maturity is passed by those who can accept suffering while continuing to work for a better life in whatever ways they may find acceptable. The crises that contain new opportunities are everywhere for adults. The theological insight that makes spiritual awareness possible is to know that God is in every place, in suffering as well as joy.

The middle years call people to readjust their view of what constitutes a successful life. This too is basically a spiritual problem. It could be a conflict between the spiritual quest and the goal of material success. The temptation, of course, is to repress the spiritual side of life in order to repress the questions. But then the meaning goes out of even the conflict and all that remains is burnout. In the middle years people can feel something of the grief of God. The suffering of Christ has new power to move them to understanding, and redemption makes sense in the face of disappointment. Grief calls us, even in our bodiliness, to transformation and hope.

A series of re-namings are underway at present in the social arena, whereby the sexuality of the elderly, the handicapped, and others formerly prevented from the experience of appropriate sexual pleasure, is being affirmed and channeled in suitable ways. Those deprived of spiritual hunger because they never tasted spiritual food are equally entitled to know of that to which the human being is called, to "have life and have it abundantly." With each step toward further integration of sexuality with spirituality, a woman lives more fully from compassion, from justice, from courage. The source of personal spirituality and the capacity for true intimacy is the same Spirit which enables us all to transcend our present lack of freedom and open ourselves to God. This openness to God is continuous with the profound self-acceptance which is performed in the love of one's bodily self.

Conclusion

If there is no incompatibility between sexuality and spirituality, and if one can discern a pattern of similar and sometimes coinciding points in spiritual and sexual development, then what can one say of practical ways (spiritual disciplines) by which greater wholeness can be cultivated? Certainly one cannot engineer one's own holiness, nor is nurturing merely a matter of techniques or exercises, but the great spiritual traditions have identified authentic ways in which their practitioners can make themselves receptive to the touch of the spirit. In our one life, both the sexual and the spiritual lives are practiced by muddling through, knowing that what is hoped for is not a product to be objectively examined, but a connecting vision in which the whole of an ambiguous life is encompassed. The connectedness that ensues in reality is experienced as wider focus, more steadfast commitment, more intense energy. Two shifts in vision become one shaft of light. In our sexual feeling and activity there is prayer, worship, and the experience of God; in our prayer is to be expected erotic feeling, insight, and (sometimes) sexual fulfillment. That sexuality and spirituality perform themselves through each other can be good news in the contemporary lives of women.

Born in Dickeyville, Wisconsin, Joan Hyacinth Timmerman has a Ph.D. in Religious Studies from Marquette University in Milwaukee (1974). Her dissertation was on the theory of God of German phenomenologist Max Scheler. This interest in systematic and philosophical theology continues to be reflected in her teaching of contemporary theologians and methodologies. She teaches also in the areas of sacramentality, sexuality, social justice, and spirituality. During her twenty years on the theology department faculty of the College of St. Catherine, she has been chair of the theology department, director of the Master of Arts program in theology, and initiator of the five-year-old Theological Insights program. *Sexuality and Spiritual Growth* (New York: Crossroad, 1992) is her third book, and completes fifteen years of teaching about sexuality and its relation to faith life and religious development.

I am He, you are She
I am song, you are verse
I am heaven, you are earth.

AYURVEDA

Relationships and Spirituality:
Taking Each Other to
Enlightenment

by

Charles Bates

*L*ove is the bonding, creative energy of the divine that organizes the universe and keeps it in existence. It is the attraction that brings things together and keeps them together, forming ever greater wholes. Human love models this bonding energy. Because all relationships are experiences of the cohesive energy of existence, the physical and psychological relationship of one human being with another can be instrumental in gaining insight into spiritual dynamics as well.

Human relationships are powerful tools for spiritual unfoldment and even vehicles for initiation into deeper spiritual truths. Over time, human encounters can transmute biological drives into profound spiritual development. All relationships, especially those that are significant to us, move us toward that development.

The deeper work of spiritual development, however, exists beyond our ability to recognize and discover it. We are drawn to it unconsciously, pulled by an inner illumination of divinity. The divine energy is infinite. The totality of divine truth cannot be contained either in one instance or in the whole of existence—it is too vast and too complex. But divinity makes a gift of itself; that gift is called life.

Life serves as a way for us to encounter the enormity of divinity within manageable pieces. Life is a theater for us to interact with the infinite divine energy in finite ways, and a way for us to remember the experiences. On its stage our self-unfoldment occurs. Through its limiting capacities of space, time, instinct, and causality, life gives us the means to make the spiritual concrete. It is this limiting that enables us to explore our spirituality and gradually assimilate what we learn, emerging as maturing human beings who are prepared to move to an ever greater sense of self.

Human relationships are one of the primary means through which we engage life. Relationships are ways of encountering what is true about the nature of existence and what is true about ourselves. The sage, Swami Rama, says, "All of life is relationship." It is through relationship that we see, one at a time, the infinite faces of divinity. Each contact holds the power of transformation and wisdom.

Relationships as Mirrors

As a culture we tend to be strongly outer-directed; we are not trained to venture inward to find the next steps of our growth. As a result, much truth lies hidden within us, in the depths of our self. Of that unknown, hidden self, there is much that must be unfolded in order for us to embody the truth of divinity.

Since we do not usually seek our divinity within, we unconsciously project parts of it onto the outer world. We then can see divinity in a sunset, in a play, in a cathedral, in another person. Whatever we see outside of us is actually a reflection of that which is already within us because we can only recognize what we already know. Thus, in seeing the divine essence "out there" we slowly realize that it is our own hidden self that we experience.

Relationships thus serve as mirrors to receive back our projections and to discover and claim those unrecognized dimensions of our self. It is here that we serve each other. The partners in our relationships become the mirrors upon which we can project and see reflected the inner potentials or unresolved conflicts of which we are unaware.

Projection is the way in which we take the yet-to-be-known, manageable pieces of life and place them outside of ourselves for scrutiny, experimentation, and eventual assimilation. Our spiritual potential is infinite; our human ability to grasp is finite. Eventually we will come to embrace parts of our potential and make them actual.

Relationship, then, is a way of claiming an inner potential that lies outside of our awareness. For example, a mentor is attractive because she is modeling behavior that is dawning in our awareness. It is through our relationship with the mentor that we first see, and eventually adopt, the mentor's valuable characteristics. While it is true that the qualities we find so admirable are actually ours, it is through the mentor that we will be able to recognize them and thereby claim them.

Projection in relationships can also be used dysfunctionally. Projecting our own aberrant qualities unto others brings a sense of expiation because this allows us to feel as if these qualities are not present within us. For example, a woman may project her fear of being abandoned onto her partner although he has no intention of abhandoning her. Her subconscious fear causes her eventually to abandon him out of defense. This behavior allows her to avoid admitting that the source of abandonment lies within herself.

Relationships are also a means of recognizing and resolving inner conflict. The drive to do so is usually unconscious. For example, it is commonly known that people with an alcoholic parent are likely to marry an alcoholic. This can be explained as an attraction to a learned pattern of caretaking within a dysfunctional environment. The adult child of an alcoholic resonates to the familiar behavior patterns of alcoholism of her new-found loved one and unconsciously resumes one side of a co-dependent relationship in an attempt to resolve feelings of failure over the inability to "heal" her parent's alcoholism.

By being present in our lives, our partners evoke, and sometimes provoke, thinking and experiences that would not be possible in isolation. In relationships, we place ourselves in situations and engender encounters that bring about a level of self-discovery that we could never create on our own. In the process of involving ourselves in relationships, we knowingly and unknowingly challenge each other to either accept or go beyond our current boundaries, dysfunctional attachments, unexamined notions, and static personal histories.

Relationships also provide an on-going opportunity to realize and expand our psychological and spiritual potency. In our relationships, life patterns play out before our eyes. We can learn to recognize these patterns as inspiration or as obstacles. As we come into contact with our best and our worst through experiences with each other, we can choose to absorb or overcome them because we come to understand the obstacles as our own. As we study ourselves through what is evoked in us by others, we can choose to live closer to the leading edge of our self-determination and self-definition.

We create our sense of self by identifying with one dimension among many possible ones. We come to identify with that dimension so strongly that we exclude the remainder as "not me." When it comes time to mature and discover the next dimension of ourselves, we often cannot see it on our own due to the blindness brought on by our exclusivity. We will then be unconsciously drawn to another person who represents what we are becoming or who embodies what we need to learn.

For example, a woman who has lived her life in a service profession, thinking herself not too bright, is now drawn to someone of high scholarly accomplishment. They become partners and over time the woman discovers her own innate ability for scholarship. Likewise, a highly conceptual, hard man might be drawn to an intuitive, soft woman and slowly begin to make her qualities of caring and nurturing his own. It is through this process of mirroring that relationships allow us to discover ourselves.

Man and Woman in Relationship

The most vital and common relationship for human beings is that between man and woman. Both exist together as an interdependent whole to generate and sustain the human community. The relationship between men and women historically has held both glory and suffering, abuse and cooperation.

Man and woman hold for each other invaluable invisible elements critical for personal and spiritual unfoldment. In essence, we truly need each other to discover our hidden dimensions. In our healing and discovery of each other we will embrace our whole being.

The human psyche, however, is a seamless whole. Like the principles of water that combine wetness, liquidity, and flowing, the psyche also serves as the seamless ground of human experience through mind, senses, and perception. When the psyche is viewed through the lens of culture, spirituality, biology, religion, or psychology, it is seen dualistically. This dualism is called femininity and masculinity and is expressed as man and woman.

Based on anatomical boundaries, culture defines what psychology will be adopted and which behaviors will be appropriate to each gender. With this pressure from culture, men and women tend to develop their faculties differently. In this way men and women are required to make different meanings out of the same reality. They end up having diverse assignments from nature and polarized assignments from culture.

Each gender has been isolated at particular points along the continuum of the human psyche. Biology aside, neither gender has a corner on excellence in any one dimension, but as a result of the historical momentum of cultural norms, each has been pressed to develop more on one side of the continuum than the other. The rich continuum of human being has thus become polarized as "masculine" and "feminine."

Biologically, the woman is gripped by surrender to nature (for example, through the functions of menstruation and child bearing), and the man is gripped by aggression (for example, through the hormone testosterone and the requirement of penetration for procreation). Culturally, however, the woman's world view is fashioned from bonding, while the male's world view is fashioned from individuation.

Looking at the masculine/feminine continuum holographically, we can see how it is possible for each gender in partnership with the other to develop and actualize the potentials that are culturally attributable to one and often culturally denied and left dormant within the other. We each have the whole masculine/feminine continuum within us, although most of it lies latent in the unconscious. It needs to be modeled in order to be actualized.

Through their relationships with each other, men and women have the opportunity to model, recognize, discover, and reconcile the difference between them by living and celebrating this difference as hidden dimensions of their own natures. Each takes dimensions of the other as the next step of development. Valuing her womanhood, the woman is free to explore qualities such as aggression, exclusion, individuation, entitlement, strength, self-validation, self-aggrandizement, independence, and power. Valuing his manhood, the man is free to explore surrender, emotion, attachment, nurturing, bonding, waiting, yielding, receiving, and vulnerability.

The Spiritual Dimension of Relationships

The magnificent possibilities for spiritual development through relationships are rarely modeled in great spiritual and religious traditions. Hinduism is one spiritual tradition that takes on this task. In the inner teachings of Hindu mythology, the union of anthropormorphized divine principles serves as a model for human relationships. The relationships between these mythological beings are as varied as the complex human psyche, thus, among many teachings, they demonstrate how relationships can be used for self-realization at various points along one's spiritual path.

Radha and Krishna, Sita and Rama, Lakshmi and Vishnu, Parvati and Siva are a few of the divine couples that model various types of female/male relationships. Radha and Krishna epitomize pure, selfless love, as well as love in separation. Because a permanent relationship between them is not possible, they have no hope of receiving anything from each other; they love in the knowledge that love is their only reward. This is in contrast to Sita and Rama's relationship of loyalty and devotion in marriage. Their union is a symbol of queenly fertility and kingly virility fostering the perfect reign of peace over all within and without. Lakshmi and Vishnu are elegance and grace. She is royal authority; he employs that authority through righteous rule. Vishnu appoints his agents while Lakshmi empowers them. Parvati and Siva represent the two poles of involvement in the world and withdrawal from it. Siva, god of extreme asceticism, and Parvati, practical household goddess, unite to live a life of reconciliation, interdependence, and harmony in sexuality and spirituality.

We learn from the divine partners that relationships are the keys that unlock the doors to our full spiritual nature. Swami Rama says, "We are already divine; we must now become human." We can do this "becoming human" only with each other. We cannot become human alone. We need each other so that we may evoke, through the mirror of relationship, the hidden dimensions that lie deep in our psyche.

Spirituality and Sexuality

One of the most profound connections in personal relationships is sexual union. Much like the universe which is in constant union, human beings long for and attempt to achieve oneness. The force which bonds the all-pervasive unity of creation is the same attraction that the electron has for the nucleus in an atom, that hydrogen has for oxygen in a molecule of water, and that human beings have for each other in relationships. This cosmic attraction is the energy of wholes.

In human beings, this attraction is manifested in many forms, chief of which is sexuality. Sexual energy is nature's equivalent to spiritual energy. The ancient science of tantra uses this energy as a means to fuel transcendence. In tantra, natural drives are encouraged to come forward in a disciplined way. Practices are attuned to biological and psychological drives, reorienting them to serve as tools to actualize spiritual potential.

Sex that is freed of mental obstacles is one of the most powerful ways two people can encounter each other in spirit, mind, and body. For a few, sexuality may not be an appropriate path, but for the vast majority, it is a powerful means of discovering our inner depths and dimensions. Released into the flame of life, sex is a gateway to the fire of spirit.

Unfortunately, humankind has made a casualty of sex. Centuries of cultural evolution and fear have polluted our ability to contact each other in truly vulnerable and expanding ways. As a result, and through no fault of sex itself, sex has become an obstacle to our spiritual development. Our personal history and societal norms often keep us frightened and separate from one another, especially on deeper levels of being. We have lost our ability to understand sex as modeling the all-pervasive divine union. In truth, we unconsciously mirror this divine union in our relationships with each other, yet we stop ourselves short of letting grace descend upon us because we fail to see the divinity in each other.

The yogic science of tantra gives us a fresh view of sex and the natural environment of which sex is a core dimension. On the path of tantra, divinity itself is tapped as a personal resource for human development. This is done through the mechanism of Vedic cosmology. As is typical of cosmologies, the characteristics of the divine are anthropomorphized in order to bring them into the human field of view. In tantra this reversed transference is used as a resource that allows the valuable qualities of the divine to be assimilated by the spiritual seeker. There are dimensions of genius, insight, power at the level of divine mystery that are essential to successfully tread the path of spiritual realization. Because these qualities, for the most part, lie outside the scope of ordinary human experience, the applied science of tantra provides routes to them. Tantra uses the relationships of goddess and god, of divinity to humanity, of creator to creature, of universal energy to every aspect of manifest nature as a route into the inner being.

In its practice, we look to ourselves, to our imagination, and to each other as living models of the divine. Tantra views all of existence as being in continual divine union. The philosophy of tantra is the exploration of the nature of that union. Tantra sets those forces into motion through external union, union in the imagination, or a combination of both. This union serves as a means to recognize, examine, and discover what is in the mind and what lies beyond mind on the pathway to the soul. Through tantra, we consciously bring the divine into the mundane in order to deepen our power of insight. As a result, we become a master through completion rather than a believer through suppression.

Our emotions are enormously powerful. They have the ability to transport us to great heights. Love, devotion, sex, and surrender are experiences that have the power to move us so profoundly that we can be transformed by them. Tantra taps this emotional intensity and by channeling it through specific devotional concentrations uses it to transport the devotee to expanded awareness. The mundane mind is affected by serving as a conduit for the experience. In this way when the devotees return to ordinary awareness, they are deepened by the infusion and experience of an expanded dimension of life.

For spiritual development, we must bring forth the whole of our beings, even that which is submerged in the unconscious. In relationship, the partners provide each other with an opportunity to actualize their latent spiritual potential by awakening and embracing polar opposites in each other and eventually in themselves. They can then each experience the entire continuum of femininity and masculinity while remaining rooted in their own femaleness or maleness.

In tantric practice, the woman sees herself as an aspect of the divine goddess of the universe. She is in union with the corresponding divine god of the universe. They represent Shakti and Shiva, the ultimate feminine and masculine principles of the cosmos, by whose union all is manifest and held steadily in existence. When this takes place, an empowering transference occurs. The woman, embodying the shakti principle, sees the man as the divine male personage of the universe, while the male, embodying the shiva principle, sees the woman as the divine female source of the universe.

As each takes the other within themselves, they become the embodiment of the principle that they represent, and awaken to the opposite dimension within each other. What was once deeply buried in the unconscious mind is elicited and discovered. She says, "Through you I find Him in me" while he says, "Through you I find Her in me." Through each other they experience wholeness.

The tantric practice of transference symbolizes and makes real the ultimate relationship: the mystical union of God and human. Through bodies, emotion, and imagination the relative as well as the ultimate is honored. Men and women become divine qualities within themselves. They worship each other as sacred beings who hold something great for one another. In truth, they embody the couple in the Vishnu Purana (1.8.15) of which it is said:

He is speech; she is meaning
He is understanding; she is intellect
He is the idea; she is the manifestation
He is all males; she is all females
He is love; she is joy.

Through the experiences of relationships, we all share in the delight of divinity making itself known in the mystical union of wholes. Having many masks, divinity is worn by those who love us enough to bear the weight of our struggle. In relationships, the divine face becomes visible shining through each of us, lighting the way on our journey to spiritual unfoldment and truth.

Charles Bates is a nationally-known consultant and lecturer in the fields of organizational development, leadership, cultural diversity and change, and holistic personal development. He is also a noted exponent of hatha yoga and body-mind integration. A member of NTL (National Training Laboratories), he is a consultant for the Gestalt Institute of Cleveland and adjunct faculty of The College of St. Catherine, St. Paul. Bates has been a student of mysticism for over twenty-two years, studying in India, Nepal, Japan, and the U.S. He conducts retreats and workshops nationally on leadership, relationships, personal development and mysticism.

He has written *Ransoming the Mind: An Integration of Yoga and Modern Therapy* and *Pigs Eat Wolves: Going into Partnership with Your Dark Side.*

In every mystical experience worthy of the name, animus and anima collaborate in an act of love.

HENRI BREMOND

Marriage and Spirituality:
Revisiting the Marriage Covenant

by

Rev. Anne Miner-Pearson

*T*here were six girls all under the ages of seven. Like many children that age, they were amusing themselves while their mothers were busy with 'adult business.' In this case, the business was setting up for a church rummage sale. Dark green plastic bags yawned open like mouths ready to spew out their contents, while tables lining the parish hall stood ready to receive the goods. The women's hands moved quickly, sorting and folding, paying little attention to the children.

There was small need to do that; these girls were entranced. A whole room of assorted goodies surrounded them: games, books, dishes, and best of all, grown-up clothes. On racks hung dresses with bows and lace, pairs of shoes waited below them, hats filled a nearby bin, purses were lined up on the table. Out of style, no longer fitting, these were someone's cast-offs, but not in the eyes of the little girls. They were the means to turn their fantasies into reality.

The children's chatter connected them as they wandered the rows. Slowly their talk formed into a plan: they would have a wedding. They would be the bride and her attendants, all bedecked and bejeweled for that most wonderful of days. Not surprisingly, the oldest became the bride and the others soon claimed their roles. Their imagination had no bounds: tea towels became veils, dresses and shoes covered shorts and bare toes, plastic centerpieces served as bouquets. No real bridal party could have held more excitement or energy. They giggled, they complimented each other, they felt beautiful as they gathered to capture the moment on a photograph.

The rummage sale is now over and the photo stands on my desk. The event may be forgotten in those young minds, but not in mine. Even at the time, it seemed more than vicarious enjoyment of children's play, more than mere observation of children constructing their world. Out of all the fantasies possible, the girls chose to enact a wedding. In spite of the failure of so many marriages around them, they were drawn to the traditional pageant of white gown and flowers, the hope of 'happily ever after.' Yet because of the changing times in which we live, because of the automatic reaction of the young wedding party to see marriage as the focus of life, and because of my own private and professional experiences with marriage, the event held an almost eerie invitation to look anew at the reality they mimicked. Through their innocence and play, they unveiled for me questions about marriage and its relationship to the Holy Other: If there is such a relationship, what does the church have to say about it? Does the voice of the marriage ceremony echo out of rummage, cast-offs from another age? Does its message no longer fit today? Is it out of style and of no use to anyone?

Like those young girls, some of us find ourselves in a church for our wedding. We share their excitement and delight, but know that this time it's for real. Or is it? Are we pretending as they were? Are we dressing up, putting on a good show because others—our parents, our friends, our tradition—want it? Are we tricking ourselves into believing that the wedding is the marriage? Those girls knew they were playing at being who they weren't. When they removed the clothes and returned to being young girls, they were refreshed and free. Does that happen for us? Or has our 'playing at marriage' left us frustrated, disappointed and empty?

I ask these questions as a woman whose life experiences no longer allow me to think of marriage as a game of dress-up. Being fifty years old may account for some of that questioning, but mostly I am affected by three critical factors: I am divorced, I am remarried, I am an Episcopal priest. These factors influence my pondering and inform my discussion of the connection between the church and marriage and between spirituality and marriage. Thus before I offer some answers to the questions arising from the young girls play, I need to say something of the bias I bring to the discussion as well as my personal experiences in the state of marriage.

Thirty years ago I stood before God and others and traditionally vowed to unite my life with another "until death do us part." I meant those words that night and believed that they would be true in all the nights and days to come. That didn't happen. Instead, some time later, a judge's words legally declared them null and void. In the midst of all the practical ramifications of a break up, like dividing furniture and picture albums, I tried hard to hold on to the meaning of two important words: promise and covenant.

Divorce ended my marriage, but it did not end the importance of those two words to me. I still believe in marriage vows and know that promise and covenant are essential to marriage or any other relationship. Yet, the deep questions surface still. How could I have broken such a critical covenant? Is it even possible to do that despite what the judge declared? And more fundamentally, what kind of person must I be to have broken such a promise and severed such a covenant?

If marriage speaks of anything, it speaks of beginnings and new life. If divorce speaks of anything, it speaks of endings and death. It is just this juxtaposition that makes divorce so difficult. People may talk of others taking divorce lightly, of 'easy divorce.' That was not my experience, nor the experience of anyone I know. There is always pain and struggle. There is always death. And the death of my marriage led finally to my struggle with guilt and forgiveness. Like a pebble tossed in the water, divorce creates rings that extend far beyond those two signing the dissolution decree. Parents, children, friends, society are injured as well. No fault laws do not erase that reality. Forgiveness is needed and it does not come easily. To name one's own and others' hurtful actions takes honesty and courage. But harder yet is the task of letting go of the hurt. Like that pebble in the water, hurts can sink very deep, creating holes that gape large and raw.

Forgiveness involves time, a conscious choice and, many times, the help of another person. For me, it has taken all three of these for the hope of forgiveness to begin to emerge as reality. Nine years have passed, and in that time, I have repeatedly had to claim that I am a forgiven person, a forgiving person. I have had to let go of hurtful memories again and again and to deny their continued hold on me. Through the healing gift of others' counsel, I also learned how insidiously resentment can permeate thoughts and actions. It poisons. It stunts growth. It prevents forgiveness from breaking through.

In the last analysis, it was the spiritual presence of a power beyond myself that finally transformed the pain and death of divorce into reconciliation and a new beginning. Within me, a healing began to happen. It was beyond my creating and beyond others' caring. The raw, gaping hole within me had started to grow together with what I trust is healthy tissue. True, the scar of divorce remains and will for all of my life. Like other scars, it may cause embarrassment or need explanation at times, but the wound no longer defines who I am.

Since that time, I have remarried. I have begun again to discover the joys and challenges of marital union. To risk again after failure is always a frightening venture and to risk after a failure as public and central as a divorce was more than frightening. I tested my capacity to trust, to trust my own ability to decide wisely, to trust that this man and I would be able to grow in our love and care for each other beyond what we now experienced.

Part of that new life has included my ordination as an Episcopal priest. This facet impacts my view of spirituality and marriage as much as my marital story. Because I stand in a particular religious tradition, my spiritual understanding of God and the human have been formed by it. All of these personal experiences—divorce, remarriage, Episcopal priesthood—have contributed to my understanding of the relationship between spirituality and marriage. Certainly, I have also been influenced by what I have learned from others' experiences. It is all this that caused me to remember those young girls playing wedding with the rummage sale clothes and to share with you how I believe marriage is an invitation to enrich our spirituality.

Marriage as Spirituality

In the Jewish and Christian traditions, it is believed that God wishes to be known within our stories. Events in daily life, signs in nature, prayers and symbols are some of the varied ways we believe that to happen. For generations, people who worship this God as Creator and Redeemer of the world have retold stories of how God acted in human life. They have added their own story to further proclaim that God yearns to be in union with them and all creation. This belief that God can be uncovered in the ordinary and everyday is important to my understanding of the place of the Holy Other in marriage.

From its 16th century roots, the Episcopal Church has held on to the Roman emphasis on the rituals while embracing the new ideas of the Reformation. That central place of ritual is still true today. Words, actions, and symbols are means pointing to a human reality commonly acknowledged; they are also pointing to a divine Reality. As the Episcopal Book of Common Prayer states it: "A Sacrament is an outward and visible sign of an inward and spiritual grace." Marriage is understood to be such a sacrament.

With this view of sacraments and the place of the priesthood in the Episcopal Church, it is not surprising that I am asked to officiate at many marriage ceremonies. Church canon requires that I meet at least three times with the couple to determine their readiness to enter into such a covenant. Most often, there are more sessions because this is an opportunity for couples to question, challenge and reflect on their relationship. For many of them, this is the first consistent, structured time they've had to do that.

Prior to marriage, however, is not the only time an examination of marital union is needed. Stresses and changes make an impact on every marriage and the ear and wisdom of a third uninvolved person becomes critical for the health and sometimes even the continuation of a marriage. I've been that third person for others, as well as sought the third person for my own marriage.

Historically, marriage evolved to legitimize a sexual relationship, to create order in the society, and to provide protection for any children born in that union. None of these concerns clearly point to matters of the spirit or an understanding of the Holy Other, but more to sociological, economic, and political perspectives. Marriage as an invitation to spirituality is not a common understanding of the institution. So perhaps this discussion of possible links between marriage and spirituality comes from affluent voices, those free to peer into yet one more layer of what is truly a multi-layered phenomenon. Once the discussion and the peering has begun, it is not difficult to uncover such links. In fact, there are many, but given my story and this space, I have chosen to suggest four that seem true to me and might provide energy for your own uncovering.

Marriage Affirms Connections

The first opening to spirituality that marriage can provide is the challenge to individualism. Much has been written about our American culture's encouragement of this normal aspect of being human. This nation's past is deeply rooted in the soil of the individual. Immigrants from other countries sought our shores in order to express personally-held religious and political convictions. Families faced physical hardships and economic poverty so that their individuality might not be oppressed. These roots are still nurtured and proclaimed as important. Certainly for me as a woman priest speaking in a still predominantly male institution, the voice and rights of an individual are central. The same is true in the institution of marriage.

It is as two individuals that we make the decision to marry. We are reminded of that individuality at the very beginning of the ceremony as the officiate repeats the names of the man and woman. There is nothing that speaks of our individuality as much as own names; there is nothing that more clearly denotes us as separate and different. (Just remember the last time someone called you by the wrong name!) Our names very clearly declare us unique creatures.

Yet we also know that to be human is to recognize and accept our deep and life-giving connections with others. I disagree with the common notion that you and I are traveling on two different paths and that if we happen to meet well and good; if not, that is fine also. Such a credo distorts a critical dimension of what it means to be fully human. It denies the spiritual reality of our deep, abiding connection with others.

Marriage constantly reminds us of our deep connection with another and, perhaps because it is so obvious, this truth is often overlooked. In deciding to link our life with another, who we will be is forever altered. For example, we do not strike out on a career path without consulting our spouse. Relocation is not an individual consideration. How we spend money, time and energy—on what, with whom and when—just doesn't ruminate in our heads and hearts alone. There is always the other's ideas, opinions and feelings with which to reckon.

Marriage is about connecting. It connects not only the two people making mutual vows, it also creates the connection of two families, often two very different families. Our marital vows make that connection for us. If our wedding ceremony is performed in a religious setting, a connection to that particular tradition is made as well.

Our name reflects many of those connections. For most of us, our name was given to us at our birth. It links us to a family, a story, an identity we did not choose nor completely make. Our name says we are more than what we have made of ourselves. We are our mother's, our father's, our ancestor's, our land's, our culture's. Our name confronts our human tendency to think we ever create ourselves or really stand alone.

The truth that our names carry our historical identity particularly undergirds women's recent struggle with naming, especially naming themselves after the marriage ceremony. In my first marriage, I willingly followed the culture and exchanged my last name for that of my husband. In 1962, no other thought occurred to me. But as the second wedding day approached nearly twenty years later, my name became an issue not only for me, but for my husband-to-be. Since my family name so connected and linked me with those of my past, how could I deny that link by changing my name? On the other hand, didn't I want my name to speak of my commitment to a future reality with the man I loved? The next question easily followed and was quite disturbing. If my name needed to show this commitment, then why shouldn't his name show the same? I asked the question aloud and it set him struggling with the importance of his own name.

The incident proved to us that all the difficulty around naming and names in marriage is more than liberal pot-stirring. It is an opportunity to look at the spiritual realities beneath the obvious. Whether we choose to keep our birth name or to create a new name, names point us to the spiritual reality of our connection to others—human others and the Holy Other. Those long lists of 'begats' in both the Hebrew and Christian biblical passages we tend to skip over are name reminders which link and bind one to another.

The Jewish and Christian understanding of the Holy Other is God who names. Thus the name is holy and sacred. By God's naming of chaos, the void is transformed into creation. By God's Word, salvation is offered. Names are a way God connects holy power and love with the creation. Names are a way from the lover to the beloved. In both scriptures there are stories of radical new beginnings occurring in people's lives, of turning from a way of life without an awareness of God's presence to a new life where God is centered. In many of these stories, such a change necessitates that a new name be bestowed by God on those involved. That new name becomes a sign of the connection with the divine, a connection to the past and to the future. Our names, too, can be a sign of the spiritual reality that connects the individuality of the one who holds it and the human and divine reality beyond.

Marriage Teaches Commitment

Beyond connecting our individuality with another's, marriage also teaches commitment. Our modern culture values commitment about as much as it values connection. Examples of our fickle national personality abound. Today's latest fad in fashion, food and fun is only that: today's. The customary gold watch for twenty-five or fifty years' employment in a company is a rarity as we work our way from one firm to another, one profession to another. Serial marriages mirror the same trend.

Always quick to sense the national mood, the *New York Times Magazine* recently examined this reluctance to commitment in marriage. A sprawled Levi-clad male body adorned the cover to announce the article: "Why Wed? The Ambivalent American Bachelor." Not since the depression years, when there was economic reason for hesitancy, had so many men decided not to marry. Although many reasons surfaced, fear of committing to an unknown future with another was a repeated strong response. There's no doubt about it. Those ambivalent American bachelors are right. Marriage means commitment to the future, an unknown future, for of course, all aspects of the future are unknown in any commitment.

When Dick and Sharon exchanged their wedding vows twenty-one years ago, neither knew that in two years Dick would be a quadriplegic. His life was drastically changed. Along with the remodeling of the kitchen and doorways of their house, Dick and Sharon's marriage faced its own adjustments. As Sharon said, "I didn't sign up for this and I'm not sure I can commit to this change." Dick surely echoed those words. Neither had signed up for this reality in their lives, but they had signed up for a future together. The car accident had wiped out the neurological connections to his limbs, but it hadn't wiped out the commitment they made to each other.

Every wedding service proclaims the couple's willingness to commit to the other, "forsaking all others" as the consent says in the Episcopal service, "...from this day forward for better for worse, for richer for poorer, in sickness and in health..." These are more than romantic sentiments. They poetically circle around the word commitment, designing a life that includes both joy and pain, light and darkness. After the accident, Sharon and Dick entered that circle in a new way with an opportunity to plunge into the center of the very meaning of commitment.

They learned. They learned about wanting to leave. They spoke the forbidden words, in anger and frustration, in tears and gentle letting go. They learned about their limitations to do and be all they wanted to do and be for themselves and for the other. They challenged each other's self pity and held each other in compassion. As two individuals and as a couple, they turned around and around in the reality of commitment like a dog trying to find a comfortable place to rest. At times there was no rest, only the seemingly endless turning.

Yet because they allowed themselves the possibility to come apart, they came together. Because of their commitment, they learned to trust the other. They learned they could trust the future together. They had lived in the chaos and had asked the most painfully difficult questions they could think of to ask, and they kept asking them until they could hear the answers. They had accepted the challenge and now they could believe the support. Their commitment in marriage was real.

The same lessons that teach us our capacity for commitment can also open us to the committed Presence that is part of the Holy Other. In story after story scripture tells us that God is faithful. By covenants with Noah, Abraham, and Moses, God chooses a people. Promises of land and prosperity are given as evidence of the bond between the Holy Other and humanity. I will be your God, the Holy Voice speaks, God for you and your descendants for generations to come. Though few in number, they belong to the Lord and receive divine love and care. Even their unfaithfulness does not change the covenant. They choose to worship golden calves and complain in the wilderness, but God remains faithful. God can be trusted; God is consistently a never-failing, loving presence.

For Christians, God creates yet another covenant. This covenant binds a people not by the birth of successive generations, but by baptism. This covenant also reveals God's faithfulness. Such divine constancy is part of God's nature and is true no matter the state of our human faithfulness to our Holy Partner.

The revelation and belief in God's love, however, does not guarantee our commitment to that relationship any more than our commitment to our partner in marriage is guaranteed. Nor is our divine/human commitment without its struggles and lapses. Yet, just as in commitments between humans, a structure is created in which and through which trust can be tested and deepened. Because that partner, either mortal or divine, will be there tomorrow, truth can be spoken and honesty can be risked. It's possible to push the boundaries of who we can be and of what our relationships can become. It's all right if the edges are brittle or fragile for the center is firm and strong. The center undergirds our courage to change and grow because there is steadfast love sustaining us.

A rosy picture is described here: love, trust, courage to grow and change. Life has moments and sometimes seasons like that, but life is not always that way. To greater or lesser degrees, we all have all been touched by cruel hands, heard abusive words and been oppressed by control and manipulation. Life is not synonymous with love. We do not receive loving care every time we act in trust. Often, we are wounded, abused, broken in our bodies and in our spirits.

Marriage Offers Healing

It is always such a wounded person who stands with another wounded person to exchange marriage vows. However willing we might be to connect ourselves to another, however willing we might be to commit our future with another, we each bring a past that contains hurt and pain. There is no therapy that completely erases the past. It enters with us into the relationship along with all the joy and promise.

But marriage is also a place for two more spiritual gifts: new beginnings and union. Through marriage, partners can become healers for the other and for themselves. It can be a bright mirror, revealing a healing and healthy view of life. By becoming a healer for the other, they become a healer for themselves as well. Each wounded person can experience a new beginning, created out of the darkness and chaos of the past. The new rising from the old, light from darkness and order out of chaos are gifts from the Holy Other. For many of us, they are gifts given through marriage.

In the Hebrew stories of creation, the Exodus and the Exile, God is pictured as creating new life out of the void, chaos and oppression. Christians tell of this same action of God through the Easter story of Jesus' crucifixion and resurrection. The power of the Holy Other continues to work in the darkness of human life to bring light. Creation is not a one-time event, but a process begun and sustained in the womb of God. Made in the image of God, we are created to participate in that ongoing creation story.

Marriage Creates Union

Entering into that creative healing process can offer us the spiritual gift of intimacy and union. If we want healing to happen we cannot stand at the edges and cover over our center. We must enter the darkness. We must risk touching the depths of who we are with ourselves and with another. For any new life to begin and be born, we must be willing to be vulnerable.

Marriage offers us a relationship in which to take those risks. With our bodies, we dare to be naked and grow old together. Through the full range of emotions and life stages, we can feel both the ecstasy and despair within us. In this joining of our bodies and minds, we can be moved toward intimacy. We can experience moments of true union when wholeness and reconciliation become real. We can experience the divine gift of union.

In the process of marriage, something new will be created. The self can be carried into the mystery of the other. This mysterious union is something we could not have created on our own or by holding on to ourselves. It could only happen as we offer that self to another. Through that union we do not lose our identity, but paradoxically discover more fully who we are.

The discovery and union provided by marriage opens us to discover and unite with the Holy Other. By connecting and commitment, by healing and union, we become willing to lose control and to trust the Other as the center of our lives. It can occur when we risk entering the mystery of the Holy Other through marriage. It can occur when we are willing to stay connected and honor commitment. It can occur when we become part of another's healing. It can occur when we open our hearts so that we might be more fully aware of the Holy presence within us and our partner. To so act is to invite intimacy with God as the very Source of love, life, and light and to more deeply unite with that source through our marital union.

Born in Kansas City, Missouri, the Reverend Anne Miner-Pearson has a degree in education from the University of Kansas and a Master of Divinity degree from Seabury Western Theological Seminary, where she also received the outstanding preaching award. Anne has a long career of service to the community, working in children's education, human resources and public service. In 1985 she received the YWCA Minneapolis Leader Award, and the Founding Feminist Award from the Minnesota Women's Political Caucus in 1986. She was interim rector of St. Mary's Church from 1984-86 and is now the rector of St. Anne's Episcopal Church in St. Paul. The mother of two children and wife of an Episcopal priest, Anne is currently pursuing her doctorate of ministry in preaching from the Association of Chicago Theological Schools.

*That Power who exists in all beings
as the Mother,
Reverence to her, reverence to her,
reverence, reverence.*

BHAGWAD PURANA

Motherhood and Spirituality:
The Path of Love and Service

by

Qahira Qalbi

ove spirals forth from the womb of Being; and so it is that each of us, every living creature, comes to this earth plane. The life force, issuing forth, is never so strongly felt as in the woman giving birth to her baby.

All my life I have had a quiet and deep gratitude that I was born a woman, but it seemed to be a privilege, especially, to be a mother. The experience of conception, which is the power of love; of pregnancy, the power of feeling; and birth, the power of thrust, is a course in motherhood and humanness both. There is an infusion of Spirit that fits us for the work to come—rearing the human race. We have heard the expression "the spirit moved him," or "the spirit moves in us." Never is this more true than in the whole drama of childbirth.

The womb was designed through eons of time to contract and expand and, with a hundred pounds of pressure, eject its nine-month tenant with powerful thrusts. Women are infused with this power; it is our inheritance from the universe. This all-pervading, permeating force is the breath that breathes us. Moment by moment we are filled with the very spirit we seek. It is the original impulse behind our every action: our birth, love-making, running a business, cleaning the house, building a bridge, getting out of bed in the morning, and most of all it is the triumphant spirit instilled during childbirth.

When the womb begins its contractions, and as they gradually get stronger and stronger, the woman experiences a cosmic power that seems to be beyond her, yet in a real way is her. The power is tangible, yet by control of the mind and the breath she can experience a partnership with spirit, even more, a oneness that is akin to a great initiation.

Tsultrim Allione in *Women of Wisdom* says that "initiation is an active choice to enter into darkness".[1] So does the woman birthing her child enter into the darkness of creation, the darkness of pain, the darkness of possible death, by choice and love in order to bring forth a new light into the world. Initiation is always a step into the unknown.

There are many steps taken into the unknown, and we may notice that some of these come unbidden, unasked for, and unexpected, like birth and death. An initiation is also the beginning of something new, something different, a chance to do something in a way it has never been done before, like our marriage, a new business, beginning a spiritual path. Other important initiations are our first tooth, our first step alone, beginning school, a severe illness, retirement, the death of a spouse or loved one. In each we are free to do things in traditional, tried-and-true ways, or we are free to explore and expand the horizons of humanity's knowing. So it is with childbirth.

Before the swimmer has ever braved the ocean waves, he knows but little of the feeling of vastness, the enormity and power of this ocean being. The same is true for the woman facing the birthing of her baby. Both are prepared by their interest in what is to happen. This step into the unknown, if there be no fear, is part of the fabric of our being. The pioneer, the explorer, the scientist, the mystic, all are within us awaiting the command, "Go!"

The mother to be has read, listened, contemplated, meditated, and drawn from within herself some primordial assurance that she, too, as her ancestors before her, can give birth. This assurance and the calming peace it brings can be deeper than she has ever felt before. If the ill winds of 'old wives tales' do not frighten her, then the joy of anticipation sets in, together with a delight in the coming of her child.

During birth itself other qualities are being forged in the woman as surely as steel is forged in the fire. There is patience in the process and endurance and fortitude in the face of the strong and stronger-growing contractions. There is diffusion of the sudden panic that arises after an intense contraction, and surrender to the assuring voice of the one who reminds her of her breath.

No one can sufficiently capture in words the euphoria, the gratitude, and the total delight which can follow a natural birth. The 'high' of these moments is spiritual to the utmost, while remaining utterly physical. Although difficult times may follow, this experience of bliss has been woven, it has been 'stamped,' in the woman's being and she will always be able to recall it.

Many qualities develop as the mothering career stretches into months and then years. Following the first uncertainty is the certainty, the quiet knowing, that she knows better than anyone the subtle nature of her child. The healer within us all is nurtured in the mother by the growth of her child. Especially when her child is ill, the mother's love pulls gradually from within her the knowledge of how to be healing. Hazrat Pir-O-Murshid Inayat Khan, a Sufi mystic of this century, said this about love:

Is love pleasure, is love merriment? No, love is longing constantly; love is persevering unweariedly; love is hoping patiently; love is willing surrender; love is regarding constantly the pleasure and displeasure of the beloved, for love is resignation to the will of the possessor of one's heart; it is love that teaches man: Thou, not I.[2]

A baby is totally dependent, yet it can call forth from us years of service and mold our personality to love as surely as a skillful craftsman. The cry of a newborn pierces the heart as deeply as a heartfelt prayer, and slowly but surely the mother and father who love become obedient servants. In the Western world we shy from the word 'obedient,' yet my Benedictine friend, Brother David Steindl-Rast, reminds us that the Latin *obaudiens* means "thoroughly listening." Again the Sufi mystic says, "The best way to love is to serve."[3] Obedient servant: what better training can one receive on any spiritual path?

The words of the beloved Sri Swami Rama, "You can never know how much God loves you until you have a child,"[4] reminds me of the phrase so often given in consolation to someone going through the fires of life: "God tests most those whom he loves most." Certainly parenthood is not only a very real spiritual path; it is a test, an initiation. Since nature itself is a sacred manuscript, can we find there an analogy of this trial by fire called motherhood?

Let us for a moment enter the consciousness of a lump of coal hidden deep in the bowels of mother earth. What does this lump know of diamondhood? Certainly nothing. It is black, soft, burnable, quite dispensable. But the divine alchemist is at work: pressure is applied for centuries on end; heat, tremendous fire, unimaginable initiations are going on unseen, unheard, undreamed. And finally, after eons of time, the insignificant lump of coal is transformed. Did the alchemist love this lump more or less to subject it to such tortures? Will the diamond lack forgiveness remembering all it endured? No, it probably will be too grateful for the loving care it receives as a diamond.

We humans are exquisite. We are free to feel any way we like about our past or future, about our joy and pain. Many people seem to have chosen bitterness, anger, resentment, self pity. It is hard to imagine that anyone would willingly choose this, yet we experience it in ourselves. Could it be that we have, as free human beings, fallen into a trap of unknowing? Have we forgotten that pain brings transformation?

> Out of the shell of the broken heart,
> Emerges the newborn soul.[5]

The experience of childbirth cannot help but change a woman and prepare her for what is to come. At no other occasion is another human being so thoroughly and completely a part of us as during pregnancy. The woman is led step by step along the path of love, and anyone who is close to her is invited to walk along.

We speak often of good mothering, conscious of the child's highest good, but good fathering is equally essential to mankind. Men have wished they could also have the experience of giving birth, but they can gather its portent only vicariously, the depth of its meaning only through relationship. But by osmosis the father is also changed, especially when he lives intimately with the mother's process. Feeling, through love, the father has a spiritual experience akin to his masculine nature. He takes giant steps in his awareness to all life forms and most especially to his own inner mysterious nature—the divine feminine. We are all designed to blossom forth as humans with a perfect balance of these two forces— masculine and feminine, the sun and the moon. The tremendous experience of birth is a catalyst for this balancing transformation.

Often young mothers feel they are missing something 'spiritual' in their life because meditation, sacred dance, retreats, and group prayer are difficult to do after the birth of their child. But spirit and matter are not separate; they are opposite ends of the same pole. Matter may be called dense spirit and spirit fine matter; in other words, matter is a state of spirit. The invocation of the Sufis is a reminder of this oneness:

> Toward the One
> the perfection of Love, Harmony, and Beauty
> the Only Being,
> united with all the illuminated souls
> who form the embodiment of the master
> the spirit of guidance.[6]

Thus bearing and rearing a child is a glorious spiritual path because it makes us guardians of the most exquisite product of spirit into matter that exists: a human being. We are all created in the image of the Only Being. When a baby comes into our midst, God, the formless Only Being, is again born in form. Our soul is to God very much what the sunbeam is to the sun. Everything is spiritual, comes from spirit, returns to spirit. The sunbeam is not less an expression of the sun though it shines only briefly on our kitchen floor. Spirit is no less than spirit though it lives briefly as us.

"Mothers don't need to meditate." When I first read those words (so long ago I have forgotten where), I cried. How could it be? I have since lived to understand their meaning and their truth. Mothering is a meditation, the most complete concentration. Caring for a child is transformative: an immature, somewhat selfish, childlike creature called a bride becomes (through a process of pregnancy, labor, and mothering), a mature, mostly compassionate, keenly perceptive, Madonna-like woman.

Physiologically speaking, there are hormones called prolactin and oxytocin, produced by the body during gestation and nursing which predispose a woman (mammals) to create a place (nesting instinct), and to 'mother' her young and even the young of other mothers. Nature readies us to feed and protect and want to care for the young of the species. Emotionally and mentally we are more alert and 'tuned in,' and should sacrifice ourselves, generally, for the good of our children. How many mothers who could not swim a stroke have dived into a pool to save a small child? And no one will ever know the endless hours mothers spend by the side of a sick or injured child. These characteristics, of course, do not belong only to the woman who has reared a child, but to all humans who have the opportunity to mature and unfold their hidden qualities of nurturance.

Growth is getting in touch with one's limits, one's failings, often painfully so. We know too keenly the times we did not measure up, did not come through with flying colors, but instead weakened, ran away, lied, or fell short of what we could have done. But we learn soon enough that there will be another chance, an opportunity to do it again and better. In the mothering career those times come often and sooner, rather than later. So mothering is an intensive, exacting art which makes of the artist a creator, sustainer, healer, and forgiver.

Nurturing

One of the most obvious spiritual practices on the path of motherhood is the development of the woman's ability to nurture. From caring for her helpless baby, through the years of the child's growth, the woman expands her ability to nurture to include all living beings.

For some women having babies and rearing children is an integral part of their purpose in life; for others it is not. But as citizens of planet earth we are all responsible for each other. We are not only our 'brother's keeper,' we are brother and sister to each other; we are each other.

New life forms are an extension of all that has been before, with the potential for being greater—greater expressions of love. We may ask "What is love?" but when we live the answer, we need not ask the question. While rearing children we have an opportunity to daily live the answer. As idyllic as this sounds, it is the answer to the human dilemma of suffering and pain. When life is lived from the vantage point of the depths of our soul, and forgiveness and love are a way of life, when resentment cannot take root because the soil of our being is too finely cultivated to admit such a seed, then what? Then love will be all we are. There will always be problems to solve and mountains to climb, but the ways to solve and climb will evolve.

We need only trust our power within; the innate power to nurture and heal is magnified when we recognize and utilize it. We all know how a gardener nurtures plants and flowers, carefully pruning them and loosening the soil that has become crusted, giving each plant the right amount of water lest some get too little and others are drowned. There is full sun for the sunflower, shade for the violets, while others need a little of both. Bark and leaves and mulch help these to grow, while this one over here just blooms and blooms, seemingly fed on neglect. The gardener, the mother, develops the skills to care for each.

Emotional nurturing comes from one whose emotions have been tempered in life's fires over and over, deeply, in the gut level. Mothers see their children torn open and sewed together, burning with raging fevers, covered from stem to stern with poison oak. These things are mild on the yardstick of misery, but a woman who emotionally survives is strong and at moments even indomitable. She has seen the impossible happen over and over and learns truly that there exists the finest attainment of all—the spirit which lies at the foundation of her nurturing.

Love

At the turn of the century a disease called marasmus was taking the lives of hundreds of babies in orphanages. Care for them was given—diapering, feeding, bathing, and so forth—yet they were mysteriously dying. Somewhere along the way an observation was made: those babies singled out to be rocked and cuddled and given individual attention had a very high survival rate. It was discovered that mothering love was the missing ingredient.

Love is the key to growth. Love is spontaneous, creative. A woman truly learns about love when she becomes a mother. She learns that it cannot be dealt out in portions, but is always giving, and more than is asked.

St. Paul, in the letter to the Corinthians says it this way:

> Now I will show you the way which surpasses all the others. If I speak with human tongues and angelic as well, but do not have love, I am a noisy gong, a clanging cymbal.
>
> If I have the gift of prophecy and, with full knowledge, comprehend all mysteries, if I have faith great enough to move mountains, but have not love, I am nothing.
>
> If I give everything I have to feed the poor and hand over my body to be burned, but have not love, I gain nothing.
>
> Love is patient, love is kind. Love is not jealous, it does not put on airs, it is not snobbish.
>
> Love is never rude, it is not self-seeking, it is not prone to anger; neither does it brood over injuries.
>
> Love does not rejoice in what is wrong but rejoices with the truth.
>
> There is no limit to love's forbearance, to its trust, its hope, its power to endure.
>
> Love never fails. Prophecies will cease, tongues will be silent, knowledge will pass away.
>
> Our knowledge is imperfect and our prophesying is imperfect.
>
> When the perfect comes, the imperfect will pass away.
>
> When I was a child I used to talk like a child, think like a child, reason like a child. When I became a man I put childish ways aside.
>
> Now we see indistinctly, as in a mirror; then we shall see face to face. My knowledge is imperfect now; then I shall know even as I am known.
>
> There are in the end three things that last: faith, hope, and love, and the greatest of these is love.[7]

How does a woman grow while mothering? Let us see.

Situation	Mother Growing in Love
A. Baby cries and cries, falls asleep after mother walks the floor with him for hours. Mother is exhausted, sleeps an hour. Baby awakens crying.	A. Does: get up, hold and nurse the baby, walk some more, even for days and nights to come, until she is quietly resigned. Could: scream, cry, shake the baby, etc.

B. Toddler being toilet trained relieves himself while grandma glares reproachfully. Mother frustrated.

B. Does: lead the child to the bathroom assuring him he is all right, and the carpet can be cleaned up.
Could: yell at toddler to show grandma she is punishing him.

C. Seven-year-old girl lies about breaking Mommy's favorite antique teapot which she accidentally broke. Mother is sad and angry.

C. Does: assure the child that she is more important than the teapot, even though it was precious, and so need never lie.
Could: smack the child for lying. Take the child's birthday money to pay for the teapot.

D. Teen comes home three hours after curfew, no call home. Mother waiting, anxious and fearful.

D. Does: listen patiently to his side of the story. Tells him she's happy he's safe and how worried she was. Reminds him to call collect. Perhaps share a snack before going to bed.
Could: explode, yell, ground him for and a month and not really listen.

E. Son, a passenger in auto accident, in intensive care, head cut open and bleeding, teeth jammed in jaw, two legs broken. Four other teens also hurt. Mother standing at bedside in emergency room.

E. Does: stand by her son and tell him he's in good hands and that she will stay with him. Reassure other children until their parents come.
Could: fall apart, faint, dissolve in tears of anquish. Talk of suing the driver.

There is probably no closer or more intense relationship than mother and child. This very flesh and blood, now alive and moving around, is dearer than one's own self. It is the future you. No human quality goes untouched, often stretched past the limit. Love grows under severe conditions, because it pummels, exalts, crushes, refines, and defines our beingness. If we are anything at all, we are love.

Love in abundance comes to the woman who has given in abundance. It is awesome. As the years flow by mothers think little of all they do; they just do it. Finally, all the seeds they've planted come up everywhere and in everyone from the family members to the train master in India. One day a 'window' opens, only a crack mind you, a 'window' to how much God actually loves us, and it is as if a tidal wave poured in: incomprehensible, totally overwhelming, shattering. And love, cultivated through the years of nurturing, now must be for everyone, everywhere all the time. No more, no less. An always-known idea becomes a reality.

Gentleness

In this world there is nothing softer or thinner than water.
But to compel the hard and unyielding, it has no equal.
That the weak overcomes the strong,
That the hard gives way to the gentle,
This everyone knows, yet no one acts accordingly.[8]

A mother will soon find that because she loves her child, she will temper rules with freedom, firmness with gentleness. The greatest form of power is gentleness. True gentleness comes from selfless love. It is tuning deeply to another person's feelings and acting out of regard for them. In honoring another person's pride we are honoring our own. In speaking gently rather than shouting, in listening quietly and long enough, we bring to an angry, troubled situation the mercy and compassion to heal the wound. Out of gentleness and harmony will come what most of the world longs for: peace. What better reason for mothers to raise their children gently?

Guidelines, law and order, rules and regulations all have their place, and in an unnatural, life-in-the-fast-lane society, they are needed. But there will come a time, and for some it is now, that mutual trust, faith, and unconditional love is a reality. When we will live from the depths of our being rather than on the surface, we will find the need for authority vaporizes. Some might think this Utopia, might find this to be the ideal, the goal for human unfoldment. But it is rather the beginning. The fact of having a human body does not necessarily mean we are fully human. 'Hu' means, in part, divine—embodying the Godlike qualities in manifestation. 'Man' comes from the Sanskrit *manus,* which means mind. When we are truly human we will live life in harmony with the divine mind, which will guide us towards perfection. There should then be no more killing, no more pollution, no more harming each other. We will guard every person's pride, love our neighbor as ourself. All axioms will be part of our everyday life—not the end of living, but the real beginning.

We know this intuitively when we look at our children and plan for their future. Our children are us in the future. Where does all this expansion of love lead to if not a more superb person? We have been told through the ages: "The past is gone; the future is not yet here." Then the only reality that is upon us is now. The only hereafter is 'here' after we transform to still another form of light.

The Sufis are fond of saying, "Die before death and resurrect now." We are all dying every moment, dying to our own fears, our own false concepts of ourselves, our own limitations. But we know this already, haven't we been told? Let us die willingly and resurrect gloriously, spiraling into the future, consciously joining all those who believe and trust in the ultimate goodness of humanity, and serving with love and patience those who do not. The Sufi mystic, Jelalludin Rumi, says it beautifully:

> From the moment you came into the manifest world a ladder was given that you might escape. From mineral substance you were transformed to plant, and later to animal. How could this be bidden? Afterwards, as man, you developed knowledge, consciousness, faith. See how this body has risen from the dust like a rose? When you have walked on from man you will be an angel, and done with this earth your place will be beyond. Pass, then from the angelic and enter the Sea. Your drop will merge with a hundred Seas of Oman. Leave him you called 'Son,' and say 'One' with your life. Although your body has aged, your soul has become young.[9]

Understanding

Daily living with children and watching their efforts to grow and learn gives us a deep understanding of their struggles to match our steps, follow our example, learn, expand. There is so much for a woman to note; she cannot help but grow in understanding. When love guides the teacher, she is so much more able to see the problem clearly, and guide usefully. One cannot help but note that the many choices of life are at our disposal. By teaching and guiding her child, a woman learns to choose more clearly:

create	destroy
nurture	shatter
cultivate	undermine
love	instill fear
patience	impatience
understand	belittle
serve	ignore
selfless	selfish
tolerant	intolerant

Even more important than the love we give our children—all children— is the bridge we are building to the future. What we do here and now will be, must be, surpassed. The idea of future, the perception we have of time and space are in reality eternity. There is something thrilling, awesome, about the thought that eternity is not out there somewhere waiting for us, but is now, this very moment.

We need not look forward to it; we are living eternity now. These truths are gently instilled in our children at quiet times. During the course of everyday life, spiritual food in the way of guidance, listening, loving is constantly there.

Now that my children are older, the truths I taught them are coming back to me multifold. One of my children said, "I listen to what I say to other people and I know it's what I learned from you!" The greatest joy comes from seeing the seeds of love and beauty sprouting through the next generation.

The saddest moment is seeing history repeat itself because lessons were not learned: the child that follows in the drinking parent's footsteps; a child abuser who was himself abused. There is a line in a Sufi prayer, "You, my Lord, will right the wrong."[10] If there is anything at all good we can do in this life, it is correcting in ourselves the mistakes our parents made with us, in not perpetuating a way of being that we realize was not helpful to us as we were growing. Motherhood is a time for appreciating and reevaluating. The mother remembers how she was nurtured by her mother and father, and also remembers what she didn't like and what hurt. It teaches courage to do things in a different pattern from our parents, our grandparents. It takes wisdom to know what to keep and what to discard. But we don't need to fear being perfect. Our children will have our mistakes to correct and their children theirs. But we will accelerate the process of perfection. We will realize the purpose and fullness of Jesus' words, "Be ye perfect, even as your Father in heaven is perfect."

Conclusion

The desire of life to reproduce is stronger than the limited human will to fulfill human desires, no matter how noble. There are those who have no inclination to have a child; they should be respected. But for the many who long for a baby, our love and encouragement is deserved. The world can never have too many loved and wanted children. We are witnessing in this day what happens when young women choose a career over and above a family. To do this is neither right nor wrong, good nor bad. There is no need to judge the decision; it is the result which is interesting to witness: women in their 30's and 40's bearing their first child, women seeking a man who will father their baby without marriage, women hiring surrogate mothers to bear their children, multiple births due to the use of fertility drugs.

There is an age to come when humans are human and we live as we are designed to live—free from the bondage of self—when our lifespan will be marked once again in the hundreds of years. Peace will be a way of life, and war a distant memory. There will be no need for birth control or talk of population explosion. There will be balance, in ourselves and in our world.

But we cannot wait until this comes about. Dreams are for those who sleep. We must live the future now. We must live as though it has already happened. This means each person's unique ideal of the future will be the way the present is lived. As we pursue the ideal, the ideal is manifest. Then comes the realization spoken of by Hazrat Inayat Khan, "Shatter your ideal on the rock of truth."[11]

Our ideal is limited by our understanding of what Life/God is. As we are willing to explore further horizons, so will the ideal change, grow, be refined. We only know as much as we need to know of life's great mysteries. The more we do realize the more responsible we must be for what we know. As we integrate our ideal, we are illumined by it. Others are encouraged and inspired to live more idealistically.

The spiritual mission of the human being is to make God a reality. Not only do we entertain many religions, but each of us in ourselves is a religion. To come to blows over religion, or God, or whatever we choose to call the nameless and formless, spaceless and traceless, the very breath that we breathe, is so unnecessary. Yet more wars are fought over God than all other reasons put together.

The imprint of peace begins in the womb and even before—in the life lived in unworldly spheres. A further impression of peace is part of the 'coded information' in the mother's voice as she sings her lullabies. We are all a product of our realization; all that makes us laugh and cry tells the secret of our knowing or unknowing. So the babe at the mother's breast is teaming to work for its food; it feels the human body as its comfort and thus experiences satisfaction.

On a spiritual path one may discover that the feminine principle embodied in motherhood is a stepping stone to our Christ-self, our Buddha-self, our divine self. Being a mother physically is not necessary to uncovering our illuminated self, or else most childless masters, saints, and prophets would not be remembered today. So the state of motherhood lies as a seed within us all. It is the qualities of love, compassion, patience, tolerance, service, enhanced by motherhood that lead to illumination. A friend once told a story about himself. His job was routine and he knew it well, so he would have conversations with God while he was working. One day he asked God why he couldn't be illuminated like others (who were writing books about their illuminations). God answered, "You are already illuminated. What are you doing with your illumination?"

The greatest resource the world (and perhaps the universe) has is the human being. All praise to parenthood and those pioneering mothers and fathers who burn in the light to give light to the world. The essence of spirituality is the spiritualization of matter and the materialization of spirit. What finer resource material than babies; what better guardians of this divinity than mothers!

It is the answer to this very question which predicts how much more light and insight we receive. Like the horizon it is endless, always more and more and only less and less as we forget who we are and why we're here. Have you noticed how matters of life and death make us think more about these great questions? When your good friend dies, don't you suddenly want to live life more fully?

It is also true when a new baby comes to live with us. Things that were once important no longer are. A deeper meaning to life makes our life richer and fuller.

Qahira Qalbi, also known as Jalelah Engle Fraley, was born July 10, 1933 into Sufism. Both her parents, Bhakti and Fatha Engle, were on the Sufi path, and her father was secretary to the great Sufi mystic and saint, Hazrat Inayat Khan.

Involvement with La Leche League International, childbirth education, Right to Life, Hospice and especially the teachings of the Sufis, have given Qahira a life-supporting view. She is a Minister in the Universal Worship, a healing conductor in the Sufi Healing Order, and for the past eleven years has guided individual and group retreats on behalf of the Sufi Cirder in the West. She has headed Sufi centers in Los Angeles and the vicinity since 1970. Qahira has traveled to New Zealand, India, Europe, and Israel and leads tours to some of the special places in the world for Sufis, such as Turkey and Egypt.

Married to Tansen-Muni for thirty years, Qahira is the mother of six children and the grandmother of four. She and her family live in a small avocado orchard in southern California where she guides individual retreats whenever she is not traveling.

Handle even a single leaf of a green in such a way that it manifest the body of the Buddha. This in turn allows the Buddha to manifest through the leaf.

DŌGEN

Food and Spirituality:
An Interview with

Abbess Koei Hoshino

bbess Koei Hoshino was interviewed by the editor at Sanko-in, a beautiful, old wooden Buddhist temple in the quiet outskirts of Tokyo where the nun is head of the temple (Jushokusan) and master teacher (sensei) of the art of Zen Cooking (shojin ryori).

Jushokusan, will you speak a little about the history of this beautiful temple?

The history of this temple goes back to the period of the northern and southern dynasties (1336-1392), so it is quite old. During the age of Japan's civil wars (1482-1558) it burned down. The present buildings in which we sit were restored in the year nine of showa (1934), about fifty years ago. So we trace the physical aspect of the temple. But we also trace another aspect of a temple—that of the lineage of the jushoku, the head of the temple. The lineage of the jushoku of this temple goes back to Kyoto. All have been trained at the chief temple of the Rinzai sect of Buddhism in Kyoto, the Donke-in, also known as the Bamboo Palace, founded in 1439. My teacher, Abbess Soei Yoneda, also received her training there from the age of seven. And it is from the unique tradition of cooking of that temple that my own work derives.

What is shojin cooking?

Shojin cooking is the vegetarian cooking developed by Zen Buddhist monks and nuns as an aid to improve their practice of meditation and spiritual life, through eating only the simplest and purest foods. The word is composed of the Chinese characters for "spirit" and "to prepare."

Is there a difference between the shojin cooking of the other temples and that of this temple, Sanko-in?

Yes. No doubt you have heard about Zenkojisan. They were princesses, the daughters of the Japanese emperors, who entered temples in Kyoto, which was then the capital of Japan. These temples had the title gosho, meaning a kind of palace, because of the princesses who lived there, either voluntarily or by force. The temples considered it a great honor to have them, and special foods were prepared for the royalty who often was the abbess. Thus, the food from these temples, including the Donke-in temple in our lineage, was a blending and interweaving of the culinary practices of food for royalty (gentle, elegant, refined, beautiful), and the traditional Zen ascetic discipline (simple and direct). For us it is an important and unique point since our temple cooks food for the public as part of our teachings of Buddhism.

So for you food preparation is an integral aspect of your spirituality?

Oh yes. Every day we rise at 5 A.M.; every day we practice meditation and read the *sutras* (dialogs and sermons of the Buddha); everyday we carry out the chores of the temple, and every day we prepare, serve, and eat food. Cooking, cleaning, doing zazen, sleeping, bathing, sitting, all come under the term gyojuzaga. This is a Buddhist term which means, "the four cardinal behaviors" of walking, standing, sitting, lying. Every aspect of life is spiritual practice. In Zen we say, "always, everyday life." This means that everything in life is training. That's how I have lived my life. So I never think of cooking as something separate from spiritual life.

What principles do you use in preparing and cooking food?

Ingredients are selected and prepared with the guidance of the three virtues, balanced with the six tastes. Zen prohibits the killing of any living thing and so we do not use meat, fish, eggs, or dairy products.

Please explain the three virtues.

The three virtues, or the three qualities, are lightness and softness, cleanliness and freshness, precision and thoroughness. They are listed, along with the six tastes, in the *Zen'en Shingi,* the oldest regulations for a Zen monastery, written in 1102. There it tells us that if the cook neglects the three qualities and the six flavors, it cannot be said that she serves the community.

And what are the six flavors?

They are difficult to translate, especially the last, but the six tastes are bitter, sour, sweet, hot, salty, and delicate.

In ordinary non-vegetarian cooking it is said that there are five tastes: sweet, salty, sour, bitter, and spicy. Those are the general tastes we experience. To this, Zen cooking adds one more to make six. It is *Tanmi.* We can translate it as a delicate taste, a quiet, and gentle taste.

So what does this really mean when it comes down to eating a meal? During the meal we experience the first five tastes and enjoy them. But after the meal, we experience what we call "aftertaste." It is a feeling, a mood of gentleness and quietness, along with the usual feeling of satisfaction. This is the sixth taste.

Do you mean that food alters one's consciousness?

Oh yes. It's a completely spiritual thing. If you are disturbed about something, if you're angry, you won't notice something so subtle. But the sixth taste, the feeling after the meal, is really the most important point of the entire meal.

It seems, then, that the cook is a key element because her spirit will also be in the food.

Exactly! It is necessary to be in a certain pure spiritual condition or psychological state to cook correctly. Of course since we are human, our thoughts change quickly and we may not always be able to maintain that state. But we should always try to achieve that purity when we prepare food.

Is this purity evident in the taste of the food as well?

Oh yes, it comes out in the taste of the food. That is why cooking is part of one's spiritual practice, part of one's training. Zen teaching says, "Allow yourself and all things to function as a whole." When we eat food prepared in this careful way, with the six flavors, then we receive three graces from the food. First, we become healthy in mind and body; second, we have the ability to be thankful for all things, and to maintain that state of mind; third, we are able to work for others with our mind and body. We will be able to give to others. Those are the virtues we receive.

Sensei, when you prepare food, do you think of those who will eat it?

In the beginning of the process, I think of those who will be given the food to eat. But then, as the process of preparing food takes over, there is *mu* (nothingness), as we say in Zen. I don't think of anything. The mind enters a state in which it is not caught up in anything. It is then that one is able to do one's best in cooking. So, if you are thinking, "Let's prepare this well for others" or "Let's offer our affectionate heart in preparing this food" you will know your practice is still shallow. When you are doing your best, you get to the point where you are just doing you best, not thinking of it.

Can you give an example of this state of mu or nothingness in cooking?

All right. Let us use the dish called sesame tofu. It is a difficult dish, made from ground sesame, water, and arrowroot. It must be stirred for a very long time, and it is hard work. When you are stirring and stirring with all your might, enough of the heavy batter for fifty people, it's so hard that you want to give up being a human being! But in the midst of the stirring you are not thinking of anything. All your attention is on the sesame. You just keep stirring and watching until the heat begins to soften the mixture and it becomes elastic. You just keep looking into the pan and stirring until the sesame tofu tells you what to do. It gets heavy again and then soft again until suddenly the surface swells up and leaps forward making a clear sound. It tells you that it's ready. Then as you quickly respond and remove it from the heat, a wonderful delicious aroma comes floating up and you know with your whole body that the sesame tofu is done.

You see, you are cooking something difficult over a very high flame, so if your attention wanders even a little, if your mind jumps to something else for even a moment, the sesame will burn. So you put everything you've got into it. You are completely one-pointed on what you are doing. Do you understand better?

Yes, Sensai, you've made it wonderfully clear. Though you are speaking of focusing on sesame tofu, you mean we should apply that same careful attention to everything else.

Yes. It applies to everything: selecting the ingredients, chopping the vegetables, cooking the food, laying the trays, setting out the chopsticks, arranging the flowers, spreading the cushions. This complete attention is what constitutes the spiritual practice. It must be understood not just with your head, but with your body. Our tradition insists that cooking involves the whole person. For hundreds of years the Zen monks and nuns have been taught to wash the grains of sand from the rice with such attention that not a single grain of rice is washed away. At no time may we allow our mind to wander as we clean the rice. This spiritual attitude to preparing food—being totally present to what you are doing—is valid anywhere in the world and in anything you may do in your daily life.

I have noticed that much attention is placed on the aspects of the season in your way of life, in the types of food you prepare, and in the decoration of the temple. Is this so?

Yes. One of our rules states that the monk or nun who is the *tenzo,* the cook for the community, must take care to choose produce of the four seasons. I think we Japanese are very sensitive to the four seasons; certainly it is a central point in Zen. When we live in each moment we cannot help but be aware of the fresh green leaves and wonderful breezes of spring, the sunny flowers and grasses of summer, the red and yellow trees of autumn, the pure white snow of winter.

The changes refresh us. The beauty inspires us. A shoji screen opened to see the pink flowers of the cherry trees in the garden is a delight; a spray of green pine and a few cones arranged in a vase cheer our hearts on a cold day, a glance of a bright red branch as we look into the autumn garden makes us happy. So should we cook. We should be surprised by the food and moved in our heart.

But only the quiet mind can see the real things and be moved by them. Look now at this tape recorder. It is rectangular, right? And this teacup is round, yes? And in this stove the fire is red. We don't make a mistake and think that the flame is black or that the teacup is rectangular. Our training is to really know that this is red and this is round. What does this mean? If your mind is always fussing about things, if your mind is continuously busy, if you often think of things that irk you, if you think a lot of heavy thoughts, you won't be able to see things clearly; you won't be moved by the beauty of things.

Therefore you have to always be training your mind. You must always maintain your mind so that you see things clearly. For instance, the buds on the willow trees come out fresh and green. Everyone who looks at the buds thinks that they are fresh green. But the point is to really know that they're fresh green, to know it clearly. In Zen we have the saying, "The flower is red and the willow is green." To be able to perceive that clearly, one must constantly practice awareness.

And cooking, requiring awareness, is thus part of that practice?

Yes. Some of us are very skillful cooks, some of us are very awkward. It does not matter. It is only important to put all of yourself in the cooking—all of yourself. All of yourself must be at that very moment, so that you have the sharp, quiet mind needed for cooking. The problems of the troubled world must not come in at all. Nothing should be allowed to disturb the cooking.

Sensei, may we return to the idea of the seasons? How do we practically relate to the seasons in our spiritual practice of cooking?

The obvious thing, of course, is to cook with seasonal ingredients. In our modern world seasonal products are often available year round. Yet serving frozen green peas in January is not the same as serving sweet, young, green peas, fresh out of their pod, in June.

In shojin cooking we are guided by the five methods and the five colors. This helps in seasonal variations also. The five methods refers to the ways of cooking. They are: boiling, grilling, deep-frying, steaming, and serving raw. The five colors are green, yellow, red, white, and black (that is, purple). We try to balance these variables with vegetables and sea plants according to season. Of course the shapes and colors of the dishes are changed according to season as well, and a small branch of flowers or leaves is an extra enjoyment for the eyes.

We try to include the entire person in the joy of eating food. First we experience the environment of the room in which we will eat. Then we see the food served. We see the color, the shape, the contrast to the plate or bowl. Then we smell the aroma of the food. Then we feel in our mouth the textures of the different courses. Each texture will produce a different sound to our ear when we chew the food. And of course we taste the various flavors as we eat. Balance and harmony in all of these elements is essential so that the important sixth taste, the aftertaste, the feeling we receive from the food, is achieved.

Sensei, it is considered one of the natural functions of women to nurture. This seems part of her nature as well as part of her spirituality. Does your work in cooking for others relate to this aspect of womanhood?

In a broad sense, yes. But to just cook without meaning is not at all the same as cooking for one's spirituality, so that one becomes rich in heart. The latter way of preparing and serving food is the way of nurturing.

When it comes to food, it's the same the world over: it's women who do the cooking. When we examine various religions we find that those engaged in ascetic practices are not those engaged in preparing the meals. Usually the ones who prepare meals do not do the spiritual practices. All the priests of the various religions, including those in Japan, have others to do their cooking. It is only in the Zen sect that the priests also cook and consider it part of their spirituality. So in most places of the world the preparation of the food is given to the women.

How can we learn the deep spiritual significance of preparing food? Where do we begin?

Ah! One must begin where one is. Now I am sitting here. It does not help me to turn now to the right, now to the back, now to the left. I find myself here. I must not think it would be better if I were facing a little more in that direction.

The place in which you find yourself now is a given. You must not complain that you are not in another environment. So first of all you have to do your best within those limits. And when you do your best in your given environment, you will succeed.

For example, let's say you are making a stew, a dish which exists everywhere in the world. You find that you don't have any carrots. Well, then you must try to make the stew as best you can compensating for the lack of carrots, perhaps by adding another ingredient. In cooking, this problem comes up frequently and the solution seems to develop naturally. If we do our best, we will succeed. This is very important in cooking, as in life.

Next, you must have a strong desire for spiritual growth. Speaking in Buddhist terms, we say you should arouse this *hosshin,* good resolution. Then you must have an awareness of what is involved in cooking. This we have been discussing. We need this awareness also.

Often we feel that cooking so many meals is a drudgery, and it becomes very difficult to perceive cooking as a means to spiritual development.

Yes, that seems to be true both in the East and the West. Rather than being told that preparing food is a spiritual exercise, women must awaken that fact in their own consciousness. When all is said and done, what we do when we prepare food is maintain life. If we don't eat, we die. We eat to live. Each of us has to understand really well that by preparing food we are sustaining life, which is something very important, something wonderful, something precious.

This life we maintain is the life of the mind and spirit as well as the life of the body. The spiritual life is naturally fostered by living and working the way we have been discussing. We know deep inside that it is true.

Let us take the family as an example. A woman wants her children and her husband to be healthy and happy. This is her fondest wish and her constant prayer. She wants them to grow in health and happiness, she brings her prayer into reality by making good food for them. The food is very important, but the prayer, the feeling behind it, is more important. We must value and nourish that feeling. The Sanko-in's motto emphasizes this point: *Chori ni kometa aijo—* Cook with love.

Every day you prepare and serve such meals. Then the day comes to an end and you look at your sleeping children, you look at your husband. You feel love for your family and I imagine you feel how wonderful it is. You don't need to dwell on things or ponder things in a certain way. Intuition is enough, and intuition will guide you.

While eating the temple food I was inspired by the great variety and freshness of the vegetables, the exquisite beauty of the dishes. But I wonder about those who cannot afford the best ingredients. What about them?

Once again, you must do the best with what you have. When you can't get the best ingredients, you do your best within the limitations. That is the guiding principle. As in all of life, you must be flexible. And if you are poor, then make up for it by being rich in heart.

For breakfast we nuns have a bowl of rice gruel and one pickled plum. We might also have a slice of pickled radish. The Western parallel might be a single slice of bread. Even so, we are rich at heart. Eating becomes training— learning to eat one's food appreciatively, as if it were much.

In meals there are two sides to the issue: those who make the food and those who eat the food. Up to now we've been speaking of the cook, but let us now touch on the other side. Here the important point, as we have said, whether one is rich or poor, is that we eat so as not to die. We need only a certain minimum in our stomach each day. That gives us a feeling of satisfaction. The one who eats the food needs to accept with a loving heart that which is given, and see that receiving the food is also part of spiritual training. We learn gratitude, appreciation, how to accept love, while gaining energy from the food.

If you don't have much, you mustn't become pessimistic and say there is nothing you can do because you can't afford much. There is always something you can do. You must begin to think how you can make something good and beautiful with what you've got. Let's say you have only one slice of bread and some milk and you must feed four people with it. You wonder what to do with it. Remain open and think with love. If it were me, I might tear up the bread into pieces and put it in the milk and make a warm soup of it.

When you do your best to prepare food with the desire to give those you love something tasty to eat, then strange to say, it always turns out delicious. Things like this are cause for great joy.

On this topic is also the idea of waste. In Zen cooking we are very careful about not wasting anything. Remember the daikon radish you were served? Well, daily we serve this dish at the temple. We peel the radishes and make the pickles. When you have thirty to forty guests a day the peelings pile up so high! I thought that was wasteful. I looked at them for a long time and decided we must do something about is. So I began to do research in pickle making. After learning the process, I realized it would be good to pickle the peelings in rice bran and salt and push them down in the mixture with the pickles. We did this and got very delicious pickles. Just eating plain rice with those pickles on it is very good. And I feel that the peelings, which were normally thrown away, are very happy to have joined the group of food!

This type of thing has power to make us confident in our thinking. When we put energy into what we do, we will be successful. Remember that preparing food is training for the spirit.

I should like to ask one further question, not directly related to cooking, but according to your words, of great import. What is the role of zazen (meditation) in your spiritual life?

Since I entered a temple where zazen was the specialty when I was young, it was said that when we did zazen our minds would become very calm and that a wonderful power would come forth in us. We were taught this way, and I practiced so. But I really did not know—really know with my whole being—that it was true until recently. My abbess, Soei Yoneda, was very kind to me and actually brought me up to this life since the age of eighteen. Fifteen years ago she had a heart attack and was told she would live only another six months. She had diabetes and heart trouble. Thanks to our lifestyle, our spiritual practices, and our vegetarian diet, she was able to live for another fifteen years. Nevertheless, I viewed her loss as something terrible and feared the day of her death more than anything. As she was nearing death, I was very sad; I was actually frantic. My position in this big temple, however, means that I must guide everyone else. So I had to do something. I did my practice of zazen very much then. I sat down to meditate, my sadness suddenly went away and I experienced deep peace. Meditation supported me through those days and has supported me since then.

I feel that my training was wonderful, and even though I am still green at it, I am glad I have been trained this way. When I give myself up to the protection of Zen, then any sadness, any anger, any joy, have no influence over me. I am not bothered by anything. I am able to become my self really, not disturbed at all. Zazen is the place where we experience the truth that our entire life—our praying, our working, our cooking, our playing—is all one.

Venerable Koei Hoshino is abbess of Sanko-in, a Zen nunnery and temple in the Koganei area of Tokyo. She chose to enter the world of meditation, work, and strict training in 1951 when she was eighteen years old. Hoshino began studying as a novice in the Rinzai sect of Zen Buddhism under the abbess Soei Yoneda. After completing her novitiate in the temple and her studies at the university, she assisted the abbess in forestalling the closure of the temple by offering the temple's unique vegetarian food to the public as a means of propagating Buddhist teachings. Later, as assistant abbess, she helped Abbess Yoneda in writing *Good Food From a Japanese Temple,* a book of recipes and philosophy. Named abbess after the death of her long-time teacher, Abbess Hoshino performs the temple ritual, teaches meditation and Buddhist philosophy, and continues the work of preparing food for temple guests. She also is the only teacher of traditional shojin cookery in Tokyo. Abbess Hoshino is the founder of the International Vegetarian Association, and in that capacity travels to many countries discovering other vegetarian traditions and promoting the principles of food preparation she so lovingly practices.

*Creating is the place where the human spirit
shines its brightest light.*

ROBERT FRITZ

Creativity and Spirituality:
The Gemini of Greatness

by

Anne Durrum Robinson

*I*n 'sky-talk' the constellation of the Gemini is often referred to as 'the heavenly twins.' That same appellation might well be used to link creativity and spirituality, for the two qualities bear a startling kinship. Like the constellation, I am an identical twin, having had as my womb-mate an exceptionally creative person. I have also been surrounded by a bevy of creative folks: a daughter, a niece, an inventive husband, two nephews, and now a gaggle of creative grandchildren. Since the early '70's (the calendar's, not mine; I am now in my late ones), I have been engaged in studying and interpreting for others the human brain/mind/spirit and their incredible powers. I am currently a consultant in Human Resource Development, offering workshops to clients in business/industry, government and academia—nationally and, occasionally, internationally. In the course of this extensive and fascinating work I have repeatedly observed that the same underlying principles govern the enhancement of creativity, the hastening of healing, the acceleration of learning, and the slowing of aging. I have likewise seen similar golden results accompany the addition of true spirituality to the human dimension.

I give broad scope to the concept of creativity. In its narrowest sense it can be defined as bringing into being something that is new to the creator. Someone else may have produced the same new concept, thought or object. That fact, however, demeans neither creator so long as neither has imitated the other. In the extended range of creativity I include a list from William Miller's excellent book, *The Creative Edge:*[1]

- Idea creativity: insight, solution, concept, new connection or perception
- Material creativity: finite creation such as a report, manual, ad, machinery photo, music, picture, costume
- Spontaneous creativity: 'light-bulb flash,' sports move, pun, cartoon
- Event creativity: meeting, conference, procedure, holiday event, party
- Organization creativity: work team, committee, system, structure, group
- Relationship creativity: new way of handling a relationship (personal or work), collaboration, cooperation, win-win negotiation
- Inner creativity: inner shift in perspective, goal, outlook (where you, not the situation, could change)

By spirituality I am not referring to some specific set of rules or dogmatic core of do's and don't's. Those caveats belong to religion and are fine in their place, for they enable us to draw the boundaries of our personal belief systems. But true spirituality means a consistent seeking of union with the Highest Overall Mind, whatever name one chooses to give it: God mind, Creative Intelligence, Cosmic Consciousness, Total Knowing. It seems to me that any purportedly spiritual outlook which tends to be overly rigid or fundamentalist stifles the creative spirit. It leans too heavily on reason and logic. It draws stiff, unalterable boundaries. It limits imagination's flight and fancy's freedom. It overemphasizes territoriality to the detriment of spontaneous interaction.

I think, for example, of a young woman in a workshop I had on the brain/mind who got up and left class when I mentioned that we would talk about dreams. Mystified by her abrupt departure, I followed her into the hall. There she told me that her religion didn't allow her to discuss dreams. "You do believe in God?" I asked. "Oh, yes." "But," I said, still puzzled, "Who do you think gave you the wonderful ability to dream?" She wouldn't answer, just refused to return to class until we had changed subjects. I couldn't help remembering all the artists who have dreamed beautiful paintings, all the inventors who have dreamed solutions helpful to humankind. Just think of Elias Howe and the story of the sewing-machine needle. Howe had tried and tried to figure an effective way to thread the needle. Not until he dreamed of being captured by wild natives carrying spears with holes in the end did he determine how he could successfully solve his problem.

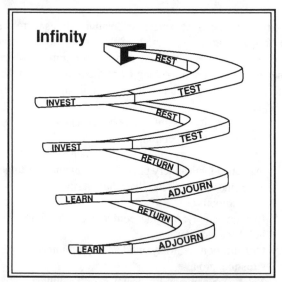

While I plan to discuss further ramifications, I can sum up my feeling about the linkage between creativity and spirituality in one finite example. I usually begin workshop by giving door prizes. In sessions on creative thinking the prize is sometimes a small, gold-plated charm engraved with the initials U.R.U. Plainly the U means 'you' but the letters themselves stand for "You are universal" and "You are unique." The universality ties the recipient to his/her spiritual universe; the uniqueness, to his/her own unmatched expression of it.

In all the participant materials for Whole-Brain Creativity workshops or for sessions on Accelerated Learning the drawing of the "Growth and Learning Spiral" is included. A spiral is often designated as the most perfect geometric figure because it makes a complete circle, yet advances with each rotation. The spiral leads to infinity. In growth and learning such a smooth, rising orbit shades each turn into three related steps: learn, adjourn, return; or invest, test, rest. In creative or spiritual advancement one must take in information, use it in one's own way, then incubate or meditate on it for a time before adding to one's general wisdom or knowledge store.

A consideration of brainwave frequencies and brain dominances may show us why some spiritual and creative approaches are more productive than others. Continuing research in the brain/mind field denies simple approaches, but a quick discussion can serve to show why, although left hemispheres are absolutely essential for whole-brain functioning, the right ones may be more in tune with truly spiritual aspects.

Our brains are composed of cells called neurons which constantly fire bursts of energy at different frequencies. These frequencies automatically change as our activities change.

BETA (14 to 28 cycles per second) is the frequency in which we spend a large part of our working, coping day. In that range we are being bombarded with information from our five normal senses: seeing, hearing, tasting, touching, smelling. These are the senses that are telling us what is happening around us, here and now. Beta is an essential frequency for operating in a complicated world, but if we stay in it without respite we are opening ourselves to over-stress. It is a frequency often fraught with anxiety and competitiveness. I think we can say that Beta is akin to the conscious mind and to the left hemisphere which is primarily concerned with facts, analysis, logic, time, sequence—a rational, no-nonsense look at the world and its workings.

ALPHA (7 to 14 cycles per second) is the second major brainwave frequency. It is lower, slower and more tranquil than Beta but still offers full awareness, either diffuse or focused. Alpha is akin to the subconscious mind and to the right hemisphere which, as a rule, prefers a visual, musical, spatial, intuitive, visionary approach.

In the early 70's I received a national grant from Women in Communications, Inc., to do subjective research on Alpha and creativity. Because of its more relaxed receptivity, I found this lower brainwave frequency to be more open to creative thinking.

At about the same time, Drs. Elmer and Alyce Green of the Menninger Foundation in Topeka, Kansas, were conducting clinical research on THETA, the third major brainwave frequency. They, too, found the lower frequency to be more conducive to creative thinking. Theta (at 3.5 to 7 cycles per second) is so low and so slow, however, that unless one is a Yogi or Zen master, long-time meditator or on a biofeedback machine, Theta is hard to sustain.

From Theta one's tendency is to drop to DELTA (.5 to 3.5 cycles per second) and go to sleep.

Consequently, for most people without extensive training, Alpha may be the most helpful creative/spiritual level. It allows one to be tranquil and aware, and establishes communication possibilities among the conscious, subconscious, and superconscious minds. Alpha is easily attained and sustained. We have two natural Alpha times, namely, the hypnogogic (when we are going into sleep) and the hypnopompic (when we are coming out of sleep). These can easily and regularly be used for creative or spiritual 'tuning in' or attuning.

While I was researching the creative contributions of Alpha, I was piloting a workshop on Creative Consciousness in six major Texas cities. One of the young men in the Houston workshop was a member of a permanent prayer group. He felt that prayer was also more effective when he was at the lower brainwave frequencies because there the seeker's subconscious mind connected more easily with the seeker's Higher Self and consequently more effectively with the highest Overall (or God) Mind.

The relationship of creativity and spirituality is expressed in what I term the Creativity Syndrome. In the following chart I have placed the conscious mind on the lower level and the subconscious mind above because I feel that the subconscious is more in touch with Collective Universal Mind and with Highest Overall Mind. In the diagram Present Self means whoever one is at this moment, because about every ten years we grow or decline into a different person.

In the Creativity Syndrome concept, Present Self can have an Idea and give it out to World Mind. On the other hand, Higher Self can receive an Inspiration from Highest Overall Self and (if the channels are open) can pass that inspiration down through what I term the 'awareness window' between subconscious and conscious minds. Present Self can convert that Inspiration into an Idea and pass it on out to World Mind. If Present Self gets an Idea and feels there should be value added, it can open its awareness window and 'send up' to Higher Self for more.

CREATIVITY SYNDROME

	⇩	
	COSMIC MIND	C M
SUBCONSCIOUS	⇩	⇧
REALM	INSPIRATION	I
	⇩	⇧
	HIGHER SELF	S
	⇩	
- -
	PRESENT SELF	⇧ s
CONSCIOUS	⇩	⇧
REALM	IDEA	i
	⇩	⇧
	WORLD MIND	wm

There is no shortage of creative substance. It is always available for the asking as long as one keeps the channels open between Present Self and Higher Self and between Higher Self and Highest Overall Self.

I would like to emphasize two important A's: Attitude and Awareness. Although we've known for a long time (from personal experience) that optimists are more enjoyable to be around than pessimists, we now have increasing evidence from research that those with an optimistic attitude in general are likely to be more creative and productive as well. Certainly they are less dampening and damaging to the creative spark in others. As for Awareness, it deserves not only an A but an A+ in encouraging a creative outlook. Artists and art teachers tell us that before we can successfully paint, we must first learn to "see." The inspiring book, *The Zen of Seeing*[2] emphasizes this point; I personally underscore it.

My twin was a near-genius who could make top grades in all subjects with a blindfold on and her hands tied behind her. I could not make the same marks, but I had to eschew the blindfold, untie the hands and work much harder. After I married I decided to go back to college and take some subjects that I had found fascinating but had been afraid to attempt because I couldn't manage the high grades. One of them was an art course. It began with charcoal drawing and then went into crayons. Much later I attempted watercolor and did manage to advance from abysmal to very bad. (Limited time has kept me from rising to 'passable.') In spite of the rather low quality of my efforts, however, I found myself seeing life in more discerning ways. Colors, even in desert stretches which I would once have dismissed as boring, now became intriguing in their variety. Shapes and composition took on whole new meanings. Even ugliness and dilapidation began to have a certain artistic appeal. Everything—big or small, mean or noble—became potentially 'paintable.' With this emerging vision came an expanding sense of the spiritual origins of things and places and people and atmospheres.

When our physical brains first began to develop we evolved the reptilian brain which dealt largely with ancient memories, cultural instincts, rituals, traditions. It contributed valuable information on archetypes and age-old heritage but was not sufficient to dwell in forever. Our next acquirement was the limbic or feeling brain, one which initiates and prompts much of what we learn and do. The limbic brain can also strongly affect our perceptions of people and places, of the past, present, and future. The neo-cortex or new brain came next. This is divided into two hemispheres, just as is the limbic. The left hemisphere emphasizes sequential, analytical, verbal, time-oriented thinking; the right has as its bailiwick the interpersonal, artistic, musical, visual, spatial, intuitive, future-oriented whole. Next was added the 'forecasting' brain, which is a treasure largely reserved for the higher animals. It allows us to set goals, plan strategically, foresee, predict. We also have the hypothalamus which serves, in may ways, as our mental 'climate control.' It determines whether we meet life with a 'fight of flight' outlook or operate from a 'flow' approach, which is much more conducive to creative thinking and spiritual linkage.

Needless to say, this is a very simplistic approach to the marvel of the human brain/mind, and there are many more important parts of even the physical brain. However, I'm leading up to Ned Herrmann's metaphor for the brain, called The Four F's.[3] Herrmann, author of *The Creative Brain,* divides the brain into four quadrants: Facts, Form, Feelings, Fantasy.

In his metaphor, Herrmann recognizes the theory that each of us has mental preferences for a certain quadrant or quadrants of the four major brain areas. We may be able to work in any of those quadrants, but we often prefer or highly prefer some quadrants, use others, and actually avoid one or more. Very few people are equally at home in all four, and our preferences definitely affect our perceptions of people, places, ideas, and values. Obviously, then, they have important bearing on our creative thinking and our spiritual outlook.

Herrmann labels the upper or cerebral left quadrant as the Facts quadrant. People with an upper left preference want specific knowledge. They are prone to highly critical judgment. For them, things must 'compute,' must make sense, must be orderly. There is no room for 'giant steps for mankind' here. One-two-three should be followed by four-five-six without unexplained (or unexplainable) gaps. While Facts people may tend to be overly judgmental, they often save the rest of us from dangerous gullibility.

Herrmann characterizes the lower or limbic left as the quadrant of Form. Those who prefer this quadrant like structure, system, and effective organization. They want an intelligently assembled universe and they work hard on its efficient composition.

The limbic right is the Feelings quadrant. Those with this preference are 'people people.' Their writings might lean toward stream of consciousness, their paintings toward impressionism. They place high importance on successful, encouraging, interpersonal relationships. Their spirituality is also likely to have a high emotional content.

The cerebral right is the Future or Fantasy quadrant. Here are the way-showers, visionaries, entrepreneurs, futurists, imaginative 'what-if-ers.' These are the possibility people, often the paradigm shifters. They are the 'new theorists' in both creative thinking and in spiritual approaches.

We need all four quadrants, whether we get them in one person or several. No brain preference wears a white hat or a black one. All are essential at the right time and in the right place. Too heavy a reliance on the left, safe-keeping side may mean too much rigidity in creative thinking or spiritual seeking and too early or too harsh a judgment. Too much reliance on the right, risk-taking, dash-ahead side may lead to foolhardiness or over-credulous responses.

Let me make brief mention of four I's (which I often call "Four Eyes for the Top of Your Head) and two S's. Of tremendous mental importance, the four I's are imagery, intuition, incubation and illumination.

Imagery is the use of the five imaginative senses. We can imagine that we see, hear, taste, touch, smell. This imaging power helps us make clear to our subconscious what our conscious has in mind. We can use it to clarify what we want or need from our willing-to-help subconscious.

Intuition is a usually-sudden flash of conscious awareness of a conclusion reached by the subconscious mind. We once thought that intuition was some sort of magic, a kind of mystical 'zap' we had to sit and wait for, one that came in its own time and of its own volition. We also thought only women had this enviable source of information. We now know that most people have intuitive capability. In women the intuitive messages seem to move faster across the corpus callosum, the connecting tissue between the two neo-cortex hemispheres. One's intuitive flash may be simply the thrusting through one's awareness window of a determination that the subconscious mind has reached after putting together memory, logic, instinct, experience and information derived from other minds and/or Cosmic Mind. Intuition, however, is not the same thing as paranormal clairsentience, a clear knowing which may come directly from Cosmic Mind.

Incubation is the highly essential time we allow for the subconscious mind to explore its sources, those which the conscious mind cannot reach. Incubation is an extremely valuable step in the mental process often overlooked or omitted in both creative thinking and spiritual efforts at attunement.

Illumination is the Aha! moment of insight which comes most fruitfully after we have employed imagery, set in motion our deliberate intuitive process, allowed incubation time, and then opened our awareness window again by sleeping, meditating, relaxing, day-dreaming, night-dreaming or holding our waking Alpha time.

The two S's are perhaps an even more esoteric part of our creative/contemplative alphabet. Synchronicity is what Jung described as 'meaningful coincidence.' Very often, in creative pursuits or in spiritual journeys, one begins to notice a certain puzzling sequence of events which is obviously not based on cause and effect.[4] The series seems to be leading to a desired end or to be underscoring a necessary awareness. I have often likened the Universe to a capable cutting horse which, by a series of drives, pushes and nudges, cuts a selected horse out of the herd and moves it to another desired location.

The second "S" is the initial letter of the oriental word, *satori*. In *The Search for Satori and Creativity,* E. Paul Torrance, one of the world's leading experts on creative thinking, defines *satori* as a sudden flash of enlightenment, the highest point attainable in 'expertness.'[5] Torrance states that the attainment of *satori* involves many things: intense devotion; constant practice of even simple operations over a long period of time; concentration and absorption; perhaps intensive and long-term relationship to a teacher; and, above all, persistence. Neither creative nor spiritual *satori* is a short-term, instant gratification proposition.

As we have seen, creativity and spirituality may be likened to the Gemini of Greatness, truly 'Heavenly Twins.' Their kinship is indirectly indicated in this closing offering:

Imagine yourself standing before a broad, beautiful flight of marble steps which stretch into infinity. There is no fear in mounting these steps, although they lead to the unknown. You sense that they will take you toward your full potential and your greatest good.

As you step upon each level, you will be suffused with colored light. Accept and take into yourself the positive qualities which this light brings.

Red   vitality, progress, full-blooded life
Orange   imagination, feeling, freshness and depth
Yellow   sun-energy, high intelligence, enhanced awareness
Green   growth, reason, wisdom
Blue   tranquillity, spirit, infinity
Violet   mysticism, tenderness, understanding, union
Purple   royal sense of worth, regal opulence
Gold   richness in all things; a treasure-filled mind, heart and soul
Silver   shimmering purity, starshine on water, moonlight on snow
White   light, clear energy; healing, boundless inspiration

This is where you dwell creatively, in that pure and dazzling source, knowing that it is part of you and you of it: Creator, created, creating in a perpetual sequence, confident that, as long as you keep your channels open, it will illumine all of life for you forever.

Anne Durrum Robinson has had a long and varied set of careers. She has been a secretary, a free lance writer, a magazine editor, a broadcaster, an account executive, a university teacher, an international presenter, a trainer of professional and support staffs, a world traveler, and a wife, mother, and grandmother. She has written for and performed on radio, TV, film and stage.

She has written two books: *Never the Twain Shall Eat*, a book of light verse written with her twin sister, and *Symphony for Simple Simon*, a light-verse coloring book which has earned more than fifty thousand dollars for symphonies across the country.

Anne is currently working as an independent consultant, teaching workshops in approximately eighteen different areas.

Shine forth your light
to guide and sustain us
prolonging, O Goddess,
our days.

Rig Veda

Art and Spirituality:
Women's Words

by

Sr. Sue Woodruff

or me time flows in a spiral. Frank Lloyd Wright gave form to this image in his design for the Solomon R. Gugenheim Museum in New York City. Although I had read about this building, I was still unprepared for the actual experience of walking its spiral path, examining each piece of art from many vantage points. As I moved along, I knew the reality of spiral time in my body. Experiences and events, truths and images which occur at a given moment on the spiral appear slightly altered as I continue my walk. In his *Original Blessing,* Matthew Fox uses a similar image when he speaks of the fourfold path we all travel: the Via Positiva, the Via Creativa, the Via Negativa, and the Via Transformativa.[1] As I live and move along this path I am accompanied by women I have met.

My grandmothers were beautiful women. Both of them empowered my life with a legacy of ritual and prayer. My mother and her friends relished the sound of words, the weaving of rhyme in poetry. My teachers introduced me to their friends radiant with wisdom. Through each of these women I met others, my women friends, who share their words of wisdom, power, and beauty with me daily.

Virginia, my mother's mother, carried in her body her Pacific Northwest roots. Her French Canadian and native American heritage flowed into her prayer. Each evening after supper, Grandma chose one of us to join her in her room for her evening ritual. I treasure the memory of those intimate moments. We carried a pot of tea, two cups, and sometimes a bowl of rice with cinnamon, sugar, and milk. While the tea steeped, Grandma freed her waist-length hair from its topknot. I brushed and brushed her white mane. Meanwhile Grandma began her formal prayers with a reading from Grandpa's French Bible. Memorial cards, yellowing letters, and birth announcements marked favorite passages. After the reading came the prayers to our Mother God in the Chinook jargon of her Columbian River ancestors. Intuitively I knew that although Grandma and I might pray very easily to God our Mother, the Sisters in our parish school would not readily accept this manner of addressing God. So God our Mother remained in our home ritual.

Next Grandma led a family litany in English during which we prayed for each of her thirteen children, her grandchildren, her sister's family, other relatives and myriad of friends. Birthdays, illnesses, deaths, failed crops, journeys, new babies, anniversaries, we prayed for them all. After I had braided Grandma's hair into one long plait for the night, she would pour two cups of tea and we would share fears, secrets, and jokes while we sipped. Then with a goodnight kiss, she would send me on my way.

My other grandmother, my father's mother Ulla Belle, often lived far from us. But for a few years, she came to Oregon and lived with Grampa on a small farm near our hometown. Grampa, a nurse in our local hospital, would pick me up on his way home, and when he left for work the next morning, I delighted in time alone with Gramma. During my days and nights with with her I learned to grill cheese sandwiches, to sew on a treadle machine, to crochet miles of chains, to scatter feed for the chickens, to eat fresh peas in the garden and to delight in stories. In place of my despised afternoon nap, she substituted a new ritual. We climbed upstairs to the big bed she usually shared with Grampa. We fluffed the pillows and settled in to read our favorite books. Sometimes she read her latest novel while I browsed through her lady magazines and shopped via her many catalogs. I loved it most when she would read aloud to me. I cried over Peter Rabbit, worried about Old Mother Hubbard, laughed with the antics of Winnie the Pooh. Gramma's voice wove magic with the words of that day's lucky author.

I also treasure the wisdom my mother, Rosie, shared with me. In our neighborhood my mother and her friends gathered for coffee and conversation while we youngsters explored our friends' yard or basement. The young mothers took time for reading, writing poetry, and sharing ideas in the midst of laundry, shopping, and cleaning. While crawling under tables and hiding behind skirts, I met such women as Maria Montessori, Dorothy Day, Barbara Ward Jackson, Caryll Houselander, Ann Morrow Lindbergh. The words and wisdom of these women lived in the conversations and poetry of my mother and her friends. Later in school I would meet these authors again and welcome them as old friends.

School opened treasures for me. My imagination and spirit fed on new ideas and word feasts. Several teachers shared their love of language by reading aloud to me and encouraging me always to read. As I grew and developed, I began to treasure the wisdom and the power I found in many women's writings. Several became sources of light and strength to which I returned again and again during the years. Their words of advice echoed in my heart as I faced new situations or reflected on past experiences. Like my grandmother, I gathered the pages of my own prayer book. From time to time I would make a new friend, a writer whose work finally reached my hands through some chance encounter.

In my spiral journey through life, I am often brought to a standstill by the utter beauty of our earth. My native Oregon is alive with natural splendor. One of my favorite childhood haunts is Silver Creek Falls. I continue to be entranced by the small creek where I wade while waiting for a rock to choose me. It is a mystery how this tiny stream suddenly falls off the edge of the earth and plunges through mist and spray to the pool below filling it up and spilling over into a new creek.

When contemporary feminist songwriter Cris Williamson sings in *Waterfall,* her song about her "endless waterfall" which is "filling up and spilling over,"[2] I am returned immediately to this childhood retreat. Biblical images of living water, healing water, cleansing water, refreshing water spill in on me. I am changed and transported to another level of my being. Mechtild of Magdeburg, a medieval woman mystic, also understood this power of water falling. "Divine love is so immensely great! Great is its overflow, for Divine Love is never still. Always ceaselessly and tirelessly it pours itself out, so that the small vessel which is ourselves might be filled to the brim and might also overflow."[3] Isn't it only right and fitting that water falling releases power to light our homes since divine life falling into us releases power to light our lives?

Along with water, the earth shares great pleasure. Do you remember mixing up mud pies or squishing barefoot through the oozing mud? Working up the soil for spring planting pleasures all the senses. One of my favorite gardeners swears that tasting the soil is essential to understanding it. The smell of freshly turned earth, of land parched by summer's heat, of soil moistened by spring rain call to images of our Earth Mother deep within.

Julian, a 14th century anchoress, lived confined within a small room attached to her church in Norwich. She is hardly the mystic one would first turn to for images of earth and of pleasure. But listen to this: "There is a treasure in the earth that is a food tasty and pleasing to the Lord. Be a gardener. Dig and ditch, toil and sweat, and turn the earth upside down, and seek the deepness, and water the plants in time. Continue this labor and make sweet floods to run, and noble and abundant fruits to spring. Take this food and drink and carry it to God as your true worship."[4]

Centuries later May Sarton, a New England poet, journaler ,and novelist, in her poem, *An Observation*, notes that "True gardeners cannot bear a glove / Between the sure touch and the tender root."[5] The price for this sensitive, sure touch is a scarred and roughened skin. We "Pay with some toughness for a gentle world."[6]

A woman May Sarton met while visiting in New Mexico shares this sensitivity and reverence for the earth. Edith Warner, a delicate, shy woman from Pennsylvania, came to live at the foot of the mesa which houses Los Alamos. Her frail constitution drew strength and healing from the rough earth, the parched air, and the precious waters near her home at Otowi crossing. In her journal, Edith reveals her reverence for her adopted land:

> My friend was wrong who said that this country was so old it
> does not matter what we Anglos do here. What we do anywhere
> matters but especially here. It matters very much. Mesas and
> mountains, rivers and trees, winds and rains are as sensitive to
> the actions and thought of humans as we are to their forces.
> They take into themselves what we give off and give it out
> again. [7]

This order and delicate balance of the entire cosmos yields a harmony that offers peace and blessing for all of us. Cycles of seasons, water falling on the earth then rising in clouds to fall again, seeds dying in the dark earth waiting for warmth and new life, these images return me to my spiral path. This first cycle overflows with blessing and open hearts: Mechtild calling me to "Live welcoming to all."[8] Images for this gallery include grapes at the crush, pressed down and spilling over; the goddess with many breasts flowing with milk for her people; the miracle of people so moved to share their food that baskets of leftovers are collected.

With the blessing and support from this Via Positiva, we move into the emptiness and darkness that at times engulfs our lives. Each of us experiences these moments of pain; they form a natural part of our lives. This Via Negativa is not to be denied or avoided or glossed over. We must enter into the darkness and embrace it before we can move on and see it from a new perspective. Our medieval beguine, Mechtild, learned from suffering that "whoever is sore wounded by love will never be made whole unless she embrace the very same love which wounded her."[9] Adrienne Rich, a contemporary feminist author, in her poem *Power* speaks of the denial by the great scientist Marie Curie:

> She died a famous woman denying
> her wounds
> denying
> her wounds came from the same source
> as her power.[10]

Emptying out and letting go is a call to prepare for new growth. St. Paul reminds us that Christ emptied himself, accepting death on a cross in preparation for his new risen life. *The Reed of God*, written near the time of my birth, contains Caryll Houselander's wartime reflections on emptiness and waiting. This English woman touched the pain of my mother and many other war brides waiting for their husbands to return. In the poem *Pastoral* she speaks of Mary and of herself as an empty reed, a shepherd's pipe. Any song can pour through her. She is empty, waiting to bring music to life when filled with breath.

> Now, if you will, breathe out your joy in me
> And make bright song,
> Or fill me with the soft moan of your love.[11]

Within ourselves we experience a pull of opposites not unlike the tug between magnetic poles: emptiness/fullness, dark/light, joy/sorrow. Our challenge is to blend, to hold the tension of these opposites within ourselves. We need to transform our dualistic worldview into a dialectical consciousness.[12]

St. Paul tells of the struggle that continually wages within him. Even when he wants to do what is good, it is something else he chooses instead. Cris Williamson acknowledges this dual reality and her struggle for freedom in her song *Wild Things*. She urges a return to the darkness. "But wild, wild things can turn on you / And you got to set them free."[13] May Sarton, too, describes the inner struggle that often spills out in our actions through her poem *The Angel and the Furies*. As we strive to maintain our balance in the swirl of "sudden motions of evil" or "imitations of good" she reminds us of our humanity. "Able to bless and forgive / Ourselves. / This is what is asked of us."[14] But Mechtild shares with us a dream she had. She is offered a choice between chalices. In one hand God presents the white wine of consolation and in the other the red wine of suffering. We choose our drink. "Blessed are they who drink this wine: for although I offer both in divine love, yet is the white wine nobler in itself; but most blessed are they who drink of both, the white and the red."[15]

Here emerges another biblical image: the vine and the branches, the vine dresser who prunes so that more and better fruit will be produced. Hildegard of Bingen, a majestic woman and medieval mystic, evokes this same image envisioning the spirit as employing a pruning sword. "In the aimless, spinning soul where fog obscures the intellect and will, where the fruit is noxious and poisonous, you guide the pruning sword."[16] Hildegard incessantly draws out the greening power of trees, plants, and even people.

> When a forest does not green vigorously,
> then it is no longer a forest.
> When a tree does not blossom,
> it cannot bear fruit.
> Likewise a person cannot be fruitful
> without the greening power of faith,
> and an understanding of scripture.[17]

Remember the biblical metaphors of seeds, plants, weeds and reeds. "Have people never observed how earthly seed come to growth when it falls to the ground and is soaked by rain and dew?"[18] Should we not also expect such periods in our lives?

Anne Morrow Lindbergh is another woman I met through my mother and her friends. As a young mother, Anne learned well the place of pain and darkness, of emptiness in her life: she endured the trauma of the kidnapping of her baby son. All her money and family prestige could not lessen the pain of unending waiting. She reflects upon waiting and emptiness in her book *Gift from the Sea*. These brief mediations on shells found by a beachcomber speak deeper truths at the heart of many women's lives.

> The sea does not reward those who are too anxious, too greedy,
> or too impatient. To dig for treasure shows not only impatience and
> greed but lack of faith. Patience, patience, patience, is what the sea
> teaches. Patience and faith. One should lie empty, open, choiceless
> as a beach waiting for a gift from the sea.[19]

Edith Warner meditates on mesas and mountains outside the window of her New Mexican home as she waits for death. She is afraid and says so. An Indian friend advised her. "She had felt a fear once that I did, but she said, 'I am strong in my heart.' Surely that is better than saying there is no fear, no pain."[20] At the same time Edith also draws on the strength of her friend and of the land. In her last Christmas letter, she writes of her dying to her friends.

After weeks in a hospital it is especially wonderful to be
here in Tilano's room. Here he can rub my arm to relax
me and give me of his calm and strength. From the bed I
can see the first light on the mountains, watch the snowclouds
rise from the glistening Truchas peaks, follow the sunset
color from the valley to the sky. I can feel the mesas even
though I do not see them. It is a good place in which to
wait for the passing from a rich, full life into whatever
work lies beyond.[21]

Death is described in rich, yet simple, images by Mechtild, the medieval
beguine. Though her God says: "Do not fear your death. For when that moment
arrives I will draw my breath and your soul will come to Me like a needle to a
magnet."[22] Death is a "rippling tide of love (that) flows secretly out from God into
the soul and draws it mightily back to its source."[23] As she ages, drawing nearer to
the time of her own death, Mechtild grows imptient and reminds herself "a good
old age must be full of patient waiting and trusts in God alone."[24] At the end of
her life, Mechtild prays, "Lord God, close now your treasured gift by a holy
end."[25]

A common mystical reference to this experience of pain and suffering,
of emptiness and waiting, is the dark night. In a plaintive, mournful tone,
Williamson cries, "Where is the light?" as she wanders in the dark. She begs,
"Magnetic true-north, show me your face."[26] She describes One of the Light as a
"song of my journey, my spiritual quest for the light which I know exists for me
in this life."[27] Mechtild writes of a lantern gone out. In the dark its beauty can no
longer be seen. "There comes a time when both body and soul enter into such a
vast darkness that one loses light and consciousness and knows nothing more of
God's intimacy. At such a time when the light in the lantern burns out the beauty
of the lantern can no longer be seen. With longing and distress we are reminded of
our nothingness."[28] Hildegard ponders how we create our own darkness. "Envy
drives out all greening power! When the greedy do not get what they want, they
fall into a depression from which they are not lightly lifted. The day hurries
quickly by, they say, 'it is always night.' If happiness should stand outside, just
beyond their door, they say, 'I am accursed.' Should it go well with all they
undertake, still they would say, 'It goes badly.'"[29]

The darkness gives way to nothingness, to emptiness, to despair. Simone
Weil, a French contemporary of my mother, but a new friend of mine, says the
main value of suffering is to teach us our nothingness. "Grace wills empty spaces
but it can only enter where there is a void to receive it, and it is grace itself which
makes this void."[30] As a Jew, Simone faced the horror happening to her people in
Nazi Germany. Although at one time she was safely in America, she chose to
return to Europe, refusing to take more for herself than her compatriots had. The
young woman undermined her precarious health and died in Ashford, Kent on
August 24, 1943 of pulmonary tuberculosis and starvation. Adrienne Rich
commemorates Simone's life, work, passion, and intensity in the poem *Leaflets,*

in which a woman is pictured distributing fliers in the pouring rain. The inherent poetry of a life lived wide open, innocent and sincere, is praised and acknowledged.

The theme of suffering and nothingness is further explored by Annie Dillard. After writing her Pulitzer prize winning *Pilgrim at Tinker Creed,* Annie moved West to an island off the coast of Washington State. The fruit of her isolation is *Holy the Firm,* a weave of reflections, insights, and the story of Julie Norwich, a child who is badly burned and airlifted to a hospital. We are forcefully reminded of being created, of living in a world which seldom makes sense. "I sit at the window, chewing the bones in my wrist. Pray for them: for Julie, for Jesse her father, for Ann her mother, pray. Who will teach us to pray?"[31]

What is our response to pain, to suffering, to the dark, to the emptiness and nothingness? We wait. Wait in silence. We embrace the dark then let it go. Into the silence comes the sound of birth, according to Caryll Houselander. One waits empty and open like the beach waiting for the gift of the sea, says Anne Morrow Lindbergh. Each foam-capped wave shelters dark spaces, observes Adrienne Rich. A leaf falling from an autumn tree teaches the art of letting go, writes May Sarton. "If I can take the dark with open eyes / And call it seasonal / Love will endure."[32]

All agree that in some way a new birth comes from this experience. Creative energy is released. This next phase is the Via Creativa. For me this part of the path highlights the image of God as Mother implanted in me as I joined my Grandmother in prayer. God as Mother was not foreign to her native language. For years this image grew inside of me, nourishing my meditation and prayer. Then one day She broke free and emerged from the paint I spread on a canvas. Her form in this painting has a special place of honor in my room and in my life.

As my life unfurled, I followed the path marked out for me, meeting other women who treasured similar images. In Santa Fe I finally came face to face with a woman who had previously existed only as a legend. Meinrad Craighead brought a series of circular Mother God images to our offices. The vivid colors, rounded forms, interplay of darkness and light, left me silent.[33]

Another woman whose creative energy astounds me is Judy Chicago. Opening day of her massive Dinner Party exhibit is a cherished memory. Symbolic plates using graphic female imagery honor thirty-nine related women. Equally impressive is the historically appropriate runner stitched for each woman. A place is set for Hildegard of Bingen. Her plate carries a stained glass motif. The runner is a reproduction of Hildegard's own drawing of the cosmos, a distinctly feminine egg shape incorporating the four directions with the elements: earth, air, fire, water.

Dorothy Day was a very special woman for my mother's circle of friends. Her newspaper, The Catholic Worker, brought her to their homes. Dorothy and her lover, Forster, were going to have a child. This very fact caused her to reflect on being made in the image of God, a co-creator of this world.

Forster loved nature with a sensuous passion. I have always felt it was life with him that brought me natural happiness, that brought me close to God. His ardent love of creation brought me to the Creator of all things. I cried out to him, 'How can there be no God, when there are all these beautiful things?' God is the Creator, and the very fact that we were begetting a child made me have a sense we were made in the image and likeness of God, co-creators with Him.[34]

Centuries ago medieval women also meditated on a maternal God. Mechtild ran to God who reached out and pulled the child up onto her lap. "God is also mother who lifts her loved child from the ground to her knee. The Trinity is like a mother's cloak wherein the child finds a home and lays its head on the maternal breast."[35]

Julian of Norwich is famous for naming not only God, but Jesus also, as mother. She identifies the love of Christ with a mother's loving concern for her children. Hildegard also develops this mother image. She visions God as gifting all people with the call to be co-creators of the universe, to give birth in imitation of God, the Birther. "Just as the creation of God, that is, humankind, never ceases to come to an end, but rather, continually develops, so also the works of humankind shall not disappear."[36]

The call to co-create draws upon our capacity for creativity. Each of us knows the satisfaction of laboring to bring to birth a creation. Some women experience this in the birth of their children. Others, like May Sarton and her mother, create in their gardens food for family and friends, flowers to delight the senses. Some women recognize clearly the role they play in birthing themselves. Joanna Cazden, another contemporary musician, challenges women to take their own courage in hand and create life for themselves. "Take your own courage down off the shelf. You can sing for the world. You can live for yourself."[37]

Anne Morrow Lindbergh reminds us of the necessity for quiet and contemplation. From this overflows some creative life of one's own: an arrangement of flowers, a poem, a prayer. The importance lies in being attentive and present to one's inner life. "Quiet time alone, contemplation, prayer, music, a centering line of thought or reading, of study or work. It can be physical or intellectual or artistic, any creative life proceeding from oneself. It need be something of one's own. Arranging a bowl of flowers in the morning can give a sense of quiet in a crowded day, like writing a poem, or saying a prayer. What matters is that one be for a time inwardly attentive."[38]

Then, lest we become too self-oriented or introspective, life continues to flow out. We continue our spiral journey by examining our reality and responsibility as a communion of people. This part of the path is called the Via Transformativa.

We are interconnected and need to recognize our need for interdependence. With the advances of technology, our world, indeed our universe, is shrinking. We must all live together in our global village. Cris

Williamson recognizes this interdependence in her song *Sister.* "Born of the earth, a child of God just one among the family."[39] We need to lean on each other, to be there for each other. Naomi Littlebear's song, *Like a Mountain* rallies peace workers on many continents. "You can't kill the spirit. It's like a mountain, old and strong: it loves on and on."[40] Edith Warner, friend of many scientists at Los Alamos, knew that they could not easily return after the war to their own various laboratories leaving the new destructive power in the hands of the military and politicians. Nor could she return to making her famous chocolate cake. Life was different. The memory of Hiroshima and Nagasaki impelled her to search for ways to live together in peace. "So louder and louder blasts echo over the Plateau and my blood runs cold remembering Hiroshima. If the world lived here, all would be reminded frequently that we must catch up with striding science and find a way to live together in the peace that Christmas signifies."[41]

For change to occur, I must change. Adrienne Rich recognizes the energy surge that touches us as people become more conscious of themselves and each other. In her poem *The Parting: II*, a woman combs her hair seeking in its tangle the part that brings order. Williamson prays, "Open mine eyes that I may see / Glimpses of truth thou hast for me / Open mine eyes, illumine me / Spirit divine."[42]

Caryll Houselander saw with her inner eye an icon of Christ with arms spread wide over a grey London street. The Russian face, later identified as that of the assassinated Tsar, spoke so clearly to her of the unity of all people. "The austere simplicity of that beautiful face stood sharp with grief. But the eyes and the mouth smiled with the ineffable love which consumes sorrow and pain as rags are consumed in a burning fire."[43] Later in an underground train, she saw this same face of Christ in everyone she met. "But I saw more than that; not only was Christ in every one of them, living in them, dying in them, rejoicing in them, sorrowing in them, but because he was in them, and because they were here, the whole world was here too, here in this underground train; not only the world as it was at that moment, not only all the people in all the countries of the world, but all those people who had lived in the past, and all those yet to come."[44]

Holly Near reiterates this theme of unity and identification when she identifies with a Central American woman, a student shot at Kent State, and a musician tortured by the junta. Seeing herself in others she continues to sing their song, calling for justice and for freedom. "It could have been me, but instead it was you. So I'll keep doing the work you were doing as if I were two."[45]

Mechtild understands this and calls us to pour out compassion on the earth. "When we on earth pour out compassion and mercy from the depths of our hearts and give to the poor and dedicate our bodies to the service of the broken, to that very extent do we resemble the Holy Spirit."[46] Power is given us that we might serve others.

We continue our journey on the path marked out for us. We spiral round and round as we glimpse again and again from new vantage points the images of our journey. The grandeur of nature continues to halt our movement. The pleasures of our earthly life treat our bodies to new delights and enhance memories of past ones. Love overflows in open, welcoming hearts. Eyes open, we enter into darkness. We find in pain and silence the Nothingness we call God. In the dark new life seeks light. We give birth to ourselves and our creations in ever-changing forms. Together we change and grow. Together we seek to build our world in justice and love.

Along the spiral path of our own journey, we have company—women to be with us. Women of long ago like Mechtild, Hildegard, and Julian shower us with wisdom born of a simpler life lived in a closer harmony with the elements. Contemporaries of my mother, Edith Warner, Caryll Houselander, May Sarton, Dorothy Day, Anne Morrow Lindbergh, bring the light of their experience of peace and war, of creation and of emptiness. Women of my day, Adrienne Rich, Annie Dillard, Meinrad Craighead, Cris Williamson, share the insights of their lives through song, poetry, painting, and writing. Each of these women accompanies us on the spiral path as we continue to create ourselves and our world.

Sister Sue Woodruff is a member of the Sisters of the Holy Names. Sue holds degrees in Elementary Education and Language Arts from Marylhurst College and in Curriculum  Development from Western Washington State University. She has taught for several years in junior high schools, latterly in open classrooms, and has worked at planning and goal-setting for her religous community. In the larger community, Sue was education counselor at the Urban Indian Council of Portland, and later Assistant Director of the Training and Employment Department. She then became editor of *The Little Magazine* of Bear and Company in Santa Fe while writing *Meditations with Mechtild of Magdeburg,* published in 1982. Returning to Oregon, Sue served on the committee for renewal within her religious community and is currently Coordinator of Ministry for the province. She continues to find wisdom and refreshment in the words of women writers, sharing these treasures with other women and men in workshops about women's spirituality and literature.

"The learned say that your lights will one day be no more," said the firefly to the stars. *The stars made no answer.*

TAGORE

Work and Spirituality:
An Interview with

Vivian Jenkins Nelsen

ivian, for many years you have been a leader in traditional bastions of male authority—church administration, higher education—and public service, and often the first woman to break ground in each place. What is it like for women in these strongholds of patriarchy?

It can be difficult; very stressful. When they are the first in a position, or when they are breaking new ground, women have to get in there and do more of whatever the men are doing. Often they develop health problems. But men never know when to stop. They get burned out and they keep right on; they get heart attacks and they also get very crazy, very neurotic. They work sick and they expect everyone else to do the same. They never take time for personal emergencies. Work! Even death means nothing. They just don't interrupt the flow of work.

The husband of one of my co-workers died suddenly at the age of forty-two. She was thrown into shock and depression. The prevailing male stereotype is that she should cry for a day and then go back to work. When she didn't follow this pattern, one of the men in the office thought, "Well, after a month she's probably getting lonely" so he asked her for a date. The woman came to me to intervene because the man kept calling her at night, pressuring her to go out with him. When I reported this with great indignation to my own male boss, he saw nothing wrong, except that perhaps the man was a little early in asking. He thought the very best advice for the bereaved woman was to get back to work so she would forget all about her loss.

I found that such crazy things are the norm for men in the world of business. All of them are ill: high blood pressure, ulcers, all kinds of stress diseases are there, pushed down, but definitely there. And the effects of their illness become part of the work environment.

What makes the men get caught that way?

I think it is the way they are socialized, the way they are raised. School and family does that to us, and all of society reinforces it through rewards and sanctions. A few men unlearn that stuff, but it is hard to do. They must take as disciplined an approach to unlearn it as they took to learn it all.

It was very interesting for me to visit third world countries where male values are entirely flipped over. The countries could still run! On a trip to Egypt with some other business women, a few of us decided to go off exploring on our own. My idea was that we would take a leisurely, romantic ride down the Nile river, watch the birds, and just drift by, seeing the country. Their idea was "What time does the boat arrive? How long is the trip? When do we arrive back at the hotel?" We sat waiting in a grubby hotel courtyard, the air full of dust, flies everywhere, until our boat man came. The other women were so distressed because he would not tell them when we would be back that they decided not to go. He would only say, "When it gets too dark." To him time is when you get done. Throughout the trip it was interesting to see workers deal with Americans who insisted that they must know when and how long and what time. "It says here on the schedule that the boat will arrive at nine. Is that right?" And the guide would say, "Oh, yes." Of course there was no boat at nine. I asked the guide why he answered yes when no was the obvious response. "Because they need the boat to be there." So there are men who work in a different way from the American model and still survive!

In our society what is the basic difference between the way men use power and the way women use power?

I think the major difference is that women need to have relationships; we are relational-oriented. I think men are raised conversely to be results-oriented. That is the major difference. Of course you will find people on both sides, but the prevailing values are 'relational' versus 'results', 'people' versus 'thing.'

How does that manifest?

It manifests in every way possible. The difference between the male style and the female style is very real. It is telling people to do things, versus negotiating with them. It is helping people to choose what they should do rather than forcing them to do things. The female style lets people choose to do things (within certain limits, of course), rather than using authority to force them to do it and then getting all that energy pushing back at them. But men in business don't understand that, and they don't understand that the women's way is the healthier style.

      For example, my boss (male) tells me, "Don't ask employees if they want to do this. Just tell them to do it!" Or he will tell me that I delegate too much: "You should hold the power more." He feels that he is being a good mentor to advise me in that way. I will say, "I want to have a group of office staff that meets regularly so they can gripe, get information from me, blow off steam, or whatever they need. It would be entirely their group." My boss says, "Well, OK, but only if you chair the group and keep it all in control." I have heard this sort of answer a number of times in different jobs, and so I now am able to recognize it as a male pattern, a male method.

      While I worked in the church I also learned this method. In the Lutheran Church each congregation is autonomous. Each is a separate entity, although connected to the larger church. The congregations thus should have much responsibility for initiating and running things. But this is all in theory only; it is all rhetoric. The mother church tells the executives: "You have to be at every meeting, and you have to make sure that nothing gets out of control." In male structures, control is very firmly held by top authority. So I see the way men and women use power as being very different. It is a difference between owning power and sharing it. Men's notion of power is 'power over'—domination and control. Women's notion of power is 'power with'—power shared among all.

When women are working in a male dominated society, how do they remain true to their own selves?

It's hard. It is very, very hard. Women have to have a strong center within. This is difficult, however, because on the one hand the environment doesn't allow easily for growth. If I know something is right, then I must always be proving it. I can never take chances with anything; I can never make mistakes. I have to be right always because it is my way against his way. Often this does damage to the way I want to be, which is to be open, letting things happen, not always defending the growth process or the change process, and letting other people and myself make mistakes. That's why the male environment is a difficult place to be. One has to be ultimately committed to being broken!

I didn't expect you to say that! Being broken is part of the process?

That's part of the process.

Yet you still feel that there is a place for women within men's power structures?

Yes. I think that women are the only answer for the workplace. It is so necessary for women to keep the spiritual windows open. I see men and their structures on the way to real destruction—destruction of people. When we look at the workplace now as compared to ten years ago, it has improved, for sure. We can see all the effects of pop psychology: people are more moved by it and more informed by it. But at the same time I think we have a driving materialism now that we have never seen before. The baby boomers are worse than their parents were. They have focused in a very concrete way on material things—things that our parents had only in a general kind of way because they were coming out of the war years and everything was scarce. Now materialism has become so intense that we have to find another way of doing things.

Do you think women are bringing a new spirituality into the workplace and into power structures?

You bet. I absolutely know that to be so.

And the difference women are able to make is due to their psychology?

Yes. It is a very profound difference for those who acknowledge it. There are a lot of women who are now removed from the women's struggle. They do not acknowledge their own psychology. They have gotten into the workplace, and so they are now just one of the boys. They don't see themselves in any way different from men because they don't behave any way different. They wear skirts, but if the norm were to wear pants, they'd wear pants. They obey the male norms perfectly.

But I maintain that there is a battle that goes on within them whether they acknowledge it or not, and whether it is going on in the conscious or the unconscious mind. They are ignoring their own feminine psyche.

There are expectations that women will be softer than men in the workplace. Women will be the ones that others can really go and talk to. A brother dies and a man feels compelled to tell the other men, "Oh well, he was just a fool; we weren't that close." But to a woman executive he comes and says, "God, I'm really broken up over this death; I feel so bad." And the woman will understand and be able to comfort him and offer sympathy because she is a woman. Men cannot do that to men. Women get to be the shoulder, the receiver, of a lot of the pain in the workplace that men can't give to each other.

Do you feel that women should keep striving for more power in society—politics, for example—to change it?

Well, that is interesting. I definitely think some women should get into politics and need to be there, but it is hard for me to talk about because it is something I personally do not value. People are often telling me to run for public office, but I really don't want to do that. My mother is a public official and so I know what it is like. To me somebody has to do it, but there are also other things that can be done to help change the power. I know it is important for women to be in politics. I have seen old ladies and young girls talking around female politicians. I went to a party for Geraldine Ferraro and the women came up to her and cried, "Geraldine, it is so important what you are doing..." There was an amazing feeling in the group. But to be in public office takes a kind of hardness, a driving, a clawing that I do not admire in women or men. We must be realistic and acknowledge that in our system that's the way things work. That's how people get to the top. That's why I say I think it is important for some, and probably for all of us in some way.

How do you think that women should use power?

Well, women should use power the way we should all use power. That is, first of all, to acknowledge that we all have power, and then to try to work toward a model where we acknowledge other people's power—whether spiritual or intellectual or intuitive or all the other kinds of power that we don't yet respect. I think that we have to work towards really utilizing that power and sharing it. That change in the whole point of view means that things will look very different, obviously, from the way they look now.

Since men are most interested in results, in making a profit, for example, how can a woman with her concept of power enrich the man who is in his framework of mind? How can he even begin to make room for her ideas about power?

Let's use an example. When Japanese motor bikes came on the market, companies like Harley Davidson called them rice cakes! They had nothing but contempt for the Japanese and their products and methods. Guess what? The American company went into trouble. They had been a really macho, male company but they were now about to fold. They had to make a real change in the way they were doing business. So the employees bought the company and inaugurated a Japanese business model. It is now working successfully. What is important is that in a funny kind of way the Japanese model of quality circles is very feminine. This is, of course, understanding that Japanese society is terribly homogeneous and terribly male-oriented. But the model of everybody being involved on the line, making decisions along with making the cars, flex time, people being able to switch jobs, and so forth, are all things that the women's movement in this country has long said needed to happen.

What about a company that is hard-nosed, makes lots of money, forces everyone to conform, tries to put everybody else out of business, but is also really successful in that sense our society recognizes?

OK. I think that as a different model pervades the workplace and the consciousness of workers is raised and they realize that they are being limited, it will change things, even at such companies.

Do you think that there is a general change in the mentality of workers?

There is, absolutely. And more is coming, because people who came through public schools will be different. Kids don't stand in lines anymore. Kids aren't forced to go separately to bathrooms like when we grew up. All that stuff is changing in one generation just because of the revolution in ideas of some major thinkers about how the schools are run. It will be very difficult for kids who learned in an open school environment (and more and more are), to go to IBM or a similar company and have to wear a suit and conform and have someone else have so much control over them. It just will not work. So companies will simply not be able to be as rigid. IBM is going to find that they will not be entirely successful in being able to raise executives up through the ranks that are like little cut-out cookies. You see it in the army too. The army is now letting recruits have various lengths of hair and wear facial hair and have more freedom. The young people will not put up with the old ideas. We are seeing this change in a lot of ways. People know there is a different way now. It will take time with big organizations, but change will happen.

Do women pay a price by being in positions of power?

Yes, a lot of prices! Often women have to choose often between career and family. If they don't make that choice, then they have to choose between being supermom and being super-executive. I myself don't have children, but I see the strain in women around me who do.

Women also have to make a choice between being ethical and being professional. Those two are not the same thing. They are not the same. In my case the question is Can I be a good Christian and also be a good business person? Do ends justify means? Do you lie or not tell the entire truth to get what you want? The whole Ollie North syndrome goes on so much in business. You struggle every time you have to make those decisions in the beginning and it eventually becomes less of a struggle. Every time you tell a lie or hold back part of the truth, it does something inside you, perhaps not at a conscious level, but it hurts you.
One of the other things that women must deal with is the incredible amount of time one must spend in order to function well in the work world. Sixty hours a week is usual, not exceptional. Some people work eighty hours. And then you have no energy, no fun for non-work activity, because you are just so tired. I also think that because of fatigue and long hours women who are married probably curtail their sex life as well.

Being the first or second woman to have a position means that one is always on view, under tremendous scrutiny and tremendous pressure. There is a double standard in this environment and women often suffer because of it. On the one hand they have to be tough, and on the other hand they are supposed to be soft. This dichotomy, this pulling and sharing, goes on all the time. One must decide, Is this the time I should be soft or is this the time I should be firm?

Another very basic, daily problem is the testing women in power must face. There is testing by men and women both. Men especially test everything women do, every decision they make, not only the results of decisions and actions, but her right to make a decision. That is the tough part. That underlying insult is always there. If the woman is more educated than the men, that produces another tension. Men go through testing too, but not to the extent that it goes on with women. Women are always being put in difficult positions that men hope will show us at our basic. Women are still an enigma in the workplace and men don't know if they can trust us, so they do terrible things to put us in situations where they can see what we will do. Will we fall apart? stay with the gang? be a team member? run?

When I first came to the university, men kept swearing and telling jokes in very bad taste in my presence to see what I would do. That sexual harassment is very real in many workplaces. Women then go through a whole stream of self-questioning: 'Did I cause that?' In the work world it is assumed that the woman caused it; she must have sent some secret message in the way she dressed, or in the way she handled herself. This is definitely not a sexual issue; it is a power issue. The male thinks, "I can empower myself on you in a way that is hard for you to say no. If that doesn't work, then I will seduce you. And then you will say what I want you to say because I've made you say it against your will in a non-knowing way." There is an intentional 'stupidness' that men use. We like to think of it as naiveté, but it really is a power play. Sometimes when men feel threatened by a woman in authority, they will react in sexual harassment. They will pretend that women like it, but they are choosing to be naive in order to control women.

You said that women also test women in power. That sounds rather sad. Why would they do that?

The why of it is fairly straightforward. The bottom line is the assumption that women are not supposed to be leaders. The fact that we haven't experienced women as leaders causes women to absorb all the stereotypes about themselves just as other stereotyped groups do. The negative part of it is rather significant. The Women's Bureau of the Department of Labor has done some research on this. There are so few women bosses that it is a pity. So women don't expect other women to be bosses and they don't know how to behave when they get one. In the beginning, my feeling about this was a kind of confused understanding of the process. I had a real impatience with it, and when I had my first secretary tell me that she had never worked for a woman and wasn't sure she wanted to, I was determined to be the very best boss that she'd ever had. Well, that puts a strain on the relationship and it isn't the most authentic relationship one can have—with one person trying to prove something to the other and the other person trying to disprove it.

The second time that this happened, I received a letter from one of my staff people saying that I could advise her but that she would be reporting directly to the Dean rather than to me because I was a woman. Her line of reporting was supposed to be directly to me. I confronted it head-on and told the Dean I would not come to work there unless he got the line of reporting straight. It did not matter to me how he handled it, but it had to be handled. That really surprised him and he said, "Well, really we don't have to confront this. Once she gets to know you she'll love you." But that was not the issue. The staff person had a working relationship with me and it should not be based on whether or not she liked me. Her working relationship with the Dean was not based on that. So he said, "Well, it seems to me that you want power and authority." I had to reply that one without the other does not work very well. I did not want to boss the woman, but I did want to be able to ask her to do things and know that she would do them for the good of the order.

That is a long way around saying what my experience has been, but my feeling about it at this point is a very deep sadness that women spend a lot of time testing each other and carrying forth stereotypes. It leads other people to say that women are their own worst enemies, which is not true, but it does give credence to that position. I think this issue is something that must definitely be worked on. When women encounter it they have to share what they are feeling at that time with the person who is causing it.

I found that confrontation to be even more helpful. In the long run the Dean did confront the woman and told her that she was going to have to operate as if the two of us—he and I—were identical. And so she did manage that, but only because the top boss told her so. I think that had I probably told her, "Look, this is the way it makes me feel when you write me a letter like this" it may or may not have had the desired effect. But now I am much less nervous about challenging people directly about those kinds of things.

Are women's experiences in executive positions all negative?

Actually it is not all negative, but it is more of a struggle than people realize. Young women going into the workplace never have any idea about how hard it is. In my case I am always on a search for meaning, so I won't spend a lot of time on people and activities that ultimately mean nothing either in my life or the institution's life. The times when you do meaningful things balance off the negative stuff. It is less a matter of people saying, "Well, you did that job well" than saying "What you did really helped me." That is much more important for me. I would also say that I am a pragmatist, geared to action. So solving problems about things and people as they interact is very satisfying for me. To know I am doing something important, even if the system does not reward me, is very important, very satisfying.

Is there is a possibility for women to grow spiritually in the workplace?

You do or you die. You have to mature, or you get stupid. I think maturation goes on anywhere you are. I don't think the ultimate questions are any different anywhere else. They are just framed in a different way in the workplace. But you are still always dealing with questions like, Is it for your good or our good? Is it yours or mine or is it ours? Is it for the good of the organization or is it for what I want—my Rolex, my Mercedes, or whatever? Those questions go on everywhere. I have done a lot of community work and I know the same thing occurs there. The ultimate value questions are always present. How you treat others, how they treat you.

Would you consider a strong spiritual background an asset for women in positions of power?

Yes, definitely yes. And it can also be a problem. If your spiritual center says that you have to treat people a certain way in order to be ethical, and if the ethics of the workplace are different, you will be clashing all the time. If everything boils down to who's got power rather than who is right in this situation, there will be problems. If your center says that you have to do things in an egalitarian or a fair way and the workplace says that you do things based on a line order or who is boss here, and it is not all right to raise the question of rightness, then you will be troubled. But I think it's a better trouble to be in than merely floundering with no center, no place to come to. I think a spiritual center is very important from a sense that wherever you are life is dancing around. Good things are happening and bad things are happening. Your center is a way of making sense out of that dance. If you don't have a spiritual center, then often things won't make sense to you.

A week ago I went to a funeral of a young male colleague. We had worked closely on a number of projects. He was not able to see his way through some problems and so, at twenty-eight, he hung himself. His violent death was extremely hard on a young woman who was his coworker. She is struggling to decipher what his death means. His boss is also spending a lot of time worrying about her style of working with him and how she contributed to his death. So the question of personal values is extremely important. Introspection is always necessary.

I think a lot of people perceive their jobs as their whole life. Their jobs bring a lot of satisfaction as long as they are able to perform them, but when they are no longer able to work, who are they? They have no identity whatever. Because women are relational, they will not have quite the problem that men have in this regard. Men die in alarming numbers the year after they retire. I think relationships are the basic reason why; many men have not learned the social skills to develop intimacy with people. Women generally learn this early in life and continue to develop it. That intimacy, that caring, both giving and receiving back, sustains us and makes life worth living. Intimacy is a spiritual quality. It is a spiritual facility. It's something that people have worked on for centuries in a very disciplined way to learn to be intimate with their spiritual center, whatever that may be—God, the universe, the environment, or all of them.

But spirituality is also frightening for some people. I have found people in the workplace very threatened by the fact that I have worked for years for the Lutheran church. They must have thought that I was going to proselytize them. It is amazing the number of people who felt that my having a spiritual center would mean coercion for them. Yet I still believe that we all have to have our own spiritual center.

Since women tend to share power and try to establish a personal relationship , how can they avoid falling into the patrimony approach to work, the idea, "I'm taking care of my own" as Mayor Daley used to say?

Well, that is a very good question and it is something I do struggle with. In organizations as large as the ones I've been in lately, one does not have to worry about it because one cannot establish personal relationships with that many people. There simply isn't time to have really quality relationships. But there are enough people to make the mix interesting, while not dominating the organization in that way.

The problem with the patrimony approach is that it can be very seductive. It can build dependency, which is its fault. Because women are accessible in a way that men are not, the staff will bring the woman personal problems; with work problems they will say, "Fix it. Help me." It is not possible to help everybody, nor is it a style that is best to foster. You want to enable your staff to find their own richness so you give them the time and permission to be able to solve their own problems. That will then hopefully create an independence from you rather than the dependency that accessibility can foster. I have seen people who mistakenly capitalize on this accessibility. I call them Queen Bees; everyone is drawn to the honey. The queen gets rather fat and bloated from all the attention. That's not healthy. You need to be able to struggle with people who say, "Your idea is dumb" and still keep moving and working. We should not constantly need approval to keep us going. We need the ups and the downs, the agreements and the disagreements also, but all of that should be covered with an ultimate caring that lets people know that we really want things to happen in a good way for them. It is important that both of us be strong in the relationship whether in the workplace or anywhere else in life. Whenever I have a choice to make it will be for the empowerment of both of us.

Vivian Jenkins Nelsen speaks from a multi-faceted career which includes positions as university lecturer, choir director, school board president, organist, and social services

worker. Currently she is President and CEO of the International Institute for Interracial Interaction: INTER-RACE.

Active in the Lutheran Church, Vivian is Program Chairperson for Mission in Communities, involved in resourcing social justice, global consciousness, peace, world hunger, and refugee settlement. She has taught at Hamline University and the University of Minnesota and has been very active in human relations and community services, particularly for minority groups.

Vivian is a member of the National Council of Negro Women, the Prince of Glory Lutheran Church Council, the Women's Equity Action League, the Metropolitan Cultural Art Center, the Women's Affairs Advisory Board of the Minnesota State Department of Human Rights, and the Greater Urban Parish Board.

*And whoever, either now or after I am gone
shall be a lamp unto themselves, and a
refuge unto themselves, and shall take
themselves to no external refuge but holding
fast to the truth as their lamp, it is they who
shall reach the topmost height.*

BUDDHA

Scriptures and Spirituality:
Tools for Women's Spiritual Quest

by

Justin O'Brien, Ph.D.

*I*f one would interview mystics and saints acclaimed by their cultures as spiritual adepts, one would find hardly an individual to vouch that spiritual growth is easy. Still the story of their achievements fascinates us. Their vexations, their inner trials, the opposing circumstances, their impact upon society, all those ingredients that make a biography interesting, enable us to associate with their spiritual journey. Their stories reveal variations, however, that defy any attempt at neat theological categorizations. The desire to evaluate spirituality on an abstract scale by degrees of holiness is never conducted by the saints themselves, but only by their admirers or their detractors. Saints frequently live unconventional lives, breaking boundaries and forcing society to reconsider its role models. Hence the import of a saint often exceeds our expectations of the spiritual life.

The successful quest for spirituality shows such wide variations in the actual lifestyles of men and women that it is difficult to collate into fixed rules. While institutional religions understandably resist approving those spiritual approaches that do not fit their denominational standards, holy men and women have been known to embarrass church orthodoxy. So how does one learn from the ranks of holy people?

A dilemma recurs particularly in Western women's quest for spirituality: spiritual guidance can be hazardous to their self-esteem. Women frequently have to make a choice between society's cultural-religious beliefs about their gender and their own personal feelings about themselves. This vexation surfaces acutely in the awareness of women who attempt to control their spiritual destiny.

A principal source of irritation for women continues to be those historical fonts of spiritual waters, the scriptures of the world. The traditional keepers of these scriptures are men who claim the final authority for interpretation. Into this established tradition have come new dissenting voices. These voices, mostly feminine, are bringing fresh reflections upon the interpretive role that gender asserts in the composition of scripture and its social context.

For most male believers, a major basis for religious security arises from the conviction that spirituality, like most everything in the universe, is truly a man's world. For centuries the male spiritual elite—theologians, pundits, priests, rabbis, shamans, mullahs, lamas, and roshis—used their scriptures to justify their privileged positions in society. The Torah and the Gospels, as well as the Qu'ran, are considered by their followers to be divinely inspired words, but words, one should keep in mind, composed from and within the context of a patriarchal culture, and thus unavoidably reflective of those values. In the ambiance of patriarchy—a classical worldview that embraces social, economic, political, and religious values stressing male privilege and domination—it happens that women are subjugated and oppressed. While men recognize that women's lives demonstrate unique aspects in this cultural context, these differences are given only secondary consideration in spirituality. Women believers have actually achieved religious security from obedience to these conditions. Security does not necessarily promote growth.

Let us take a look at one of the principal scriptures. The Bible is not a series of scientific abstracts, but just the opposite. It narrates stories of Semitic peoples in their search and struggle for the meaning of life, covering a period of approximately 1,400 years. Their quest has been characterized by theologians as salvation-history, wherein oppressed and sinful people respond in various ways when offered liberation by a divine benefactor. The heroes of these stories have names like Abraham, Noah, Moses, David, Solomon, Sampson, Jeremiah, Isaias, Daniel, John the Baptist, Jesus, Peter, Paul, Stephen, to name a few. Heroines, in comparison, hardly exist. Since the spread of the Bible into the world it has been customary for believers, not only in Semitic societies, but throughout the Western hemisphere, to accept the patriarchal world-view it depicts as the cultural standard.

Over the centuries a great deal of social modification has ensued. The description of a Jewish or Christian wedding in the twentieth century, for example, is not the same in every detail as in the times of Moses or Paul. Yet the religious and cultural patterns of modern societies still retain the same patriarchal perspective. Women's social status and spiritual opportunities are primarily devised and approved by men. Spiritual authority and the abundance of spiritual benefices have devolved historically upon males as the primary, if not exclusive, agents of achievements and transmission. Even the God of the Bible has been traditionally imaged as male. Would it seem, women inquire, a blasphemy to imagine the divine as transcending gender? Would God be impugned by inclusive male and female characteristics? Is salvation permitted only if one accepts allegiance to God in the male role? A further question may be asked regarding the Bible as a whole. Just as the prophets in the Hebrew scriptures reinterpreted their own traditions, dismissing and rejecting as well as emphasizing and enhancing inherited values, has the time come in our period of history to place the patriarchal standard of the Bible up for debate? As the standard of social intercourse it may have worn out its welcome and, thanks to feminine criticism, we are realizing its limitations. A new quandary then emerges for those whose sole roots for spiritual values reside in the Bible. If one relies upon the Bible for every clue to spirituality, then any questioning of biblical structures sounds subversive.

For many women, the Bible is the most authoritative source for their spiritual life. As we have seen, the composition and redaction of the Bible has been the responsibility of those living within a patriarchal social context. Down through the ages this fundamental outlook has been the inspiration that male believers have recounted to indicate the proper place of women in social and spiritual life. For the most part, women have accepted this arrangement.

Yet what are women to do when frustrated by the conflict between their religious beliefs about their gender and their own self-discovery? Some assert questions that jeopardize their religious and social inheritance. They criticize specific interpretations of biblical texts that assume, and thus support, the male context of spirituality on social and theological grounds. Some discover how confining and unfair this tradition appears, and later come upon other scriptures, such as the Upanishads, which, in contradiction, exalt the feminine person.

Theological speculation and religious ritual have been derived from those texts of scripture that would indicate that women should retain a submissive role. It has been the common practice to generalize many texts and give them an anthropological import. For example, Paul's letter to the Corinthians speaks about the proper decorum and manners of women in a religious assembly:

> But every woman who prays or prophesys with her head uncovered dishonors her head; for that is even all one as if she were shaven. For if the woman be not covered, let her also be shorn; but if it be a shame for a woman to be shaven, let her be covered. I Cor. 11: 5-6

The traditional interpretation of this text is that women must cover their heads because this decree arises either from an exigency of woman's nature or by divine ordination. Since Paul spoke about Corinthian women of the first century, traditionalists would insist that his regulation must be valid today. But the expansion of Paul's remark to a local community into a universal proclamation about women's headdress makes as much sense as insisting that Paul had vested interests in a haberdashery. Other problems arise: is Paul's dictum obeyed better by the colossal extravagances of Victorian women or by the postage-size doilies pinned on the heads of the women of the Assembly of God Church? There is neither textual nor logical connection between Paul's utterance and its unconditional application to women everywhere and for all time. What are exegetes and theologians to do in the face of texts that scholarship alone cannot seem to resolve? What about texts that offer only a negative status quo about women, as well as those that would challenge this presumption?

> I will therefore that men pray everywhere, lifting up holy hands without wrath and doubting. In like manner also, that women adorn themselves in modest apparel, with shamefacedness and sobriety; not with braided hair, or gold, or pearls, or costly array but (which becomes women professing godliness) with good works. Let the woman learn in silence with all subjection. But I suffer not a woman to teach, nor to usurp authority over the man, but to be in silence. For Adam was first formed, then Eve. And Adam was not deceived, but the woman being deceived was in the transgression. Not withstanding she shall be saved in childbearing, if they continue in faith and charity

and holiness with sobriety. I Tim. 2:8-15

> For as many of you as have been baptized into Christ
> have put on Christ, there is neither Jew nor Greek, there is
> neither bond nor free, there is neither male nor female; for ye
> are all one in Christ Jesus. Galations 3:27-8

These quandaries illuminate a further problem: Just how useful is the Bible as a guide for feminine spirituality? Depicting women in scriptures is one thing; discerning her nature and possible spiritual options is another. Does belief in the Bible as God's revelation presume that it instructs women to reiterate in their current spiritual life the same socio-religious values that structured Semitic societies? Specifically, is the description of women's subordinate role an appeal to perpetuate it forever? Is this what being faithful to the holy texts means? With such an approach to the Bible it would be only logical to insist that Jews and Christians initiate holy wars, extending the pillage and rape recorded in Exodus. Obviously a civilized person would be repulsed by such an inference. But the repulsion does not remove the problem: Should believers today reinstitute the self-image and social status of men and women found in the passages of the Bible? Does the paucity of biblical stories enhancing women's role mean that this absence is normative, ethically and spiritually?

Confronting the Bible are irreversible changes in history. The cultural emergence of the nuclear age has no antecedents in biblical times; the attitudes, ambitions, pressures, and general sense of living today have no exact equivalent in the biblical world. Curiously the enlargement of women's roles and the increased recognition of new opportunities in society have been inspired less by biblical resources than by women's hard struggle in the social, economical, and political arenas. A tension unavoidably arises between the Bible's description of women and the contemporary assessment of her worth and opportunities.

When the Bible is not appraised as a manual of proof-texts to exemplify a patriarchal society, then there is room for viewing women in other contexts. Seeing many contexts for women's lives leads to a variety of moral values.

Acknowledging the historical conditions for textual statements clarifies the range for applying these statements. The Jewish community would not cast its reading of the Wisdom literature, for instance, into the political light of Deuteronomy; the Psalms are not legislation. At the same time, the continuity of the people in their history accumulates an overall context for the personal well-being of the community.

One advantage in approaching the Bible overall (its spirit of salvation rather than its cultural mores) is that it exerts a corrective pressure upon all forms of oppression. It questions the patronizing of either gender oppressed over groups in society, thereby exposing any arbitrary assumptions around treatment of those considered different than oneself.

For example, women have known the feelings of being powerless in male societies dedicated to personal freedom. One of the multiple themes taken up in biblical stories involves the perspective of the powerless. Stories of God's concern for widows, orphans, outcasts, the physically handicapped, the impoverished, and the enslaved abound. The afflicted of society are very much included in the biblical concern for justice and liberation. Women could associate their own exile from recognition by society and religious authorities with these various episodes. Thus they can draw upon the Bible's emancipation themes for stimulus to continue their own struggle for personal, social, and spiritual identity. If the Bible opposes such a sense of justice, then belief in the Bible is fruitless and destructive.

There is another unexpected critical tradition within the Bible that is not given sufficient attention as a spiritual resource. The prophetic tradition presents a host of protesters to confront the social and spiritual abuses of not only the "pagan," but of the Jewish faithful. From Amos to Zechariah there is a long list of prophets whose writings reveal a distinctive perspective that opposed the injustices of the social and religious status quo. The prophets were keen critics. They denounced society's use of religion to exonerate injustice and prejudice and to entrench privileges of power over the less advantaged.

What these writings provide in their spirit and rationale is both precedent and incentive to examine the forms and policies constituting spirituality today. The reason for resisting the canonizing of particular texts is that they themselves reveal limitations. They relate to specific problems in a specific era—crucial problems at that time, but not exhaustive of every instance of injustice. The acerbic judgment of a prophet does not necessarily extend to every form of oppression in that community. Obviously the prophets selected certain issues to denounce or praise; others they left untouched. They were sensitive to the enslavement of the Jewish people by foreign empires, but neglected to protest the Jewish family's use of slaves. Is it safe to assume that because other instances of oppression are not denounced they are therefore tacitly approved by the prophets? If this tradition is more than merely a historical episode, then its prophetic spirit is an encouragement to examine the current forms of spiritual orthodoxy for their enrichment, as well as for their deformation.

The Bible speaks to one's path when it stirs the mind and heart of life. Scripture can shake our sense of reality, stirring our longing for life, beauty, truth, and goodness. It requires less our submission than our enlargement of soul to recognize its worth. It must relieve our anxiety about the fragmentariness of living and beckon us to wholeness.

Scripture, however, cannot be the highest court of appeal for spirituality; no revealed writings can. The greatness of the Bible, as well as other scriptures, lies not in its composition and proclamations but in its power to induce the reader and listener to fulfill themselves from its message. Once, when I was completing research at a library belonging to the New Church of Jerusalem, I asked one of the church officers, an energetic and intelligent young man, if the people in the community meditated and explored consciousness as Emmanuel Swedenborg, their founder, charted it. He replied that it was most unlikely. Why should they bother since it had all been done already by their founder in the eighteenth century and was vividly described in his writings? Apparently many people are satisfied to treat scripture as an armchair traveler's brochure: read about it but don't visit.

Scripture can be viewed as one of the many important companions that we meet along the way of our life's destiny, a companion which offers us an encouraging word, suggests a route, and displays a rough map. This encounter illuminates the meaning of our experience, provided we pay attention. Our weariness with the many insoluble moments of not knowing what to do about the confusion of life can fade almost like magic. We feel refreshed. Scripture has this power to renew when it reflects our most profound desires. It is a precious map; it is not the territory. It offers only a guide to where the treasure lies, leaving the details of how to get there to us. As a trusted companion it can reveal much about ourselves but it becomes a peril when we substitute it for the private work of self-discovery.

Spiritual growth, then, does not necessarily result from reading and believing in scripture. Faith in the biblical word cannot be equated with the realization of spirituality. Memorizing a biblical text is not the same thing as realizing that text in our concrete daily life. The profound meaning and direction of life is not a duplication of biblical stories. By itself the Bible cannot serve as the sole resource for human wisdom any more than as the sole source of astronomy when it describes the heavens. At best, it is naive to use scripture as the only means for spiritual guidance. God does not reside in a book. Genesis and the Wisdom books assert that God is found by means of learning about reality. Only by engaging in life's problems, living in the world and drawing upon its values, does one begin the long, twisting road to understanding the meaning of God and of oneself.

The objective discrepancy between the biblical account of women and that of the ever-changing contemporary scene demands that women cross-examine both. They must perform the interrogation by themselves. It is a spiritual inquest, one that hopefully illuminates evidence to assess in the unending journey of self-definition.

For this task, full of wonder and pain, there are certain aids and principles that hasten the marvel of self-discovery and its attending freedom. The aids have proved sound over the centuries. They are useful only if the traveler finds a resonance with them. Not all will be suitable at once; they require adjustment to one's lifestyle. But since they come recommended by historical persistence, they are worth more than a glance.

First is the recognition that health and spirituality belong together. Taking care of one's body is imperative. A spiritual program that undermines health is spiritually destructive. It almost seems banal to mention, but it is a fact of our hectic world that women are as guilty as men in abusing the elementary requirements for sound health. Adequate sleep, nutritious food, sufficient exercise and relaxation are the staples that, if neglected, imperil one's overall health and spiritual vitality. Occasionally one has to step back and ponder: What am I doing to my body? Since my body is an extension of my mind, what I do with my body rebounds upon my mental outlook. It is amazing how melancholy and nervous behavior lessen when bodily requirements are met. Too often one's concept of spirituality includes a disregard of the body which leads to decreased energy and illness.

The second principle is one's responsibility for the formation of personal identity. Spiritual growth does not entail the vigorous diminution of the ego, for without it one could hardly entertain a serious possibility for spiritual fulfillment. One's individual responses to life and the way one judges life's experiences derive from, as well as instill, an intimate sense of identity. Self-worth and personal ambition reflect one another. When women think they should disqualify themselves from spiritual attainment out of a restrictive sense of modesty, then the result is mediocrity, a sense of unworthiness, and a threatening, scattered life. Healthy spirituality, on the other hand, instills a vibrant sense of self-direction. Forming a strong sense of personal worth is not necessarily equivalent to self-aggrandizement. The candid assessment of one's talents, together with an attitude of positive engagement with life's ambiguities, and a refusal to be less successful about life than the sages and saints are some of the elements composing the spiritual formation of personal identity.

The various spiritual practices are designed not to embellish the personality's complacency in its holiness, but to confront oneself with ever more and richer reality. All spiritual practices are attempts at personal insight which liberate one from self-imposed boundaries. The finite personality reaches out to the unknown, the infinite. The bruises incurred by growth, it seems to me, have only one ultimate reason: to bring one to the truths about life. Anything less is self-delusion, which is the biggest cause of our troubles. One struggles until shrewdness dawns.

The third principle is the recognition that one's person is not just the result of historical forces and society's standards. Persons possess a life force which may be described as inherent dignity. This quality is neither granted nor abrogated by society. People may abuse it but it is never lost. Historically, societies have been slow to recognize the broad implications of this irreversible truth and in the contemporary world it is insufficiently appreciated. But cultural roles and social mores cannot erase the priority of human dignity; it remains unalterable and must include an equitable share in the cultural good, services, and opportunities necessary for humane survival with dignity.

Women's experience of life is as important as men's. The complementarity of the sexes means that one gender is not inferior or subservient to the other, scriptures notwithstanding. A woman must trust her own experience rather than man's interpretation of it. So many assumptions are embedded in society's ways of treating people that a constant vigilance is demanded to disclose any demeaning of the sexes.

Men and women are variously interdependent among themselves and among each other. We require each other in order to become self-reliant. Society's rules are not made to establish utter conformity but to support sufficient order so that people can become themselves. Personhood does not deny autonomous individuality but realizes that it can take place better in community.

People can actually achieve more by fostering ties with a developing community.

A community, however, remains an abstraction without a material setting. We cannot exist as spiritual human beings without preserving our earthly roots. It finally comes down to the insight that both men and women are morally responsible to ensure that the universe succeeds. People are not monads, islands of sheer individuality. A certain reciprocity emerges as one recognizes how dependent one is upon clean air, pure water, nutritious crops, and the rhythms of nature. No longer a leisurely option, ecology must become a trust, an indispensable obligation, for survival.

These minimum principles are not really subject to the democratic procedure of consent. They are not a temporary preference, but a requirement of the very nature of self-consciousness in either gender. Any lessening of them in political, economic, educational, and spiritual aims or policies dehumanizes all in the community. They belong to the spiritual essence of being human and thus form a foundation for spirituality.

It should be obvious that the comprehension of spirituality, like humanity, is impossible through one sex alone. The marvel of nature is that each gender reveals those characteristics that are variously androgynous to both. How the human spirit expresses these potentials is the particular combination of temperament, character, and choices that blend into making the individual. Gradually one understands that only by nurturing personal relations with others can certain truths about individual human nature and gender emerge. In this way, individuality-in-community comes into being—a paradox but not a contradiction. The various ways society can discover to encourage interdependence upon genders protects the claim to public and private recognition of individuality. One's interactions are a telling index of one's self-regard. Hence spirituality thrives when there is a healthy recognition of diverse paths. Orthodoxy is not necessarily one-dimensional. A diversity of traditions must prevail if the value of the person is appreciated.

And so the factors are listed. All quite simple on paper and seemingly unspiritual. Yet without them to forge the journey, one makes oneself anemic on a diet of holy dreams. Christian women must resist the temptation to imagine spirituality as a holy fairy tale with Prince Jesus coming to their rescue.

Spiritual growth demands a revision of the meaning of life. It takes place in the face of real experiences, private and social. A spiritual path forces one to pass through a series of predicaments, confusions, upheavals, and readjustments to life. It's never easy. The revisions demanded for growth are more than a change in ideas. The will, emotions, attitudes, relationships, the way one schedules each day, all affect a lifestyle that embodies the uneven growth in self-knowledge. The locus for feminine spirituality cannot start in scripture. It begins in the throes of that feminine struggle that finally sees in the heat of life's trials the world's attitude that she still ought not be as free as men because of her gender. Out of this painful insight and her personal struggles of defeat and gain, however tenuous, emerges a clarifying freedom that, assimilated alone though shared with others, disposes a woman to find the ultimate resource in herself.

Spirituality always remains a personal odyssey, a life ripening towards wisdom; a life wherein one gradually loses fear of change, where insecurity and loneliness are whiffs of memory recalled in the laughter of remembrance, where a steady tranquillity feels at home amidst the chaos of ephemeral values of the day, where petty anxieties cannot touch deeply, and where one senses more and more a union with creation in its altering manifestations of creative energy. Self-discovery now becomes for her a sacred revelation, not because a church confirms it or that any bible suggests it, but because a woman matures from it into her feminine consciousness of being. The spiritual quest beckons to her to nurture from out of all this complexity of pain and wonder a personal philosophy that kindles a new awareness of life's worth and a celebration of feminine destiny. From the truth of her experience of living she may even hear echoes of the scriptures.

Justin O'Brien, Ph.D., theologian, philosopher, researcher, is a consultant in Lifestyle Management and the Director of Ethics and Human Development at Aveda Corporation. Formerly the Senior Research and Education Fellow in Holistic Medicine at St. Mary's Medical School, London, and Director of Education at the Marylebone Health Centre, he holds advanced degrees in both philosophy and theology from American and European universities. He has served on several college faculties, including Franklin and Marshall College, The New School for Social Research, New York City, Mundelein College, The Himalayan International Institute of Yoga Science and Philosophy, and ten years with Loyola University, Chicago.

A recognized expert in meditation, he draws upon his experiences of traditional disciplines in monasteries, ashrams, and hermitages in America, Europe, the Middle East, the Orient, and India, as well as fifteen years of training with Sri Swami Rama of the Himalayas. Since 1972 he has also been a faculty member of the Himalayan International Institute of Yoga Science and Philosophy.

The author of many articles, Dr. O'Brien has also written *Yoga and Christianity, Running and Breathing, A Theory of Religious Consciousness, Christianity & Yoga: Meeting of Mystic Paths, The Wellness Tree,* and *Mirrors for Men.*

I found God in myself and I loved her,
I loved her fiercely.

NTOZAKE SHANGE

Prophecy and Spirituality:
The Voice of Prophet Woman

by

Rabbi Lynn Gottlieb

*T*hey drink wine in bowls
Anoint themselves in oil
But they are not grieved over
the ruin of (my people) Yosef

Amos

There arise generations and times in which the nature of our existence undergoes yet another revelation of consciousness. As the scientist reveals the cosmos, as the artist reveals the imagination, as the psychologist reveals the workings of the hidden mind, so the prophet reveals the nature of justice in her time.

Within the Way of the Nameless Mystery, Jewish tradition believes there is a Caring whose manifestation is the prophetic voice. The prophet is one who illuminates the core message emanating from the Caring: we are commanded, called, summoned, moved to lead lives grounded in love and justice. The call to love *(hesed)* and justice *(tzedek)* is a vision of humanity which can transform violence and oppression, greed and hatred into gentleness and equality, generosity and compassion.

Love and justice are synonymous; they are two sides of the same whole. That whole, or shalom, is peace. Love and justice balance each other. They are both considered a sacred obligation on the daily path of peace. The obligation to love and justice requires certain behavior. To love is to act justly. To love is not to oppress the poor, or the stranger, or the less privileged in society. To love is not to bear false witness, or stand idly by while one's neighbor's blood is being shed, or withhold the wages of a day worker until morning. Love is manifested through deeds of righteousness. Justice, which is required for peace, is understood as the right of every member in society to a certain economic base which includes the right to own land, and the right to maintain the land of one's ancestors.

The prophet, in Jewish tradition, is a person extremely sensitive to these commandments. The prophet is sensitive to spiritual insensitivity. For within the prophet lies an open heart, a heart which is not afraid to touch pain and suffering, a heart which is called to make things right, a heart which rages against the devastation of human lives caused by evil and ignorance. This rage is not merely word, but also action. The prophet is not passive; she lives on the streets, in the midst of the people. And she speaks, speaks with a poet's voice drawing on the words of the people.

The love of the prophet for the people is a theology of ultimate concern,

and a theology of hope. Because the prophet loves life and trusts in the power of
the spirit to heal, the prophet counsels against war, against violence. "Not by
might and not by power, by spirit alone shall all people become free." Zecharia.

The centrality of justice as the measure of love in Jewish tradition
derives from our experience as slaves in ancient Egypt. Because of the suffering
of that generation were are commanded to remember what it is like to be
oppressed, and so to develop an ongoing sensitivity and responsibility to maintain
a society based on justice.

> When a stranger sojourns with you in your land, you shall not
> do him wrong. The stranger who sojourns without shall be as
> the natives among you, and you shall love him as yourself, for
> you were strangers in the land of Mizryim. Exodus 22:21

Finding Women's Voices

History, as life, is not static. A people's fate can change, sometimes for the better,
sometimes for the worse. And so the dialogue about the meaning of justice must
continue to be a sacred obligation. Jewish tradition preserves this dialogue
through the yearly celebration of Passover. We are required to tell our children
about Yitzian Mizryim, the liberation from ancient Egypt, as if we ourselves were
slaves. We must be able to show a sensitivity to the meaning of suffering, and an
understanding of redemption, and be able to apply them to issues of injustice
facing us in our current lives. Who plays the role of Pharaoh today? And who are
the midwives who resist oppression and initiate the struggle for freedom?

When the word 'prophet' is spoken, images of Isaiah, Jeremiah, Ezekiel,
Amos, and others spring to mind. In this work we reflect upon the spiritual voice
of prophet woman. Who was she? Never canonized into a book proper, how do
we find her? Who are the women who express the value of ultimate concern?
Who are the women who see through the conventions and beliefs and power
structures of the privileged classes of their time to the passionate call for justice?

It is already recognized that most women in the world suffer from the
institutionalization of male privilege in all spheres of life. This state is commonly
known as patriarchy. Jewish women have and still do suffer from this oppression
as well. Institutionalized privilege does not easily surrender its power. For the
most part, the official interpreters of Jewish law and custom have been men.
Women were not permitted to legislate, to give witness in court, to be counted in
official prayer quorums (a daily aspect of traditional male Jewish culture), to read
from the Torah in public (from Talmudic times, because of the supposed offense
to male honor), to initiate divorce, or to sing around men (because it might arouse
their lust). Our role was limited. We were designated as nurturers and providers
for the family. We did not have time for the scholarly pursuit engaged in by the
men. This inheritance of segregation continued to recent times. Within the last
one hundred years and especially in the last twenty, Jewish women have managed
a revolution in custom. We now enjoy full sacred status in all but Orthodox
Jewish communities. As we integrate ourselves into the realm of the sacred, we

ask ourselves: What is the nature of the sacred way of Jewish women?

The Prophetic Voice of Women

The impulse to freedom and the liberation of human potential is in itself part of the prophetic impulse to justice, and so forms part of the content, of the female prophetic voice. As we create an open place for ourselves, part of our work is healing the wounds caused by a long history of oppression. Healing of the wounds is part of the peace-making process. How do we heal our wounds?

So many women feel invisible. Our story is not told. We open the pages of our sacred texts and we read mostly about the lives of men. The prophet is a woman who breaks the silence of history by speaking women's names into the void. Healing is performed by giving ourselves a past, a sense of where we came from. Knowing our past gives us homelands from which to grow the future. The past gives root to our souls, helps ground our spirits in women's evolutionary herstory, and puts us in touch with women's knowledge and adventure throughout time. Yet how do we find our past? Where do we look for prophet-woman?

In search of prophet-woman we must draw on many tools of research: historical, literary, anthropological, archeological, and linguistic. We look both to primary sources within the tradition, and we also make cross-cultural comparisons, looking to the voice of prophet-woman in other traditions. In this work, I would like to examine the role of the prophet-women who were part of the Exodus tale: the midwives Serach, Yohevet, and Miriam. In this context, it is important to understand how much Jewish tradition honors oral tradition. While the Torah is considered the classical and 'authoritative' sacred text, nonetheless it is said that both the written and the oral traditions were given to the people at the moment of revelation. The oral tradition has come to include post and pre-Biblical legends and laws.

Every generation is commanded to interpret the Torah. In this process of interpretation, meaning is clarified, deepened, expanded upon, illuminated from the shadows and implications in the text. We discover the text from our own perspective as we also ground ourselves in traditional meaning. The Torah is spiderwoman—unfolding her web of meaning in each generation. The changing tapestry of tales, prayers, and customs is alive and a sign of the vitality of the people. So we turn toward the past, and begin our journey to uncover the voice of prophet-woman in the Exodus tale. Who was prophet-woman of ancient times?

Prophet-Woman in Early Israel

Jewish men did not invent the patriarchy, but they participated in its rise, long ago. Patriarchy began to dominate the world scene some time around the year 5000 BCE. Patriarchy spawned many forms, bore many societies through its head, and gradually replaced the predominant world religion which had preceded it by 30,000 years. Before the origins of the warrior kings, we find evidence that wherever people left artifacts, they worshipped the Great Goddess, the Lady of

Infinite Forms. Called by a thousand names, her icons are everywhere. She is associated with the rise of humanity to consciousness. In those times women were highly honored because of their ability to speak in her name. A woman was called prophet, or seer, when she performed certain roles. The prophet was an interpreter of dreams and events, a counselor to the people and to rulers of people. She proclaimed judgments and settled conflicts; upon her rested decisions of war and peace. As prophet-woman she led the people in celebration and lament. She was a poet; she sang the history of her people, she sang praises to the Mother of Life. As prophet-woman she presided in a holy shrine, keeping watch over eternal fires, teaching the young her craft, creating disciples for the future; she practiced the art of envisioning and making peace.

Prophet-women existed among the early Israelites. They were women of power. Devorah, Hulda, Miriam, the wise women of Avel, and Serach all give testimony to the presence of the female prophetic voice within early Jewish culture and tradition. It is difficult to know exactly how and when women lost their former prophetic status. We know that women held positions of power that were later denied them. It seems likely that women began to lose their ancient tribal powers with the onset of the Israelite monarchy. Saul persecuted women spiritualists. Over time women's spirituality was viewed as demonic and fearsome. The lives and memories of women of power were erased from history. Only traces remain. Yet from those traces we can begin to reimage women's place in prepatriarchal times. It is an act of historical irony that Jewish women are led to the forbidden icons and foreign tales to gain a fuller understanding of our own heroines. By knowing, for instance, that Queen Bee is an epithet of the Goddess, we can better understand the meaning in the name Devorah, which means "queen bee." Devorah was probably not a proper name, but a title of a woman who served as chief prophet: Devorah, or Queen Bee, who sat on Mount Tabor, Navel Mountain. The mountain, too, is a sacred realm of the Goddess, her navel leads to the underworld. She sat under a palm tree, a tree held sacred by practitioners of Goddess religion. And she was keeper of the fires: Eshet Lapidot. When we see how women from other cultures shared and performed the tasks held by Devorah, we can begin to contemplate her true place among the Israelites, and also begin to get a sense of her spirituality and the spiritual meaning of a culture rooted in positive female imagery.

Creating a Tale

In this work I would like to offer a poem called Navia, or Prophet Woman. This poem draws on traditions and images from ancient Goddess religions as positive sources of women's spirituality. This poem also draws on the Jewish sense of justice as it is related in the Exodus story and as it has become the ongoing heart message of Jewish sacred tradition. As a preface to the poem, I am including information on each of the prophetic personas which compose the poem: the midwives Shifra and Puah, Serach, Yohevet and Miriam.

The Midwives

The midwives Shifra and Puah, chief midwives among the Evriim (Hebrews) are the feminine prophetic prototypes of Jewish tradition. They are concerned with life, and are willing to surrender their own lives in order to save women and children from acts of state cruelty. Their acts of courage in the first chapter of the Exodus tale initiate the process of liberation which eventually unfolds in full. Since they were head midwives, we can assume that there were other midwives as well. Puah, or "Increase Hand Woman," and Shifra, or "Horn of Freedom Woman" are merely the two who have become visible to history. As leaders, they serve as role models for the entire community. Midwives possessed the knowledge of healing herbs to cure the body. They also possessed the power of healing the social realm of human relations. Because of these characteristics Shifra and Puah are honored and given special status among the Israelites.

The midwives are associated with the name of the mystery known as Elohim. Elohim in Jewish tradition refers to the aspect of justice within the Great Mystery. Elohim also refers to the justice of the earth. This is the justice which sides with the powerless and shows concern for those struggling to survive.

In the Exodus tale, the midwives are the enablers of freedom. The image of women enabling other women to give birth is linked to the people of Israel running through the parting seas. As the seas open, so the womb opens and sends forth new creation. What patriarchal tradition could not do in the Jewish context is make the theological leap to God as a midwife woman. The female motif of midwife, birth, blood, children, parting seas, and liberation point to divine movement and presence. The Spirit is a midwife woman, enabling us to give birth to our own freedom.

Serach—Smells of Time Woman

Serach (not Sarah) is mentioned by name in the Bible only as Serach, daughter of Asher. But in Jewish legend she holds a place as the bearer of redemptive wisdom. Serach knows secrets and she reveals them to those she deems worthy of receiving them. She reveals to Yaakov that Yosef is alive in Mizryim, and so all the family journeys toward its destiny. She knows the mysterious words which will bring on redemption so that, when Moshe returns from Madiam proclaiming himself as redeemer, he is sent by the elders to Serach, who then tests his wisdom. Serach also knows where the bones of Yosef are buried, and how to raise them up from the river Nile. It is said she worked in the grist mills of Mizryim during the enslavement period and that she was over four hundred years old when the people left Mizryim. It is also said that she did not die, but went directly to Paradise like Elijah: she leaped into the other side. Her name means "smelly" and to make sure it is properly understood in a positive light, I have called her "Smells of Time Woman." She is prophet-woman as wise elder, as possessor of the insights which come from age and experience, and so are fully crafted in their wisdom. These are the elements of Serach's tale upon which I draw in respinning her yarn.

Yohevet—Goldencloud Woman

Yohevet means "glory of Yo," which refers to the name Yhvh. She is the mother of Miriam, Aron, and Moses. Some traditions say she was one of the midwives. As in many of the tales, I find that I can expand on the tale by exploring the meaning of a character's name. Kavod, the last part of Yoheved's name, refers to the cloud of glory associated with the presence of the Mystery. In the Exodus story this cloud led the people out of Mizryim and formed a kind of house (sukkah) of protection around the people. This cloud became known as the wings of Shekinah, the feminine presence or female divine in Jewish tradition. So I have drawn a story of Yoheved, or Goldencloud woman, from the implications of the meaning of Kavod in her name. How did she receive her name? That became the question out of which the story is spun. Yoheved then is prophet-woman in her aspect of hope.

Yehoyah—God as Midwife-Woman
In Yoheved's name, Yo refers to the enigmatic description of the mystery of Yhvh. The letters form the verb "be." The form 'yhvh' indicates an active being, being in the sense of process, of unfoldment. In the Kabbalistic tradition Jewish religion came to acknowledge feminine and masculine aspects of Yhvh. This allowed me to begin looking for the feminine images associated with Yhvy. I began to see Yhvh as Changing-woman of Native American tradition, and as Shakti Lali of Hindu tradition. I began to see the feminine in Yhvh not as the tradition saw it, a passive receptive aspect which receives and reflects male energies, but rather as an active creatrix in the midst of life. In Jewish tradition the creative divine aspect is always associated with the male. To change this perspective I have changed the pronunciation of Yhvh. Although there is a tradition not to pronounce the name, we still refer Yhvh with the male formulation Adonai or My Lord. I began to see Yhvh as my midwife.

Originally the name Yhvh was a wordless cry yelled by women. The support for this is found in the name Halleluyah, or "praise yah." Traveling to the Middle East and hearing the ululation spoken at celebration and lamenting time by women, I understood the origins of Yhvh. It is a cry, a woman's cry. It has been described as sounding like the cry of birds, and the howl of wild animals. It is a sound of tremendous power and release, of strength and expression. It fits in with the understanding of Jewish tradition that the Mystery is beyond names. The cry of ululation is used by women during times of giving birth and so becomes part of the theological context of the Passover story. God as midwife crying the ululation as the sea parts and she draws her people through. So I have come to call Yhvh in the female aspect: Yehoyah, Changing Woman in her aspect as Midwife.

Miriam—Parting-seas Woman
Miriam, sister of Aron (and Moses?) is called Navia at the moment she leads the women in dance at the parting seas. As Rahel Adler has pointed out, "Miriam is identified as a prophet during a time in which a prophet is known as a miracle worker, a source of new religious knowledge, and a poet. Yet she is portrayed as the protector of her infant brother Moses and as the leader of a woman's victory

chorus repeating a song sung by Moses. The nurturitive role is stressed over the creative."

Here again we must draw on Israelite sources, and other women's materials to pull a fuller story of Miriam from what is only hinted at in the text. Again, I began by looking at Miriam's name. Although Miriam can be understood to mean "Bitter Sea Woman," it can also be understood as "Mistress of the Sea." If we associate this name with ancient Goddess religion, we come up with the Goddess as Lady of the Sea. In the Exodus tale, this image of Yehoyah as midwife woman also carries the image of Yehoyah as Sea Woman. Miriam as prophet interprets the word of Sea Woman, Mother of Life. Miriam is midwife woman and healer, envisioner and celebrant. She brings new religious knowledge. What does she see? How would she have told her story?

NAVIA: VOICE OF PROPHET WOMAN

Dedication

As I commit these words to page, my heart and mind, my voice and hands join the cry of women everywhere in the world today. We are living in times of great violence. Women from many cultures and traditions are under vicious attack by the forces of greed. Wherever we turn our gaze, whichever country we look upon we see the faces of poor women, hungry women, women with many children struggling to survive. And we know too that the spirit of women is rising, is on the move. We will not be contained. We are hearing the voice of prophet woman in our time calling us to create her web of caring; calling us to envision the rainbow; calling us to commit our lives to the peacemaking trail. As a Jewish woman, I am aware also that I must reach out to extend my spirit beyond the Jewish kinship ties to make peace with my Muslim and Christian sisters. The truth must be comprehensive, must include all of us. Male theological systems have for so long mirrored us to each other as enemies. Today, in our time, we must create a theology from our own experience and a spiritual vision which mirrors us to each other as beloved friends. We are all children of the earth. Let us, together, find the way to make peace on her ground, to make peace in her skies, to make peace in the hearts of all earthkind.

The Midwives' Prayer

We claim the right not to be driven from the land
We claim the right not to be beaten
We claim the right not to be starved
We claim the right not to be sick all the time
We claim the right not to be enslaved by an oppressor's hand.
We are strong faced women
Our eyes fill the heavens
We are not afraid to stand up

See, we are standing here today
And will not move from this place
until our children
are restored.
Yehoyah
Sacred One of birth and healing
Upon you we call
You who created the healing herbs
Your prophet-woman wears a skirt of many shells
As the sky wears stars
So may our people grow
So may our children increase.
Kol Yohevet

A new Pharaoh
who did not know Yosef
came into power over Mizryim.
He announced to his people:
"The Israelites among us are too numerous
 and strong for us
we must deal cleverly with them now
otherwise
they may increase so much
that in the case of war
they will join our enemies
and fight against us
driving us from the land."
So they appointed taskmasters over us
to crush our spirits with hard labor.
We were to build up the store cities of
Pythom and Raamses
as supply centers for Pharaoh.
But the more they oppressed us
the more we increased.
The Mizryim came to dread us.
They began to force us to do labor
designed to break our bodies.
They made our lives miserable with harsh work
involving mortar and brick
as well as all kinds of work in the field;
all the labor was intended to break us.

In those days Pharaoh summoned the head midwives
of the Evrim.
  That is the name they gave us

vagabonds, gypsies
so we wore the name and honored
the power of free roamers
My mother was one of the midwives.
The people called her Puah
increase hand woman.
She demanded that each birth become a celebration.
Somehow bread and wine were collected
shells and beads
goat hair blankets and woven baskets were brought.
We would go to the tall grass by the river
with singing and dancing
to bless the mother and father,
we would welcome the newborn child.
A new name among us
renewed hope
life extended.

Yehoyah knew the love of the midwives
and the people increased greatly
and because of their love, Yehoyah
made them great houses.

It was rumored that Pharaoh could not sleep
on the nights the Israelite women gave birth.
He would dream of us
turning into grasshoppers
and creeping crawling things
swarming over his bed,
his hands his face
He would wrest himself
from his inner horrors
screaming along
with our birth cries.
So he summoned my mother
and her sister saying:
"When you deliver a Hebrew infant
if it is a boy, kill it
if it is a girl
let it live."
My mother loved Yehoyah
and did not do as Pharaoh commanded
and let the boys live
and Pharaoh summoned them again and demanded:
"Why did you do this, you let the infant boys live?"

My mother understood his madness well
and said: "The Hebrew women are not like Mizryim women.
They deliver as swiftly as the beasts of the field.
They give birth before a midwife ever gets to them."

Pharaoh hung my mother
and my aunt Shifra.
I was a young girl, only ten years in my life.
I buried my mother's body
and planted a cedar twig
over her grave.
Everyday
I would visit her and weep
over the grave.
Because I cried so many tears
the twig grew quickly
into a tree.
One day
a morning dove came to live in the tree.
Much to my surprise,
everything I secretly wished for
the bird brought to me.
Because of the suffering
I came often to the tree
and the bird.
Here I felt protected and close to my mother.
One evening
under the full moon sky
I embraced the tree
 and felt my mother's body.
A luminous cloud rose up
and the bird began to sing
From that time on
the people called me Yoheevet
golden cloud woman
because of the seven luminous clouds
which surrounded me
wherever my footsteps fell.
It was a sign of great hope
among the people.
They said it was a sign
Yehoyah was with us.
That Yehoyah heard our cries.
Navia, Healing Woman

Once, we were nothing
but souls on the wind
until she came and gathered our spirits.
She washed our wounds
in the healing waters of her courage
until we found our tongues
singing in our mouths
our eyes
able once again
to see the spirit of the people
an eagle in our vision.

The Birth of Miriam

Goldencloud woman
gave birth to three children:
 Aron Moshe
and Mariam Navia
Parting seas Woman
born with a snake wrapped around her
a sun emerging from her forehead
horns like the crescent moon
she greeted her people
as the morning star
shimmers in the dawn
her seafires burned within.
Open
open to your vision of the waters. She sees
Yehoyah, the Midwife Woman
whose strong hands
catch us
as we are cast by the tides
of her parting seas onto earth's open shore.
As her eyes greet the light
she sees a mountain
she sees an eagle flying over the waters
she sees all the people passing through.

Kol Miriam

Navia
truthseeker seeing past
convention
through illusion
to the boney

truth.
Spiritwarrior
down into Tehom's wide abyss
you dive into her well
eat the fruit buried
at her roots
visions draw near
dreams stream through you
and your voice
wet
and open
moves image
into sound
sound into image
snakewoman
your utterance bubbles forth
flowing with words
a rushing river
of exaltations
with your long snake tongue
slender bird tongue
thick cow tongue
entoning with drum
what your mind's eye
sees.
Parting seas woman
open open
to your vision of the waters.
The future unfurls like a fern
yielding its spiral to the rain.
In the rising spring tide
comes the muddy flood waters
the people
like grains of sand along the river
carried off to distant lands
waves like wings
bearing them to new nesting grounds
an eagle in your vision.
Face east
to the yellow sun
you remember the promise of freedom
and think
the time should be now.
Too many dead
too many dead children

Navia Dolores
Bitter Water Woman
your eyes run down with tears.
Too many dead
too many dead children
you have seen their faces
flesh on fire
bodies burning like funeral pyres
you rub yourself in ashes
tear your clothing
and call to the other women
to mourn with you.
At first they are afraid
but their children are
too many dead
so they sit with you
crying like jackals in the night
a storm rages inside them
it is the rage
of Yehoyah.

What turned You
to look at me
my anger my fits of rage
my loud grieving
what turned You to look at me
I saw You in a woman
hiding herself in the fields
squatting over stone
rocking and groaning out a child
I saw you crying over her
cupping up her cries and drinking them like water
her birth blood rose to Your nostrils
the smell reminded You of Your promise
You said:

I hear the cries of the people
I will take you out of Mizryim
I will draw you forth with wonders
and a midwife's hand
I am Yehoyah
the Midwife Woman.

I offered a prayer
saying
Yehoyah
Sacred one of birth and healing
upon You we call
You who made the healing herbs
Look, your prophet woman wears a skirt
of many shells
as the sky wears stars
as the sea holds drops of water
so let our people grow
so let our children increase.

And I prophesied in Your name
I spoke to the children of Yisrael saying:
People of Yisrael
you pray to the peak of the West
to Isis and Osirus
to Horus and Re
you wait for their sweet breezes to purify you
for their soft hands to soothe you.
but their wind is foul
their hands crust and cannot heal.
We are mud carriers for dead gods
because their people offer thanksgiving to them,
while they embitter our lives.
We build their cities
fill their silos with grain
their overseers belch and sleep
while we lick up bird droppings for a meal.
They instruct us in the wisdom of their scribes

OPPOSITION TO SUPERIORS IS A PAINFUL THING
ONE LIVES AS LONG AS ONE IS MILD
obedient sons and daughters obey the gods
Only a fool does not know these things.

My kin
let us become a nation of fools
and madwomen.
Mizryim's teachings bring us death
their wisdom causes pain.
We build houses for idols
pyramids for hollow men
our sides ache
we destroy our arms at work
we are wretched through and through.
Yet you lift your face
to stone
and ask for mercy.
You stretch out your arms to wood
and beg for justice.
Can stone answer
or wood speak?
Do the gods heal our children
or comfort a mother's grief?
We serve Mizryim with silver
and lapis lazuli
we carve gods out of carob wood
and fashion ornaments of turquoise
and costly stone
we clear their way up the river to the tombs
and they cover our path with thorns
they rule over us
embitter our lives.
Listen Yisrael
rise up from your long sleep.
Let us set a table for the needy
offer our poor bread to the homeless
and set aside a day of feasting
for Yehoyah has called us
to make a path to the wilderness
where the eagle flies free.
Across the waters She will carry us
over the mighty flood waters
she will bear us
with outstretched arms
and a midwife's strong hand. Yehoyah is like
Eaglewoman
grieving like a motherbird
whose young are kidnapped from the nest.
There will be no end to her grieving

until her children
are set free.

Kol Serach

Every one thousand years
there is born a woman
who does not die
but lives
forever
she comes from the root soul
of the Ancient Mother of Days
When seven such women are born
and seven Houses rise
this circle of knowledge
will be
complete.

    With no borders between skin and soil, Serach seemed like an old weed whose thick stalk and web of tendrils reached down deep. She could not be uprooted. Her flesh was human parchment, a scroll of bones upon which life had inscribed four hundred years. Her mind was clear. Stories she remembered in detail. She knew stillness in the midst of fire and could reach into herself and draw forth just the right gift of wisdom.

    When Pharaoh, king of Mizryim, enslaved the tribes, Serach was forced to work in the grist mills. Sorrow filled the people; seeing her in chains, they feared for her life. For Serach held the memory of their beginnings, she alone knew the time of their redemption. How could she die?

    Squatting by her grinding stone, she raised her head slowly and spread her strong hands in the blessing sign. Even in the fields they could feel the force of her blessing. Even without their drums the women could hold the rhythm or tales with their grinding stones.

    Serach opened her mouth. And in the hollow of her first sound, they saw a moment held forever, Yehoyah in her fire, Yehoyah in her word, Yehoyah in her soft eyes. Each listening heart became a letter in her word, became the breath between the letters, became the light in the breath of all beginnings. With this light they could remember the first fluttering fires of creation, streaming into time and space like blood, pulsing into the open space of her abyss. With that fire they beheld the story of the people on the path to the city of peace.

She said: "The homeland is earth, but it is also a dream." She said: "Each one of you will come to understand the gift you must craft within yourself as an offering to Yehoyah. For this gift is need for the dream." Then sitting there she raised the grinding stone above her head and smashed it on the ground, shattering the stone into six hundred thousand pieces. She moved her hands over them like two birds hovering over the abyss. And the fragments became birds and the birds flew to us, each one carrying a mirror. "Gaze upon this," she said, "and you shall see the face of eternity in all which meets your gaze." As each one turned their eyes to the mirror it melted into their foreheads, and each one saw Her, in a moment held forever. Yehoyah, the midwife woman, would enable freedom in their own time. And in that mirror they saw Serach, suddenly an eagle, flying into a small opening in Her seam. That was the last they saw her in Mizryim.

But they say she wanders. And she has been sighted throughout the world at the birth of children, where people still believe that souls of great compassion send blessings to an open heart.

Rabbi Lynn Gottlieb is a story teller. She has been working in her field since 1973 when she began serving as rabbi to Temple Beth Or of the Deaf and the Hebrew Association of the Deaf. She began writing and performing stories of women in the Bible in 1976, and has continued to travel throughout the United States, Europe, Canada, and Israel, telling tales with chant, story, and sign language, as well as leading rituals in peace-making and Jewish celebration.

Since 1983 Rabbi Gottlieb has served Congregation Nahalat Shalom (Inheritance of Peace), which she helped found in Albuquerque, New Mexico. Lynn Gottlieb was ordained by Rabbi Zalman Schacter and Rabbi Everett Gendler in 1980 in New York City.

She is currently working on a book entitled: *Shekinah Coming Home, A Guide to Jewish Women's Mysteries*.

If you don't breathe, you die;
If you don't pray, you die spiritually.

<small>Soren Kierkegaard</small>

Prayer and Spirituality: The Language of Love

by

Mary E. Giles, Ph.D.

s I struggle to begin this essay on prayer I appreciate the discomfort of St. Teresa of Avila when she was instructed by religious superiors to write about her inner life for the edification of her sisters and the lay folk who sought her spiritual guidance. The natural reluctance to reveal intimate aspects of ourselves was sharpened in Teresa by the fact that, even though she was intelligent and spiritually perceptive, she was not theologically educated. She realized all too well that the Catholic Church took seriously Paul's injunction that women not teach; those who dared speak in Teresa's day often had to explain themselves before the inquisition. Teresa, however, was encouraged to teach by her divine Mentor whose instruction was infinitely superior to a degree from the university of Salamanca or Alcala de Henares.

Obeying the direction of her superiors, Teresa wisely chose not to venture outside the bounds of personal experience. Even when she refers to an event in prayer as happening to "a woman she knows," we recognize Teresa. She stunned the theological distinctions of learned men as too clever for her and of little profit to the uneducated women for whom she wrote. Let theologians write about prayer in their correct (and dull) language; she, Teresa, formed an appealing vocabulary for the stuff of everyday life, brightened by images of groundhogs and water wheels and palmetto plants.

I first heard about St. Teresa of Avila when, as a graduate student of Spanish literature, I was expected to sample what literary critics consider to be some of the finest prose written in the Spanish language. Teresa, who lived from 1515 to 1582, was typical of women in Spain at that time in that she received little more than a rudimentary education. After her famed spiritual conversion around the age of 40, Teresa was inspired to work for the reform of her Carmelite Order and, gifted with mystical experiences, she was directed by her religious superiors to write for the edification of her sisters and other devout souls who sought to journey inward in prayer.

Untrained as a writer, Teresa nonetheless emerges in her writings as something of a literary genius. Among her major works are the *Life,* the *Way of Perfection,* the *Foundations* and the *Interior Castle.* Such is the wisdom of her mystical literature and its power to move men and women to deeper love for God that in 1970 the Roman Catholic Church proclaimed her, along with Catherine of Sienna, as the first women doctors of the Church.

Intimidated now by the subtlety of the subject and aware that others are more qualified than I to write of prayer, once again I appeal to Teresa, first to define a point of departure, second for the courage to persevere in the task. The starting point I discern in her example of writing out of personal experience; the courage, in submitting my understandings to the wisdom of Teresa and other "authorities" on the language of love.

Returning to that moment years ago when I was inspired to pray, I consulted the autobiography of Teresa and her Interior Castle, a work of remarkable artistic maturity as well as a cohesive elaboration of the journey in prayer which she had outlined in several chapters of the *Life*. I resolved to follow her advice about "mental prayer," a kind of praying which, she explains in the *Interior Castle*, begins the journey inward. Indeed, says Teresa, we cannot enter the castle of our soul and embark on the journey to its deepest center where soul and God are united in intimate loving unless we practice mental prayer:

As far as I can understand, the door of entry into this castle is prayer and meditation: I do not say mental prayer rather than vocal, for, if it is prayer at all, it must be accompanied by meditation. If a person does not think Whom he is addressing, and what he is asking for, and who it is that is asking and of Whom he is asking it, I do not consider that he is praying at all even though he be constantly moving his lips.[1]

We need remember that in Teresa's day women were not encouraged to think for themselves in religious matters, including prayer. Mindless recitation of formulaic prayer was the order of the day, even in convents which were supposedly dedicated to cultivating the interior life. Teresa was espousing dangerous teachings, for a woman, yet she was given to understand in her own twenty-year odyssey of turning inward to God that mental prayer was the essential first step for her nuns, and for all of us, if we are to advance in loving God.

Mental prayer is commonly known and practiced today under the rubric of "meditation," but when I was casting about for direction in prayer, meditation was associated with Eastern religions rather than Christianity. So everything Teresa said about mental prayer was news to me and very helpful. I was immediately attracted to mental prayer, in large part because years of academic study had trained me in the art of paying attention, which is the point of this prayer.

I emulated Teresa in the practice of picturing events in the life of Jesus Christ, particularly his passion and crucifixion. For example, I would see myself present at the crowning of thorns, imagine my feelings, relate the event to my own life, and reflect on its meaning in the larger arena of human endeavor. As a beginner I found mental prayer effective because there was something for my imagination and reason "to do."

Even though it was easy for me to quiet my body and emotions and concentrate on images and thoughts, I did not presume that mental prayer was a subject to be mastered in a given period of time. I did not consider mental prayer in the same category as the preterit tense of irregular verbs in Spanish. Teresa's repeated advice to continue prayer indicated that here was an indeterminable content that would require indefinite practice; thus I applied to prayer the principles of repetition and regularity which undergird teaching and learning.

Prayer may not be of definable content, but in one major respect its practice is similar to both academic learning and art. Prayer, study and art require increasing concentration. In a course on English literature, as students learn about authors, works, movements and how to analyze literature, not only the nature of literature but also its critical methodology become more and more sophisticated. The demands of analyzing a tragedy by Shakespeare are clearly greater than those implied in the study of a fairy tale!

The same need for rigor and concentration is evident in art. Could we imagine a Leonardo da Vinci taking up brush and paints one day and the next creating the Mona Lisa? Granted, he was a genius, but even the most gifted must train their talent and submit to long, arduous practice to find and refine their artistry.

Prepared by years of academic discipline, I heeded Teresa's counsel to practice prayer. I did not slavishly imitate the details of her practice, however, for our lives were very different. She was a nun in a convent in sixteenth century Spain; I, a modern woman with the responsibilities of wife, mother, and teacher. Gradually, through experimentation, a pattern evolved in which I set aside for prayer a large part of Friday mornings and, as possible, a short time each day, except for Saturdays when all the family was home. I did not have a cell as Teresa did, but the area in our bedroom where I studied functioned as my is prayer space. I sat on the chair or the floor for prayer and used the desk for writing in the spiritual journal I had begun. The atmosphere was as conducive to prayer as it was to study, with an entire wall of windows that opened to a restful view of the garden and hills beyond. A time and space for prayer suited me because the sense of routine was assurance that in my already busy schedule I would pray regularly.

In retreats and workshops over the years I have always stressed the need for a specific time and space for prayer because these factors were helpful to me. When women objected that it is extremely difficult to find time each day for prayer, especially if they have small children at home (one woman said the only time she could pray was when she took a bath), I would reply that usually we make time for what we really want to do. That response is valid up to a point: I have come to see that some women are imprisoned by the very routine which freed me from negligence, procrastination, and apathy. More spontaneous than I by disposition, some friends of mine pray "on the wing," like humming birds at the flower—which is not to say that their mode is better or worse than mine. It is just different. Nor do they fail to pray regularly; for these spontaneous prayers, regularity means that they pray frequently rather than at a set time in the same place.

The recognition that practice can take different forms points to the fundamental truth that prayer is unique. Spiritual guides through the centuries say over and over that prayer is different for each person. Prayer must be different because it must be unique and it must be unique because each person is unique. The point is simplistically obvious, yet confusion threatens to cloud our understanding as soon as we outfit ourselves with guidelines, principles, and road maps, which in a multitude of ways suggest that what tradition calls the "straight and narrow" road is also uniform.

The fact of uniqueness means that each of us is destined to create rather than imitate prayer. Only if we are liberated from preconceptions of what prayer should be can we create modes of praying that at the moment are the just right expression of our love for God. Freedom in prayer means that we must push beyond rote recitation of words and search out meanings for ourselves, that we speak to God in our own vocabulary, that we listen to guides like Teresa but not strain to imitate them. Freedom means that we are to be adventurers of the heart, charting the strange, "fabulous isles" of which Teresa's spiritual friend, St. John of the Cross (1542-1591), sings in his *Spiritual Canticle.*

This adventure is risky. We are bound to take wrong turns in prayer, now trying a method that is ill suited to our temperament, now clinging to one prayer when God calls us to another. But these are matters to be found out; what is important is that we travel by the compass of the heart, alert to the desire for God that initiates the journey and enables us to persevere when we cannot see the road ahead.

Rather than suggest techniques for mental prayer, therefore, I prefer to recommend a disposition that is beneficial to prayer in general. The disposition is for solitude. In our society where the marketplace sets a mood of frenzy and prizes efficiency and profit, there is little encouragement to nourish solitude and silence. Watching students rush on and off the campus, juggling incredibly heavy and conflicting schedules of classes and jobs, I am not surprised they have neither time nor taste for solitude. Even their study goes on in noise—the noise of worry over grades, requirements for graduation and prospects for well-paying jobs.

We can nourish solitude in many ways. I find inspiration in nature and animals. Recently I was walking across the campus in the late fall afternoon when I caught sight of a furry gray squirrel skimming head-first down the trunk of a tree. Rather than walk by with a thought of "how cute and picturesque," I stopped to watch the squirrel complete the downward journey, scoop up a nut and sit upright with bulging cheek and bright eyes. Then he caught sight of me. No movement. I looked at the squirrel; he looked at me. Then his buddy started head-first down the trunk. Midway he stopped. The three of us looked at one another. Aware of a presence behind me, I turned to see a student who had stopped. Now four of us watched one another. Suddenly a cool October breeze swept across the back of my neck and stirred the leaves on the ground. Did I imagine the conversation or did the squirrel poised on the trunk actually say to his buddy, "Get up here with that nut, friend; we've got lots of work ahead of us." I realized I had interrupted a serious enterprise. I walked on, leaving them to their nut-gathering. It was a small moment, but briefly I saw the world through the eyes of a creature other than myself.

For several months mental prayer was so satisfying it never occurred to me that prayer could be other than what I was doing: consciously quieting myself and focusing my imagination and reason on a subject. I was confident that with mental prayer, devotional reading, and attendance at church liturgies, my relationship with God was splendid.

Although I had read in Teresa's writings about prayer further inside the castle, my reality was limited to the entry hall. The words I had read about prayer in the inner mansions were just that—words.

One evening I went to my 'prayer space,' settled in the chair, read a short passage from Scripture, and closed my eyes to imagine the scene selected for meditation. Or rather I was about to close my eyes when suddenly I felt them close and my entire being became quiet, more intensely quiet than I had ever accomplished previously. No image, no thought; just a quieting as if I were wrapped in stillness. I had not caused this wonderful quieting that moved through and around me. The experience lasted perhaps fifteen minutes; then the quieting lifted as unexpectedly as it had dropped around me. Something marvelous had occurred, but what, I didn't know.

Some days later I was reading in the *Interior Castle* and came upon this passage:

> First of all, I will say something (though not much, as I have dealt with it elsewhere) about another kind of prayer, which almost invariably begins before this one. It is a form of recollection which also seems to me supernatural, for it does not involve remaining in the dark, or closing the eyes, nor is it dependent upon anything exterior. A person involuntarily closes his eyes and desires solitude; and, without the display of any human skill there seems gradually to be built for him a temple in which he can make the prayer already described; the senses and all external things seem gradually to lose their hold on him, while the soul, on the other hand, regains its lost control.[2]

I recognized the experience as mine and understood from Teresa's explanation that for her this unsolicited quieting (called recollection) marks the entry into a subtle mode of praying which, because it is out of our control, is described as "supernatural." Even though we know there is the phenomenon of recollection, and even though we quiet ourselves in readiness for it, we cannot make it happen; recollection takes us by surprise.

Until this event my awareness in prayer was of what I was doing: quieting the body, saying words, imagining scenes, evoking emotional responses and scrutinizing concepts. Now, in the silence of recollection, I was made aware of God and God's activity; that activity was simply stilling, quieting, silencing me.

This experience of recollection made me acutely aware of another truth of prayer, one almost obscured by my efforts to pray: Prayer is relationship. In a relationship two persons are in a process of being present one to the other. In the abstract that truth is obvious, but in practice it is a truth we do not always honor or know how to honor.

In prayer we miss the mark of relationship in two ways. First, as beginners, we can be so intent on what we are doing and how to do it, as I was with mental prayer, that we become self-absorbed, losing sight of the fact that prayer is a conversation rather than a monologue. Second, we make of God an object by bringing to prayer expectations about who God is and what God is to do for us. I assumed, for example, that God was a someone "out there" and "up there" to listen to my prayers and grant requests. The consequence of making God an object is that we cannot see God as God is, that is, not until by God we are stripped of the expectations, needs and cravings that stand between us and the Beloved.

The latter observation suggests that God and our relationship with God is mystery; our senses, emotions and reason cannot catch and contain the presence to whom we stretch out in prayer. This mystery we also discern in human relationships. On marrying, a man and woman embark on a journey of creating their relationship. They may set out with notions of what a marriage should be, but they will discover that the real circumstances of living day in and day out with another person make a lie of preconceptions. A man and woman as individuals undergo uncontrollable psychological and physical changes which the relationship being created through them cannot not reflect. Under the stress of change preconceptions and the expectations they fuel shatter. Thus at no given time can a man and woman define their relationship as a "this" or a "that." Relationship is mystery—that which in this moment is being wrought in word, gesture, and the thousand ways we are present to one another.

This relationship being created with God through prayer is also a mystery. I cannot see now into the deepest corners of my being or know the person of ten years hence whom I am becoming, nor do I understand the One with whom I relate in prayer. My faith is that the moment of relating somehow is creating a living unity—a God-and-I. In prayer I do not produce a commodity; there is no package tied with the ribbons of reason which I hold aloft in proud ownership: "This package is my relationship with God." How-to manuals to the contrary, relationship with God, like human relationships, has nothing whatsoever to do with production or analysis. The point is that praying is creating love for God, and this creating and this loving are mystery.

On this journey in mystery we are bound eventually to travel without agendas, time tables, specific destinations or such known modes of transportation as mental prayer. What we can know is that we are destined for the stars and beyond, to travel in the space ship of the heart.

Thus caution is "thrown to the winds" insofar as time and specifics are concerned. There are no five-year plans for loving on the journey, nor are there in human relationship. We do not sign up for a twelve-month friendship or a five-year love affair. We plunge into friendships and love affairs and relationship with God for the duration of our lives.

In the months and years after the first experience of recollection, I came to discern in it two qualities which proved to be reliable indications whether prayer was given by God or my own activity. The first quality was its unexpectedness. I did not expect to be quieted by God that day I was about to gather myself inward for meditation, nor subsequently would I anticipate the moments when God drew me ever more intimately inward. The second quality was discernible in the effects of the prayer: refreshed, joyful, peaceful, and above all, caught in wonderment that something so beautiful had happened to me.

A further indication that the prayer is genuinely from God is a sense of certitude remaining afterward which nothing can eradicate. To this day that first experience of recollection is as vivid as the day it occurred, as is the conviction that it came unbidden, an indescribably lovely gift from God.

If that certitude is absent, then I must ask myself the "hard questions." Was I truly surprised? Had I been reading anything or talking with someone about something that could have triggered the event? Was I truly humble, or was there a voice whispering, "You deserved the favor"? If even a little hesitancy creeps into my reply, I should admit that somehow, consciously or otherwise, I authored the experience.

The question of whether an experience originates with God or in us as the work of wish-fulfillment or an overly active imagination is difficult to answer, particularly if we do not have help in discernment from a spiritual director. I am sensitive to the need for spiritual directors because in retreats and workshops on prayer the question inevitably comes up: "Where can I find a spiritual director?" I would like to have a list of directors available; alas, directors are scarce, more available to the religious, of course, than the laity. Nonetheless we are not entirely without spiritual direction if we take for a friend a volume like the *Interior Castle* or *Contemplative Prayer* by Thomas Merton or the perennially reliable two-part treatise by St. John of the Cross entitled the *Ascent of Mt. Carmel* and *Dark Night of the Soul*. For those who are unsure if they should remain with mental prayer I recommend the latter works, in which St. John gives concrete signs for discerning if God is calling us from meditation to contemplation.

Contemplation is the traditional term in Christianity for the reaches of prayer beyond meditation where we do not initiate or govern the prayer but are recipients of God's loving. Recollection is for Teresa and her generation the lowest rung of the contemplative ladder, but it is nevertheless "supernatural" prayer because it comes outside the natural mode of knowing which involves the active use of our senses, imagination and intellect.

The experience of being made quiet is akin to a consciousness which I call attentiveness. Attentiveness is an attitude of being alert to, receptive to, open to. In contrast to "paying attention" during which we push outward to grasp something with the intellect, in attentiveness we are being opened...to what we are not sure.

Attentiveness has a counterpart in activities other than prayer just as concentration or paying attention do. Sometimes in the classroom I "see" in students the transition from paying attention to being attentive. Recently in a course on medieval culture we were discussing the theological significance of the Beatific Vision which crowns Dante's journey in *The Divine Comedy*. As the students grappled with terms like 'trinity,' 'incarnation' and 'redemption' I could see the turning wheels of their attentiveness. Sensing their struggle with the strange vocabulary, I stopped talking, took up the text and began to read. Dante's poetry swiftly overtook me; I felt poised with the poet before the circles of light wherein he is inspired to see the mysteries of his faith. Attentive to the poem, I became attentive also to the students, hearing stilled their wheels of concentrating. No explication, no questions, no discussion intruded on our attentiveness. When the reading concluded with Dante's completing his journey and turning earthward to share the vision, we remained quiet for several minutes, nourished by the poet's gift—his language of love.

So also in prayer there is this transition from paying attention to the words of a prayer or the meaning of a passage from Scripture as the wheels of analysis are stilled and we are brought to rest in a prayer over which we have no control, a prayer that is simply waiting on God.

The transition, unfortunately, can be complicated by our attempts to cling to mental prayer out of habit or fear of the unknown or because we think it is the right thing to do; we do not understand that God is calling us to a subtle conversation. Thus the question of discerning the transition is important. For assistance in discerning this step from meditation to contemplation, let us look at the thirteenth chapter of Book Two of the *Ascent of Mt. Carmel* where St. John says that if the following three signs are present at once rather than successively, then God is calling us to supernatural prayer:

First, we no longer can meditate or use our reason. That is, no matter how strenuously and for how long we try, we simply cannot pay attention. The mind will not function as it has in the past, and the effort to force meditation can cause headaches and even nausea.

Second, we have no desire to fix our meditation on other particular objects, exterior or interior, and derive no pleasure from prayer or other activities. We do not have a distaste for prayer that is alleviated by a substitute activity such as going to the movies; rather we have lost our taste and ability for mental prayer and know not where to turn.

Third, our only pleasure is in being alone, alert to God. Let us listen to St. John:

> The third and surest sign is that the soul takes pleasure in being alone, and waits with loving attentiveness upon God, without making any particular meditation, in inward peace and quietness and rest, and without acts and exercises of the faculties— memory, understanding and will—at least, without discursive acts, that is, without passing from one thing to another; the soul is alone, with an attentiveness and a knowledge, general and loving, as we said, but without any particular understanding, and adverting not to that which it is contemplating.[3]

If we cannot meditate, if we take no pleasure in meditating on God or anything else, and if we want only to be alone, resting attentive to God, we should cease trying to meditate and remain quiet. Our alertness to God, our attentiveness to God, our receptivity to God, our being open to God—this attitude or condition in itself is prayer: God is speaking the divine language of loving in words that are not heard and gestures not seen or felt. Instructed in loving, all we can do and are to do is "listen," for what and to what we do not understand.

This loving, this prayer, is "dark" because we do not understand it with the senses, imagination or intellect. Thomas Merton wrote marvelously clear descriptions of contemplation:

> Contemplation is essentially a listening in silence, an expectancy. And yet in a certain sense, we must truly begin to hear God when we have ceased to listen. What is the explanation of this paradox? Perhaps only that there is a higher kind of listening, which is not an attentiveness to some special wave length, a receptivity to a certain kind of message, but a general emptiness that waits to realize the fullness of the message of God within its own apparent void. In other words, the true contemplative is not the one who prepared his mind for a particular message that he wants or expects to hear, but who remains empty because he knows that he can never expect or anticipate the word that will transform his darkness into light. He does not even anticipate a special kind of transformation. He does not demand light instead of darkness. He waits on the Word of God in silence, and when he is 'answered' it is not so much by a word that bursts into his silence. It is by his silence itself suddenly, inexplicably revealing itself to him as a word of great power, full of the voice of God.[4]

Many have been inspired by St. John's treatise to write their own accounts of the dark way that God takes us as we move more discretely in prayer, but no one has mastered the master of the dark night in his gentle proddings on the mystery of God's quieting our physical-psychological being and conversing with the soul in the language of silence. St. John realized that this language causes us pain at the outset because we strain to interpret the darkness that overwhelms us. He realized that darkness in prayer is a dimension of the larger darkness that overtakes us as we are weaned from relying on people, institutions, rituals and theologies that mediate the divine presence. He realized that God pulls us into an intimate embrace where there is no room for an idea of who God is or a person to mediate God's reality. God is drawing us out of the consciousness wherein we see God in a flower or a lover or a painting or a priest or a liturgy and pulling us into a higher consciousness in which all particular and specific items are seen in God. The shift in perspective is radical; shattering comfortable ways of knowing about God and plunging us into knowing God as God is. Of course our mode of prayer is affected, and of course the forms of prayer that were solacing and useful (mental prayer, for example), no longer serve. The old forms were specific in nature because we molded them from the clay of our experiences, but God's prayer does not fit into those forms because the clay of the divine is altogether different. The darkness we experience in prayer as well as in other aspects of our lives where we are accustomed to seek God—liturgy, symbols, people—is both the measure and nature of God's love. And the darkness, St. John reminds us, is painful until by

God's grace we are able to see the darkness as light. St. John assures us that "although this happy night brings darkness to the spirit, it does so only to give it light in everything; and that, although it humbles it and makes it miserable, it does so only to exalt it and to raise it up."[5]

I stated that when I first experienced recollection I was in no way anticipating it, and that even though I may have read of the experience in Teresa's writings, I was not conscious of it in days and weeks preceding the event. The fact that we are reading spiritual descriptions of the inner way as a guide for ourselves, however, presents the possibility that unconsciously we would like to imitate the path set forth. As much as I admire and love Teresa, I remind myself that her prayer is hers and mine is mine. If I allow her example to dictate my steps rather than inspire them, I am bound to stumble. I must find my own path which, though it may run parallel to hers, will not overlay it.

One area where our paths run far apart is that of the extraordinary phenomena with which Teresa often is identified. I refer to visions, locutions, trances, flights of the spirit—the many phenomena she describes in the rooms of the castle between recollection and the spiritual marriage of the seventh and last mansions.

Why was Teresa's prayer characterized for several years by these phenomena? Why did she see Jesus and hear his words? Why was she enraptured with effects which she vividly describes?

> For when He means to enrapture this soul, it loses its power of breathing, with the result that, although its other senses sometimes remain active a little longer, it cannot possibly speak. At other times it loses all its powers at once, and the hands and the body grow so cold that the body seems no longer to have a soul—sometimes it even seems doubtful if there is any breath in the body. This lasts only for a short time (I mean, only for a short period at any one time) because when this profound suspension lifts a little, the body seems to come partly to itself again, and draws breath, though only to die once more, and, in doing so, to give fuller life to the soul. Complete ecstasy, therefore, does not last long.[6]

The simplest answer to the question of why Teresa suffered ecstasy is that God chose to love her this way. Scholars have also sought psychological explanation in her emotional temperament and dependence on senses and imagination in prayer.

St. John warns that the way of a Teresa is fraught with danger. He saw all around him in sixteenth century Spain evidence of the perils that beset those who relied on what they saw with their physical eyes or eyes of the imagination, or heard with the physical ears or ears of the imagination. He saw men and women in and out of religious life who were so smitten by the prospect of seeing angels and conversing with Jesus that they imagined supernatural beings in astonishing detail and chatted with them aloud in self-induced trances. John saw also how pride and envy divided convents and monasteries where the religious sought to outdo each other in length, intensity, and detail of their visions and confessors boasted to one another about the feats of their spiritual charges.

The prudent course of action, St. John advises, is to resist the phenomena, and failing that, to disregard them when against our will a vision overtakes us or we are enraptured out of our senses. What need have we of revelations, St. John asks, when for the Christian the ultimate revelation has been given in Jesus Christ? And do not trouble yourself, he says further, that God will be offended if you resist, for if the experience truly is a divine favor, you are powerless to reject it. Moreover, God sees deeply within your heart that your desire is intent not on specific favors limited by particular forms but on the formless darkness that more and more we intuit is God as God is.

John's advice is as sound and welcome today as it was four centuries ago. Superstitions may change their garb, but they do not disappear; the twentieth century has its share of superstitious beliefs in prophets and visionaries and cultic leaders who betray us with their emphasis on precisely that which we must leave behind in our journey to God. That is, we must drop the baggage of expecting and relying on particular experience such as visions of the end of the world or revelations whispered distinctly in the ear of a self-proclaimed prophet and travel unencumbered through darkness.

In the case of Teresa, whose journey for many years was marked by the phenomena St. John warns against, let us remember that they were a stage which she had to endure. When Teresa is drawn into the innermost recesses of her soul, described in the seventh mansions, therein to meet her Beloved in the beautifully simple union of the Spiritual Marriage, the extraordinary phenomena cease. Her life in the seventh mansions is a harmony of all her energies—physical, emotional, intellectual, and spiritual—and she is a unity of loving with her God. Her prayer is as simple as the unity of the active Martha and contemplative Mary who symbolize these mansions.

Like all prayer, contemplation is limitless, growing from simplicity to simplicity and purity to purity. By simplicity I mean that the senses, imagination and intellect are bound into the single thread of attentiveness. Purity means that prayer has been cleansed of specific intentions: We love God for the joy of loving and nothing more. As we move from simplicity to simplicity and purity to purity our awareness is deepened and heightened, as is the quality of our love, so that at any given moment we are freed from specific intentions and made single-hearted in our attentiveness; at this moment our prayer is perfect. But another moment comes when the simple is more simple and the pure, purer, though we do not consciously make comparisons with the past or hope for greater things in the future. The moment is complete, hence perfect, in and of itself, and in this completeness we rejoice without thought for the past or future.

Although we cannot control contemplation, we can dispose ourselves to it. The way I dispose myself to contemplation is to read slowly several times a short passage from Scripture until a line or phrase attracts my attention. Then I close my eyes and aloud or silently repeat the phrase, addressing it to spiritual friends whom I 'meet in prayer.' It may happen that suddenly I am absorbed and suspended, not speaking, thinking or moving, my entire being for a moment caught in God. The experience can last for only a second or for several minutes. Usually I am aware of going in and out of absorption, as it were, somewhat like a swimmer who comes up for air. The experience may last for as long as an hour. Sometimes even after having gone about my other activities, I am aware of being absorbed, as if I were doing and speaking from within a bubble of quiet.

I have had to learn not to strain for contemplation. Contemplation is so nourishing that we would like it often; so there is the temptation that we try to make it happen. We can't. I also have learned that psychological rubbish surfaces during contemplation. St. John knew that obscene images and sexual stirrings can occur during prayer, and he advises us to disregard them as much as possible for they are temporary and must be endured. They are no reason to stop praying or cease disposing ourselves to God's prayer.

I mentioned meeting friends in prayer. Several years I ago at a retreat, another woman and I agreed to meet each other in prayer. On Friday mornings we would think of each other as our companion in loving God. Over the years many women and men have joined us. I do not invoke the name or imagine the face of every person whom I know to be present on Friday mornings, but I find that each week one or two friends are particularly vivid and so with them I greet in general all others who are meeting in prayer.

One benefit of this companionship in prayer is that knowing others are praying with me strengthens me to pray when I might succumb to the lure of reading a book or going for a hike. But the greater benefits are those I cannot discern, the ones that issue unseen from the fact of prayer itself. They lighten days when my praying falls victim to the deluge of family and professional obligations and pour into the stream of grace that enables me to pray at all.

Spiritual friends are praying friends, whether we sit together in silence or from a distance gather as one in love. For women today whose lives are immensely rich and complex and who do not have the institutional support that was Teresa's, we must create ways of helping each other on the inner way. We all need at least one person with whom to talk about prayer and pray with. I am blessed with several such friends, most of whom are "secular" rather than religious.

Of course opposites such as secular / religious and contemplative / active break down before the force of Unity which through prayer is being realized in loving God. More and more I am aware of this truth as teaching, study and writing as well as relationship with family and friends are becoming prayer. In my commitment to inspire in students love for beauty, truth, compassion and goodness through our study of literature, art, philosophy and religion, each day I am aware of being absorbed, as it were. As I teach and work individually with students I feel as if I am acting from within an absorption that stills me to distractions and magnifies my concentration and attentiveness. I am not aware of addressing specific words or thoughts to God, but nonetheless I know I am praying. The method and meaning and context of prayer have been transformed from moments of concentrating on God and being made attentive to God into an unbroken moment of awareness within God. This awareness is not being aware of, say, an idea or person or activity, but rather it is a keen sense of purpose—that life is meaningful, that all of my being is meaning, that praying is the expression of awareness of meaning. I create with God meaning through every word, gesture, and thought.

The increasing awareness that life has purpose does not mean, however, the end of suffering. I find that for prolonged periods I may experience spiritual dryness when God's presence seems to have been withdrawn from me, in prayer as well as in other aspects of life. It is easy to commit myself to silence and adoration when I the feel desire to pray, but when the light of desire seems to be extinguished, prayer becomes distasteful. During one of these dry times I read that all God asks is that we wait. Well, I told myself, that is something I can do—I can wait. So much of my praying is simply a waiting. But this waiting is not like waiting for a bus when we expect the arrival of a specific item at a specific time. No, this is a waiting of a radically different nature. This is waiting with no expectation whatsoever.

I suppose that the simplest praying is this waiting, devoid of form and barren of expectation. I'm discovering, too—or rather, it is being discovered to me—that in such waiting the present moment emerges as sacred. Jean-Pierre de Caussade, an eighteenth-century priest in the tradition of St. John of the Cross, writes in a beautiful little volume entitled The Sacrament of the Present Moment that "Our souls can only be truly nourished, strengthened, enriched and sanctified by the bounty of the present moment".[7] Prayer, then, is to wait in the present moment in the faith that God is revealed in the smallest happenings, the most subtle stirrings...and in the most grievous afflictions.

I ought not end this essay before sharing a word or two of feminist inclination, since this is a collection of writings about women and spirituality. Is there something unique to women as prayers? Frankly, I don't know. If I subscribed to the theory that women by nature are receptive and intuitive, I could make the case that women are thus predisposed to contemplation. However, from the perspective of uniqueness, the case is weak before it is argued.

The prudent, generous and wise course is to acknowledge the fact of uniqueness. God calls us to love as the unique person each one is. What can be said to apply to all who hear the call is that the journey in prayer takes us through darkness into the light wherein we see ourselves and God in a wondrous simplicity, a unity of loving.

Mary Giles, Ph.D., writer and teacher, holds a doctorate in Romance Literature from the University of California, Berkeley. She has taught Humanities, Spanish, Medieval Cultures, and Religious Studies since 1964 at California State University in Sacramento. Mary is the founding editor of the quarterly journal, *Studia Mystica* and the author of many articles on literature and spirituality. She is a frequent speaker at both scholarly meetings and at religious workshops and retreats. She also leads retreats on prayer and women's spirituality. Her translation, with critical introduction, of Francisco de Osuna's *Third Spiritual Alphabet* is part of the Classics of Western Spirituality series published by Paulist Press. Her other books include *The Feminine Mystic: Essays on Women and Spirituality, When Each Leaf Shines,* a theology for women's ministry, and *The Poetics of Love: Meditations with John of the Cross.*

Mary is a wife and mother, devoted to her family. In her leisure she enjoys riding her horses and caring for her other animals.

I am the greatest truth of all, nothing beyond.

CHANDIDAS

Introspection and Spirituality:
Women and Mysticism

by

Bernadette Roberts

7 f we were to remove all mention of women from the history of the world's major religions, the history of these religions would not undergo the slightest change. If, on the other hand, we removed all mention of men from the history of the world's major religions, these religions would cease to exist. What the history of religion reveals is that the evolution or revelation of religious truths, philosophies, and theologies is no different today than if women had never existed, and that the presence of feminine mystics and holy women has never altered the course of religious history or changed its direction in any way. As an historical reality the absence of women in the evolution of religious revelation is a curious phenomena, and one of the questions it raises is the extent to which these religions truly reflect a feminine consciousness, its needs and goals.

That we have always assumed our religions were equally representative of the feminine psyche is an assumption that finds no footing in our religious histories. As solely representative of the masculine consciousness, what this history suggests is that we may not yet have the complete story of the human psyche in its encounter with the divine. Defining religion as both the quest for ultimate truth and the experiential revelation of that truth,[1] a totally masculine revelation poses the question of whether or not there is a difference in the way ultimate truth is experienced and interpreted by women and men respectively. As with any one-sided representation, our religious history leaves open the possibility there may be another side to truth, a side that may have been unrecognized, ignored, or otherwise judged incompatible with the masculine psyche. If there is another side, however, we cannot look to our religious histories to find it. History has posed the question; it does not answer it.

In searching for an explanation of our dominantly masculine religions, there is at least one place we know not to look, and that is to the Godhead, Absolute or Ultimate Truth, which, being void of all distinctions, cannot be said to be either female or male. Being beyond distinctions, the divine would not account for any particularly male or female revelation, experience, or insight. While our religious history would seem to justify the belief (held by many) that revelation of the divine to the male psyche is proof of its predilection or affinity with a masculine God, this view not only contradicts an absolute without distinctions, but automatically excludes women from the possibility of a definitive revelation of the absolute, in which case religion would be a hopeless pursuit for women. But since we hold that the absolute transcends the distinction of gender, we must look to something less than absolute to account for our masculine religions; look instead to that particular faculty in human beings that experiences the divine, namely, consciousness, self, or psyche. As the unique experiential faculty of all human beings, consciousness is not only responsible for our religions, but responsible for all distinctions and differences that we know of. In our view, the true distinction between men and women is one of consciousness. Thus our primary goal is to point out that particular factor in the psyche that best defines this difference. If there is no distinction between the masculine and feminine psyche, then we have no explanation for the masculine dominance of religion apart from a religiously based suppression of women.

Although it may be tempting to view the evolution of religious history in terms of an unconscious (or conscious) cultural view of women as inferior beings, this explanation does not really get to the heart of the matter. For one thing, this view is not justified by the facts of history; women may have been overlooked, but there is nothing to verify their actual suppression or silencing. Even if we insist on this notion we would still have to account for the reason underlying this suppression, account for its psychological and religious basis. Then too, without an intrinsic distinction between the masculine and feminine psyches there would be no reason why women were not equally represented in our religious histories and involved in the same areas of its evolution. But if we are dealing with two different psyches, and, as we will be pointing out, two different levels of religion, we move beyond the merely conditioned level of consciousness to its unconditioned origins, directly to the source of our psychological and religious differences.

Viewing our religious history in the light of an intrinsic distinction yields a different insight than if this history is viewed as an unconscious cultural suppression of women. Bringing to light the 'other side' of truth (other than the one generally represented by the masculine psyche) yields valuable insight into the nature of consciousness and the distinction between its masculine and feminine experience. Somehow the old argument that in the end truth must be the same for all is not very convincing when ultimate truth reveals itself to men only, or when men only have defined it, taught it, propagated it, are its sole authorities, and historically have defended it with outright wars. Those who do not find this a curious phenomena or who cannot question such a 'truth' should probably not read any further. We are addressing those who seriously question their past and present religious history, and who are open to the possibility of another side to truth, a side discoverable through the recognition of an intrinsic distinction between the masculine and feminine psyche.

The fact that this distinction has never been fully recognized for its religious implications or brought to the fore in our religious histories, does not mean that women have necessarily and whole-heartedly understood or endorsed the masculine revelation. On the contrary, their historical silence may indicate the opposite—namely, they have never gone along with it. In the depths of their psyches they may never have been able to do so. The women mystics who appear in the pages of our religious histories could hardly be expected to differ with the predominant religious view when their very recognition was unconsciously dependent upon this conformity. Even then, women mystics had no position within their traditional religious framework. Thus, if they saw anything that might have contradicted this framework, we can be certain not to have heard of it. (As the more illiterate members of the society, they could hardly have checked up on what was being written about themselves).

At any rate, we are not accusing men of suppressing a side of truth or revelation they do not know is there, or a side they may be incapable of grasping. On the contrary, we hold that the revelation of the divine to the feminine psyche may not be wholly understandable to the masculine consciousness, for which reason it has been largely ignored, not taken seriously, or simply brought into conformity with the masculine psyche. At the same time, the fact that the masculine mentality (along with its particular view of women, or ignorance of them), has dominated our religious histories, not only suggests the male's greater psychological need for dominance, but more importantly, suggests its greater need for religion. These two needs, religion and dominance, are not entirely unrelated, as our history reveals. What we have to face is the fact that any truth that must be vigorously guarded and defended has less to do with the divine than it does with the psyche's experiences and understanding of the divine.

Thus while religion can rarely be reduced to the divine or absolute truth, with a few exceptions it can almost always be reduced to the human psyche and the extent to which religion serves its needs and purposes. There is nothing the matter with this, of course, so long as religion is not exclusive in its services, or so long as it serves one and all without distinction. Whether or not our religions have done so is one of the questions raised by its history. Our point is that the masculine psyche, which has dominated the religious scene, does not attest so much to the divine as it does to its own psyche—its particular mentality, needs, goals, and so on. But before we pursue this line of thought any further, we must first say something of what we mean by 'revelation' and how it is used in our present context.

As we know, revelation is always the experiential disclosure of the divine (truth or absolute; it has many names) to an individual subjective consciousness. We have no way of knowing, of course, if the experience of one human being is the same experience of another. We cannot get under each other's skin, and even if we could, we would immediately lose all knowledge and experience of ourselves, in which case we would be nothing ahead. At best, then, all we can speak of is the 'similarity' of our experiences without making claim to having had someone else's exact experience. Although we may say that every experience of the divine is a revelation of sorts, yet the notion of revelation usually centers on the disclosure of something new to the individual experiencer, or is a hitherto unknown truth, a universal revelation.

As ultimate truth, a universal revelation would be unmixed with any masculine or feminine discriminatory elements because the divine is without discriminatory elements. Thus the particular gender of the experiencer would be a matter of total indifference. If we look carefully at our religious histories, however, we discover that universal truths of such a totally ageless, nondiscriminative applicability are exceedingly rare; at least there are very few I know of. More often than not, what goes by the name 'divine revelation' bears the stamp of discriminative consciouness in some form or other in that it pertains solely to an individual consciousness (male or female) or to a particular religious, racial, or cultural group of people. Like the divine, however, the hallmark of universal truth would transcend all such discriminatory factors as well as the purely external, historical circumstances that would otherwise limit its applicability to all people. That we have few such truths indicates that somewhere along the line the medium has gotten in the way of the revelation.

Looking at our religious histories, the absence of the feminine medium suggests that either universal truth has not revealed itself to woman, or that its revelation has not been recognized, grasped, or understood by the masculine psyche. The reason for this we think is obvious: we are simply dealing with two distinct psyches. Thus the feminine revelation may not have served the masculine interests and its view of how things should go or 'be.' But whatever the reason for the dominance of the masculine revelation, one thing we know: women as the discoverers or revealers of universal truth will not be found in the pages of our religious histories.

So far we have excluded the divine and its revelation as being devoid of any distinction of gender. We turn next to address the notion of a feminine–masculine distinction based on the differences of biological or sexual functioning. In our view, use of the biological argument is more suitable to the animal kingdom than it is to the human species, because it is an argument that need not include the human species at all. We cannot give priority to our animal nature when we know that human beings are unique by reason or consciousness, not by reason of what they have in common with animals, plants, and minerals. But the fallacy of the biological argument is that consciousness itself is responsible for the gender distinction—a distinction the animals know nothing about, or would be unable to argue from their purely sensory way of knowing. Left to themselves, the senses know nothing of the biological or sexual distinctions consciousness has made possible to the human mind. Not only is consciousness the primary distinction between man and animal, but consciousness is the faculty responsible for this very distinction, and all distinctions, for that matter. In other words, consciousness is our human distinction as well as our distinguisher. This is why the search for our human differences must be grounded in our purely human uniqueness, and why the only true distinction we can speak of—between male and female—centers on consciousness and not on our animal or vegetative differences.

Unfortunately, when we turn to the study of consciousness we find that here, too, knowledge of the feminine psyche has been the historical product of the masculine psyche, a psyche that has never had the immediate feminine experience. That men have put themselves up as authorities on the feminine psyche is the most naive form of dishonesty I have ever heard of. What we have to face again and again in all honesty is the fact we can never have one another's experiences, and that what men and women know of one another is based solely on their continuous interaction and relationships. Our knowledge of one another is always outside–in, never inside–out. (Strictly speaking this one–way phenomena attests to the absolute One of the divine that can never create or give rise to two absolutely identical things, even psyches).

But if we object to men as authorities of the feminine psyche, we have to admit that until women find their own unique expression in large number and over a period of time, our masculine religious and psychological assumptions will continue to be unconsciously accepted as the only truth there is. To open up new possibilities we need to develop a new eye on old and deeply imbedded religious psychological notions, a uniquely feminine eye capable of divining those traditional assumptions that may not be working for the feminine consciousness, or that strike it as not applicable, or simply as not true. It takes a profound spiritual maturity and self-knowledge to do this.

Although on its more superficial or conscious level the psyche is largely conditioned by its cultural milieu, on its deeper unconscious level, consciousness itself is the maker of this milieu. As the mind's inherent discriminator or reflexive mechanism, consciousness creates our social, religious, philosophical paradigms, histories, and cultures. Thus we have to be careful, aware, alert, and responsible for every idea we espouse or reject because this acceptance or rejection will condition the consciousness that creates our cultural environment. So long as consciousness remains, nobody can escape this conditioning. All we can do is examine it and be responsible for it.

At the same time, we have to realize that it is the inherent unconscious function of reflexive consciousness to make the divine into its own image and likeness. Although this truth has been cleverly turned around to read that man is created in the image and likeness of God, yet we know that God has no image or likeness and thus, ultimately, neither would man—a fact that would seem to topple the argument. But the paradox of the great image-maker (consciousness) is that this reversal—man made in the image of the divine—is necessary illusion without which there would be no quest for ultimate truth.

If on some rudimentary level of consciousness human beings were not assured of an affinity with the divine, they would not bother to pursue the true nature of this affinity.[2] And without this pursuit, no one can hope to overcome the illusions that consciousness puts in the way of ultimate truth. At one and the same time then, consciousness or self is a great reality and a great illusion-maker, which means our human journey is both a passage through consciousness as well as its gradual unmasking. It is only at the end of the passage, with no illusions remaining, that the illusion-maker falls away. But in the meantime, so long as consciousness remains, it has no choice but to bring its experiences of the divine into its own dimension of knowing and experiencing. In this way, the Absolute that is All and Everywhere is brought into focus and experienced as personally subjective, an experience that is both satisfying and self-serving to consciousness. The phenomena of consciousness is nothing less than the phenomena of the divine at the service of human beings. But as to those for whom this invention has been most self-serving, well that is the story of our religious histories.

If we can understand how and why reflexive consciousness makes the divine into its own image and likeness, we can get some understanding of why certain cultural views of the divine are reflective of a masculine mentality and its particular way of knowing and feeling. We note, for example, that the divine is often portrayed with masculine attributes, behaviors, judgements, feelings, and so on; and how it always has a curious way of setting up a social order of some kind. Whether this order is that of a religious hierarchy, a caste system, or a privileged religious, racial or cultural group of people, underlying this order is the implicit (sometimes explicit) understanding that women are either inferior to men or subject to them. It amounts to the same thing. It is mind-boggling to consider how much there is in our world religions that has always been unconsciously (or consciously) self-serving to the masculine psyche. That our traditional views have been solely representative of its intellect and vision is not a happy matter when we consider that these views have been taken as absolute truth—truth on which men and women have staked their lives. But the fact that our traditional views of the divine or ultimate truth can be traced to the masculine psyche is not our major concern; rather our concern is that these views are void of any feminine representation. What difference this makes, or could make, is the question posed by our religious histories.

Earlier we stated that the total dominance of the masculine revelation points to the male's greater need for religion. To discover the psychological factor underlying this greater need we propose to look at the distinctive religious goals that the masculine psyche has envisioned for its ultimate fulfillment. As expressive of man's psychological deficits and needs, religious goals not only explain man's religions, but explain his psyche—how he experiences himself or sees himself. Thus as the vision of perfection and fulfillment, our religious goals are a revelation and expression of consciousness itself; I would even say that our religious goals are the single most important clue we have regarding the true nature of consciousness.

In looking over our religious histories I find the following goals to be universally held in common: the experiential realization of oneness with the absolute or ultimate truth; transcendence of the ego or a condition sometimes called 'selflessness'; an unbounded compassion, love, and charity that is capable of giving without receiving, or the ability to give without any egoic return. To truly attain any one of these, of course, is to attain them all.

Although these goals are testimony to a common human heritage and its vision of ultimate fulfillment, we must nevertheless question the degree to which these goals reflect similar feminine deficits and needs. Observation does not bear out an equal degree of feminine egoic and self-centeredness, self-centeredness being proportional to the experiential absence of the divine. In general at least, we do not find women noteworthy for a lack of genuine compassion, or the inability to give selflessly, or to serve others in a most hidden and non-gratifying way. Nor can we assume that women have ever felt themselves truly separate from the divine, or separate from a profound inner center of strength that they somehow know or intuit is beyond themselves. The definition of 'ego' as a sense of separateness—separate from the divine, from nature, from other people—is a masculine definition expressive of its own experience; an experience, I am convinced, that is not equally reflective of the feminine psyche. That the stronger feminine sense of oneness has been cited as evidence of a more 'primitive psyche' or a 'pre-conscious' condition, is just another egoic ruse for assuming ascendancy. But my point is this: the attributes men prize, the goals they aspire to attain through their religious framework, are innate in the feminine psyche—attributes, in fact, that best define the feminine psyche.

This does not mean women do not have to strive to perfect a native endowment, or that they have no ego, but it does mean that they experience far less problems in transcending the ego, and less need to go outside themselves to do so. Thus the need for intellectual thought and instruction, interpretation, authority, rules and regulation, rigorous ascetics, rituals and practices—perhaps ninety percent of what we know as 'religion'—are inventions of the masculine psyche and reflective of its own needs. We do not question the validity of these needs and the path it has mapped out for itself; what we question is the extent to which they are equally reflective of the feminine psyche, its needs and goals, and the path it must take.

Putting aside what may be regarded as merely a personal observation, let us look at our religious histories, look at all history in fact, to see if there is any truth to the observation we are making. What history reveals is that the male's native aggressive need for dominance has been problematic from the beginning. Religion is the recognition of this problem, for which reason it addresses itself to the need for discipline and ultimate transcendence of the problematic ego. Without this, there can be no lasting peace, no true relationship between human beings, and even no ultimate salvation. But if the religious goal of transcending the ego is both admirable and imperative for the masculine psyche, what about women? What is their true relationship to religion, or their place in its scheme of things?

Although we hold that men have a greater need for religion, we also hold that women are more innately or naturally religious, for which reason they unconsciously gravitate to its more profound level, a level that men must work to realize with greater diligence and conscious striving. In simple terms, women are more at home in the transcendent areas of religion, while men have the greater tendencey to remain on the more superficial levels of religious involvement. As less native to men, it is always a greater fete, of course, when the masculine consciousness breaks through to the transcendent level, which is why we hear more about the masculine breakthrough and why, even today, it is the 'holy men' of our various religions who articulate and propagate the transcendent levels of their respective religions.

While women have no trouble understanding the masculine breakthrough, they are somewhat at a loss to understand its earth-shaking momentousness. In other words, the masculine breakthrough acts to point out much of what women have unconsciously taken for granted; while, at the same time, this breakthrough tells us what men have never been able to take for granted in their own psyches. For women, being faced everywhere they turn with a totally masculine example and authority as well as its particular path, the response is the rather eloquent silence we meet within our religions histories. While finding themselves in accord with the transcendent level, they may not, however, find themselves in accord with the path and its particular pespective.

Here I am reminded of certain feminine Christian mystics who suffered unnecessarily because they felt bound to bring their experiences of the divine into conformity with the traditional masculine view of how these experiences should be understood, interpreted, articulated, and so on. With these impossible and dishonest demands put on her, a woman simply retires into silence—a silence that, unfortunately, has been regarded as total agreement or endorsement of the masculine perspective. We see other reasons for this silence, reasons that have yet to be brought to light. As things stand, however, it is thanks to the masculine breakthrough into the transcendental level that we have any recognition at all of women in our religious histories; without the masculine breakthrough there would be no mention or recognition of women having attained the ultimate masculine goal.

As we can see, religion can act as a double-edged sword. On its more superficial level it can become a vehicle for sheer egoic dominance and a vehicle for keeping everyone in their place. On its more profound, contemplative and mystical level, religion can be the vehicle for overcoming or transcending this same ego and its need for a pecking order. For women, this sword has historically cut only one way. Where we meet outstanding women in our religious histories is on its most profound and transcendent level. We do not meet them on the superficial level of egoic involvement or where the power struggle goes on. Thus one reason for the absence of women in our religious histories is this history's involvement in the more superficial levels of religion. While this may be more native to the masculine psyche, it is not the home ground of feminine consciousness. Clearly, our religious histories testify to the presence of two very different psyches and two very different levels of religion—the egoic and the transcendent.

When we turn to consciousness to find the origin or cause of these different levels, what is needed first of all is a complete overview of consciousness. As our unique human experience and way of knowing, consciousness is a multifaceted system that can be studied from a number of perspectives, from the purely physiological to the metaphysical and on into the unknown. In these few pages, however, we cannot hope to cover this ground. Thus what follows is primarily focused on the phenomena or experience we call the 'ego.' As I see it, the more dominant male ego accounts for the major distinction between the feminine and masculine pysche; and, in turn, the transcendence or nontranscendence of the ego accounts for the two different levels we find present in our various religions.

As the unique property of all human beings, consciousness, on its most basic level of structure and function, is no different for men than it is for women. As the reflexive mechanism of the mind, consciousness is the mind's ability to bend back on itself, and in this unconscious action the mind not only knows itself but, at the same time, puts its subjective stamp on all incoming sensory data. Without this subjective stamp the intellect could not develop. In the developmental process, this stamp is increasingly colored with cultural perceptions, values, and judgements which play a large part in conditioning either a masculine or feminine consciousness. But the reflexive mechansism, which is the knowing self, is only one side of the coin; the other side of consciousness is an entirely different dimension of experience, a side we know as the 'feeling self.' While this second side is not reducible to the reflexive mechanism, it nevertheless functions in conjunction with it to compose the entire experiential field of consciousness and its unitary functiong. Together the knowing and feeling self make up our entire human dimension of experience. It is in the particular dimension of the feeling self, however, that I find the major distinction between a masculine and feminine consciousness.

The unconscious action of the reflexive mechansim sets up the subject-object poles of consciousness, responsible for the object-self and the subject-self.[3] But in this same unconscious action of knowing itself (which is a looking into itself), the mind automatically gravitates to a mysterious 'point' in consciousness where the subject-object self converge to a single non-dual experience. It is at this point of convergence that we experience the origin and essence of the feeling self. The most profound and subtle experience of this point or feeling self is one of simple 'being' or 'life.' We call this experiential point the 'center' of consciousness; and from this center there arises various experiences of energy, will power, emotionality, and other subtle feelings. This center is also responsible for the experience of psychological and spiritual interiority, a sense of within and without, and the feeling of being a discrete entity or separate physical form. Altogether this center gives rise to a pervasive experience of life—psychic, spiritual, and physical life—and this all pervasive experience is the feeling self.

Prior to its falling away, shattering, or transcendence, this center of consciousness is what I call the ego. Although in the developmental process this experience (feeling self) takes on an increasingly masculine or feminine expression, we must remember that the experience itself is prior to its cultural expression, which expression varies from culture to culture. In other words, consciousness or the feeling self gives rise to culture and its religions. It is not the other way around.

What I call 'ego' then, is the initial center of self or consciousness which, in experience, is the will or self-energy unconsciously centered on itself. What irreversibly initiates the transforming process is the sudden falling away of this center (a shattering that is painful to the will) and the subsequent encounter with a void in its stead. This hole or void in the center of consciousness effects the totality of consciousness—every aspect of the knowing, feeling self—to bring about a totally new type of awareness, a radical change of consciousness. From here on there can be no will or self energy (ego) centered in or on itself. Instead all is centered in the divine.

Adjusting to this event is the journey to the bottom or innermost center of our being or void, also the highest center, where the divine reveals itself as our abiding true center and the center of all that exists. From here on, the unconscious reflexive mechanism of the mind not only bends back on itself, but also bends back on the divine, the true center that has replaced the ego center. At this point of realization we also learn, solely in retrospect, the difference between the ego-self and the true-self, the old man and the new man as the masculine saying goes. But just as we do not know the ego-self until it is gone, so too, we cannot possibly know the true nature of the true-self until it, too, is gone.

First, however, we must realize the true self in its oneness with the divine, and live it thoroughly in the ordinary events of life, before this oneness—self and the divine—can ultimately fall away. This falling away is comparable to Christ's own death. But since this final death heralds the end of our human journey or the end of our passage through consciousness, it is not our present concern. Rather, our first concern is to come into our mature state of oneness or transcendence of the ego, for it is only after living this egoless state to its ultimate completion that we can even begin to discuss our final eternal state or ultimate human destiny.

Our view of the ego, defined as self-centeredness or as self-will unconsciously focused on itself, is different from 'ego' as it is defined, say, in the Hindu tradition or in the psychological paradigm of Carl Jung. For the Hindu the ego is the jiva or individual self that has not yet realized its oneness with the divine, or realized its true identity as the divine. This ego or individual separate self lasts only so long as this realization is absent. But once realized, all experiences of an individual self as separate from the divine or separate from anything else that exists simply falls away. Thus for the Hindu, the realized or transcendent state is void of ego, individual self, or jiva.

For Jung, on the other hand, the true individual self only emerges in the transformed state. Here the ego (which Jung regards as the totality of self-consciousness) is united or integrated with self (the totality of the unconscious). In this view the ego never falls away because it is responsible for all man consciously knows about himself. It is the totality of reflective self-consciousness as distinct from the unconscious, or all man does not know about himself, or has yet to learn. Thus what Jung identifies as ego—the totality of reflective self-consciousness—the Hindu indentifies as a false or illusory condition or state of consciouness. For the Hindu 'true' self-consciousness is more in the order of 'feeling-being' rather than the mind's reflexive mechanism, which seems to be Jung's sole notion of self-consciousness. For the Hindu, true self-consciousness is divine consciousness, the experience of divine Being, is itself consciousness.

What Jung only vaguely got hold of or missed altogether, is the fact that self-consciousness is present in the unconscious before it ever rises to the level of consciousness. Thus true self-consciousness is on the unconscious level of the psyche, and not merely on its conscious level. What this means is that the entire system of consciousness, all its levels including the conscious (ego) and unconscious (self), is self-consciousness. Man's entire experience of psyche or consciousness is the experience of self on some level or other. This fact not only accounts for the contunuity of consciousness across its various levels, but tells us that self-consciousness goes right on whether we are aware of it or not. In a word, nothing can be said of consciousness that cannot be said of self, and all self words are but expressions of this uniquely functional experience we call 'consciousness.'

At first sight the crux of the difference between the Hindu and the Jungian view of ego seems to lie in their different view of the individual. Where the Hindu means the experience of an entity separate from the divine, Jung means the experience of an entity who has realized its oneness with the divine, at least symbolically. The difference is not merely semantic, however. Everything depends upon the articulation of their respective experiences. Thus, for example, I did not encounter any recognizable experience of the divine in Jung's writings, but did, in fact, recognize this experience in certain Hindu texts. For the Hindu, Self is the divine in subjective experience and the only uniquely 'One' there is, not to be confused with the experience of the egoic one or individual. For Jung, on the other hand, neither the unconscious self nor any aspect of consciousness is regarded as truly divine; at best it can only symbolize the divine. In fact, Jung never admitted to any divine at all, even beyond consciousness. All told, we cannot honestly compare his definition of ego and self with that of the Hindu, when by definition and experience, they are not speaking of the same thing. The lesson, or course, is that we must be careful about brushing off our differences as 'merely semantic' when truth lies in the different experiences that underlie the use of similar words.

My view of ego is somewhat different from both of the above. While I hold that the entire system of consciousness is the essence and true nature of self, yet I hold that it is not divine, but like everything else that exists, it is also not separate from the divine. Consciousness is that human faculty of function that brings an otherwise infinite all-pervasive divine into focus and centers it in experience of 'being.' Without this faculty, the divine would not be a specific experience; it could not be focused on within or without. In fact it could not be known to the human mind at all. While I do not agree with Jung that the ego is responsible for our entire sense of self or self-consciousness, I agree that the ego is the immature, superficial center of consciousness. And while I concur with the Hindu view that the true center underlying the ego is the divine (and not merely the unconscious or 'self' as defined by Jung) I do not agree that the ego is an illusion of a separate self. On the contrary, if prior to the realized or transcendental condition the ego has not already experienced, glimpsed, or intuited its oneness with the divine, it would not go in search of its perfect realization. Thus it is neither accurate nor sufficient to define the ego as the experience of separateness when, in fact, the ego may have continuous unitive experiences prior to its permanent dissolution in the realization of oneness.

In the yin and yang theory we have the view that consciousness is composed of two different energies, and that the best of all possible lives is to live with these two energies in perfect balance. As I see it, however, consciousness can only be a single energy—single in its origin and its ending—but which, in turn, can generate a number of different experiences of energy. If we call the singular feminine energy the 'yin,' and the distinctive masculine energy the 'yang,' we can understand how these two energies were discoverable: by the sheer contrast of men and women in their encounter with one another. So long as we are the living embodiment of an energy, we can only take it for granted, but when we meet with a dissimilar energy, then we can no longer take our own experience or energy for granted. Thus it is in the encounter and relationship between men and women that we not only recognize our own distinct energy but recognize the 'other' type as well, and the difference between the two.

Without denying the attraction between these two energies or the fact they can learn from one another, we deny that these energies can ever be experientially exchanged or shared. What balance can be achieved between them is soley on the basis of the feminine-masculine relationship; and however useful this may be in the process of realizing our identity, it can never constitute that identity. Those who rely on the feminine-masculine relationship for their identity will sooner or later be left with no ground to stand on, for in the process of discovering the true self we must surrender all relationships through which this identity was hitherto known. Only the divine can give us our new identity.

As a specific energy, or as consciousness' own experience itself, the yin and yang are innately distinct. Even after the transforming process, when consciousness has attained what many people consider to be its highest state—transcendental, unitive, or God-consciousness—this distinction remains. The unique balance achieved in this transcendent state, however, is not between two opposite energies, but between a single unified energy (individual consciousness) and the divine.

In contrast to the experience of consciousness, which is the experience of energy, experience of the divine is one of 'no energy.' Thus the unitive or transcendental condition is the balance between a positive and negative experience of energy, where the divine (no-energy) curtails the egoic energy of consciousness by the sheer void or non-existence of that egoic energy. Thereafter it is the void or no-feeling that keeps the feeling self from exceeding its proper mean, or keeps it from experiencing excessive passion, desires, and so on.

It is important to keep in mind that in experience the divine is a 'still-point,' not an energy point. The experience of energy is always and everywhere our 'self'–consciousness or psyche. The notion that the divine is energy or consciousness is just another example of consciousness making the divine into its own image and likeness. Although the divine truly touches upon consciousness and moves it, this movement belongs to consciousness. We might liken the divine to a stone thrown into the quiet pond of consciousness. The stone moves the waters, but the moving waters are not the stone. The cause is not the effect. The illusionmaker, however, has always tended to mistake the moving waters for the divine and to believe that its experience of the divine is the divine. But this is why the falling away of the illusion-maker or consciousness is equally the falling away of the divine. When, at the end of our journey, consciousness or self falls away, the first thing known is that all experiences we had believed to be the divine was only the self. This is a shocking revelation, but also a great truth that is revealed.

Because our present interest in the ego is its expression in a religious context, we will assume that the ego has chosen to pursue the greatest good it knows or experiences, which is the divine or ultimate truth. One of the first mistakes we make is the religious belief that this whole-hearted turning to the divine is all that is required, or that having set our hearts and minds on the divine we are therefore automatically relieved of the ego and its self-centered existence. Until the divine has shattered the ego, however, or shattered this energy in pursuit of its own desires and its own vision of the divine, we are still unconsciously wearing our religion on our sleeve; it is still superficial and self-serving.

Unfortunately, the vast majority of religious people spend their lives on this egoic level of religion and consciousness. What happens when there is no transformation is very subtle: unknowingly the ego uses religion to preserve itself, defend itself, change the world for itself, and thus religion becomes the servant of the ego, its cloak and its mask. This is the most powerful position the ego can possibly assume, because it is all in the name of the divine and ultimate truth. And other people believe it. Once again, we have to face the historical fact that religion can be as destructive to human beings as it can be helpful. Whether the ego is transcended or not depends upon which way the sword cuts.

The reason so few religious people go through the transforming process is because it is obviously not self-serving to do so. After some well intended beginnings, the ego finds religion so comfortable, secure, and self-rewarding that it sells out to this beginner's level and goes no further. Thus there is no transformation, and no true religion. We need not detail how this lack of egoic transformation and transcendence has affected our religious histories; with one exception, it is the whole of this history. The one area of exception is the contemplative dimension of egoic transcendence, which alone represents the truth and profound depths of religion. We do not hear about this dimension in our churches and temples, however. Those who run them not only find this dimension personally threatening, but the idea of common people getting hold of this profound dimension is often viewed as threatening to the status quo. The unspoken fear, of course, is that the experiential revelation of the divine to subjective consciousness will somehow contradict the traditional belief system. In this matter, not even the divine is to be trusted to get it right. For this reason experiences of the divine beyond the egoic level (sentiment, devotion, emotionality, and so on) are often regarded as suspect and out of the ordinary line up, not wholly to be trusted.

One egoic ruse that keeps us from aspiring to the contemplative dimension is the view that this dimension is a special gift of the divine (or a special placement of birth, as in the Eastern religions), given to a few privileged souls or saints. By putting the transcendent dimension and its saints on a pedestal and out of reach, religion can otherwise maintain a common mental, experiential dimension, the one-dimensional level so typical and indicative of egoic consciousness. Another ruse is the view that contemplatives live in a world of their own beyond the pale of ordinary society; their lives are often seen as selfish, antisocial, and therefore useless to anybody but themselves. This myth is contradicted, of course, by the fact we would not have heard of the profound transcendent level of our religions if these people had not stepped forward to help others realize the same. That there is no value for the 'unseen' or for what cannot be tangibly demonstrated, is a paradox of the egoic level of religion.

Whatever the ruse or rationalization used, the outcome invariably works to maintain the egoic level at all costs. We must not think, however, that this is done consciously or with mal-intent. On the contrary, the ego is ignorance personified. Ego consciousness is not something apart from ourselves or something we can put our finger on within ourselves. Rather the ego is the entire (immature) personality and consciousness, everything we know about ourselves, our entire experience.

Thus so long as we are living it, we cannot possibly know anything of an 'egoic self.' All we have to go on is the recognition that all is not perfect within ourselves, a recognition that should clue us in to the necessity of going deeper within to find a more perfect dimension of existence. That so few realize it is absolutely imperative for every human being to make this journey attests to the failure of our religions.

Putting together what we have said so far, it should be obvious that the absence of women in our religious histories is no great loss. That women have not been involved on the more superficial or egoic levels of their respective religions is indicative of the difference between the masculine and feminine psyches. We really cannot ask what our religious histories might have been (or would be today), if women were equally represented on the masculine level of power and authority. The fact that they are not so represented speaks for itself. Needless to say, if there is no distinction between psyches, then our religious histories would have had equal feminine representation, in which case no distinction could have been made in this area. Then too, we have to understand that it does not matter who is in a position of authority—man or woman—if this fact in no way changes our history, or if positions of authority are more disastrous than helpful. Merely to substitute a feminine figure for a masculine figure would net us nothing. What the feminine psyche does reveal is that the most profound level of religion has no need for dominance in any form, and that, as a matter of religious history and significance, the silence of the feminine consciousness speaks eloquently for religion's sole validity—its transcendent level.

While consciousness is responsible for our religions, our religions in turn are responsible for conditioning consciousness. It is imperative to be aware of this circular phenomena and to understand how it works. We must be sure to derive our religion from its original wellsprings, that is, from the unconditioned depths of our own experience of the divine, and not from a conditioned level of consciousness or any secondary source. Change on the conditioned level is merely the presence of a new idea or insight, which is incapable of bringing about true change or of having any lasting effects. But change on the unconditioned level where consciousness emerges from the divine and eventually dissolves into it involves an irreversible change, one that moves outward like ripples on a pond to effect us all. On the surface it would appear that religion has been the cause of war, unrest, and the lack of peace in the world. But if we look deeper, we find no religion there at all. Instead what we find is religion being used as the excuse, the mask, and the facade for the warring, domineering, authoritative ego.

While women cannot change this fact, they can nevertheless be mediums of the divine in pointing up the transcendent, non-egoic, contemplative, and mystical depths that alone are the.sole essence of true religion.

Bernadette Roberts has searched for answers to ultimate questions since childhood when her interior experiences seemed to have nothing to do with the Christian beliefs in which she was raised. At fifteen she realized that Christ's own interior experience was the experience of God and not merely of himself. From that point on, her own journey was one of duplicating Christ's experiences of life with God.

At seventeen she entered a Discalced Carmelite monastery where she remained for eight and a half years.

After receiving a degree in philosophy, she taught in high school, later receiving a master's degree in early childhood education. Along with the addition of Montessori credentials and four children of her own, she established an 'experimental preschool' that duplicated Piaget's developmental tasks and Montessori's initial teaching experiment. She ended her teaching career in 1975 teaching child development in a junior college.

In 1978 Bernadette had what she called 'the experience of no-Self,' which was the dissolution of both the divine and the phenomenal self experience. It was the end of the unitive state she realized in the monastic years. Because she could not find an account of this event in the contemplative literature of her own tradition or in those of the Eastern traditions, she wrote two books: *The Experience of No-Self* and *The Path to No-Self.*

*In proportion as one simplifies one's life,
the laws of the universe will appear less
complex, and solitude will not be solitude,
nor poverty poverty, nor weakness weakness.*

THOREAU

Renunciation and Spirituality:
In the Footsteps of the Wise

by

Tenzin Dechen

eople come to an awareness of a spiritual dimension in their lives by many different means—some through the experience of great suffering, some through a sense of meaninglessness, some through the experience of a moment of heightened awareness, some through a strong devotional response towards a particular being who represents or embodies a certain spiritual ideal.

However one may become aware of, or develop an aspiration towards, a spiritual path, there is generally some kind of inner movement that takes place. This is characteristically a movement away from a more negative state towards a more positive state. This type of inner movement is the embryo or seed of renunciation, which is not just a matter of giving things up for the sake of it, but rather of a movement towards a better goal.

What is Renunciation?

Renunciation is a movement away from the confines of self-centered interests towards the deeper and more fulfilling life of serving one's beloved spiritual teacher, trying to practice what he or she teaches and trying to help all those whom the teacher loves. This inner movement is a joyful experience accompanied by a feeling of freedom rather than of loss or constraint. The external movement of 'giving things up' is just what follows from the internal change. To move from love of self to love of others in any real and consistent way, however, is like trying to leap across a chasm which is a mile wide. One needs a bridge. In Christianity the bridge is devotion, where one's love of Christ is greater than one's love of oneself. Through loving and serving him, through practicing what he taught, and through prayer, one aspires gradually to develop his qualities.

Buddhist's also aspire to develop the qualities of the completely perfect, omniscient, infinitely wise and compassionate being. Such a being is known as 'Buddha' or 'Enlightened One.' The difference between Buddhism and Christianity from a practical point of view, is that there are many more bridges offered in Buddhism. Within Tibetan Buddhism, devotion is seen to be the root of the path, as one receives blessings and guidance from one's enlightened master. The guidance and teachings themselves are very extensive, and when they are put into practice they have the power to transform us.

The person whom we refer to as the Buddha, the founder of Buddhism, was born about 2500 years ago in North India. He manifested as an unenlightened being who became a Buddha through his own dedicated spiritual practice. Nevertheless, he was endowed with very special qualities from birth. He was of aristocratic lineage, and is said to have been glorious to behold, with an equally beautiful mind and character—naturally kind, compassionate, intelligent, and wise, with great charm and a good sense of humor. At the age of sixteen Gotama, as he was named, won his wife by means of a sporting contest. They married and had a son. Gotama lived with them in the family palace under the care of his very protective father, who took great efforts to keep his son from experiencing or witnessing any of the gross sufferings of life.

Gotama, however, was not at ease in his life of sensuous pleasures at the palace. He felt a need to visit the outside world. On four occasions he secretly ventured out with his carriage driver. On the first occasion he saw an old man; on the second he saw a man stricken with sickness; on the third he saw a corpse; and on the fourth he saw a monk with a shaven head and yellow robe, radiant with inner peace. Gotama was deeply moved by these sights. He realized that what he saw on the first three occasions were the inevitable results of birth in the world of suffering. What he saw on the last occasion indicated a way to free oneself from the craving which leads to such birth. These four sights are known as the 'four signs,' and it is these which led to Gotama's renunciation of the worldly life.

A life which is centered around fulfilling one's desires may bring temporary pleasures or happiness, but in the long run it only binds one to the wheel of suffering existence—continually revolving from rebirth to sickness, old age, and death, and again to rebirth, by the force of the momentum of ego-grasping. Blindly engaging in life perpetuates ego-grasping which again leads to rebirth in a form pervaded by suffering. The only thing that can cut the root of all suffering is the wisdom which realizes selflessness.

With the determination to achieve this aim for the sake of guiding all beings to enlightenment, Gotama renounced his worldly life. He secretly left the palace at night, and once far enough away, cut off his long black hair and exchanged his princely robes for those of a beggar. He sought teachings from a number of different sages and quickly mastered all that they had to offer. Not satisfied with these attainments he set out on his own. For six years he meditated and practiced austerities which were so severe that they almost led to his death. Realizing that this was useless, he once again accepted food and renewed his meditation practice. Finally, through the power of his meditative wisdom, he attained enlightenment. After this he set about trying to help others deliver themselves from suffering.

It may seem from this overview that renunciation means giving up one's home, job, clothing, and other material possessions, just like the Buddha did. This is completely missing the point. Renunciation is not merely a matter of an external lifestyle. Sometimes it can be very helpful to adopt a so-called 'renounced' way of life but only if it functions to develop or strengthen the inner realization of renunciation. Abandoning pleasures and comforts does not necessarily lead to spiritual development, and can at worst be harmful. For example, if one's craving for certain comforts is too strong, or if one lacks any clear purpose, renouncing the comforts can cause more misery and confusion to arise in the mind. This would be totally counter to spiritual development. So we need to understand what renunciation really is, and then see how it is helpful, indeed necessary, for any real spiritual development.

Renunciation literally means "to abandon." What is it, on a spiritual path, that we are trying to abandon? According to Buddhist teachings, what we hope to abandon are suffering and the causes of suffering. True Sufferings and True Causes of suffering are the first two of the Four Noble Truths which the Buddha taught after his enlightenment. The third is True Cessations, which refers to the permanent abandonment of different levels of suffering (eventually resulting in complete enlightenment), and the fourth is True Paths, which are the spiritual practices and training that lead to true cessations.

Renunciation, in the Buddhist sense, has two aspects. One aspect is the recognition of, and the wish to abandon, True Sufferings and their Causes. The other aspect is the recognition of, and the wish to attain, True Cessations. In order to fulfill these wishes, one must practice the True Paths.

What is Suffering?

First of all we need to understand the nature of suffering. This may sound strange given that there is so much suffering in the world: so many wars, so much starvation and sickness, so much general dissatisfaction, depression, and loneliness. However, all these things that we experience to a greater or lesser extent, or that we see going on around us, are only one type of suffering. In Buddhist terminology this is referred to as the suffering of misery. Even a slight headache or a little emotional discomfort falls into this category. This kind of suffering we can easily recognize, and quite naturally wish to avoid, without any spiritual training or insight. The other two types of suffering are more difficult to understand as suffering, and much more difficult to develop the wish to avoid. For this we do need spiritual training and insight.

The second type of suffering is known as the suffering of change. This includes everything that relieves us from pain and satisfies our desires. What we call 'pleasure' or 'relief' is simply the movement from one form of suffering to another. If we are hungry and eat some good food, this relieves us from the suffering of hunger and satisfies our desire for experiencing pleasant tastes. If we continue to eat, however, our stomach will eventually become very painful and even the delicious smell of the food will make us feel sick. The food in itself is not a cause of happiness. It is relative to certain conditions. What underlies these types of suffering is the third type, which is known as pervasive suffering, or the suffering of composition. Pervasive suffering is the fact that our bodies and minds, and everything which these bodies and minds come into contact with, are composed of aggregates which are contaminated in the sense that they are products of our delusions and past actions. As such they are ready to give rise to the suffering of misery at any moment, regardless of our present circumstances. Due to the influence of delusions within our continuum, we have created negative actions in the past which have left negative potentials, or seeds, on our mind stream. All that is needed is for certain circumstances to be present, and these negative seeds will ripen, giving rise to unpleasant situations and painful experiences. There are no external methods of preventing this from happening. Future experiences of suffering and misery are bound to arise in one form or another, at one time or another, unless we have completed the task of removing the causes of suffering from our continuum.

The real causes of suffering are delusions: ignorance, aversion, craving, etc. Ignorance of the true nature of our self causes us to see everything from the point of view of a solid, subjective, self-existent ego-entity, thus giving rise to the strong feeling of 'I' and 'mine.' We naturally grasp onto this 'I' and look to its well-being. We spend our lives continuously trying to make it feel comfortable in every possible respect. If anything comes along that threatens the comfort or well-being of this 'I,' we feel aversion towards that circumstance or person; we want to fight it or run away from it. At all costs we don't want to diminish the comfort of the 'I.'

By reacting in this way we create negative actions of body, speech, and mind—actions which are motivated by craving for pleasant things and aversion towards unpleasant things. Even if we manage to create only virtuous actions, we still create the causes of contaminated aggregates, merely because we experience this fabricated 'I' as being a self-existent and solid entity. Until we have removed the causes of this misperception, our continuum is not pure. So it is important to aim to purify the delusions themselves.

Removing Suffering

We may wonder if it is ever possible to remove this root delusion of ego-grasping ignorance which causes suffering. Because the delusions are not of the same nature as the mind, it is possible to remove them. The nature of the mind is clear, like the sky, and delusions are like the clouds which obscure it. Although they have been within our mindstream since beginningless time, the delusions are like the dust on a mirror and can be removed. The job of removing them is, of course, the biggest of all possible jobs. But it is the only job that is ultimately worth doing. A person who fully recognizes this situation and is fully engaged in the job of delivering himself from delusion has developed what Buddhists call renunciation. Such a person has no attachment for the pleasures of conditioned existence, as he can see that they contain no real happiness; his only wish is to find release from the conditions which he sees as continuous suffering. To do this one first needs to develop one's mind by gradually accustoming it to virtue. As one's virtuous tendencies increase and one's non-virtuous tendencies decrease, one's mind will become clearer and more peaceful, and one will find it easier to concentrate. The practice of virtue is based on sound reasoning, not on superstition.

According to the Buddhist view there is no person 'up there,' neither Buddha nor anybody else, who decides whether or not you've been a good boy or girl, and what you should experience next, either in this life or the one to come. Everything that happens to us is dependent on a cause and effect procedure. This is known as the law of karma, and concerns the planting of certain kinds of seeds in our continuum by engaging in virtuous, non-virtuous, or neutral acts of body, speech, and mind. It is just a fact of life that virtue leads to happiness and non-virtue to misery, both for oneself and others, whether the result is experienced in this life or in future lives.

The abandonment of non-virtuous actions is itself an expression of some level of renunciation. By abandoning non-virtuous actions one ceases to create the causes of one's own future misery, as well as, and more importantly, ceasing to create present misery for others. The abandonment of the ten non-virtuous actions is a fairly simple method of purifying negative karma and creating good karma. Merely from the point of view of wishing to protect oneself from experiencing misery in the future it is necessary to practice these. However, if one is a Buddhist one can dedicate this practice to achieving liberation. It will then act as a cause of liberation rather than merely a cause of pleasant circumstances within conditioned existence. And for a Buddhist who dedicates this practice to enlightenment for the sake of all beings, it will act as a cause of enlightenment.

The ten non-virtuous actions are: killing, stealing, sexual misconduct, lying, slander, harsh words, idle gossip, covetousness, harmful thoughts, and wrong views.

Renunciation and Vows

All committed Buddhists are to renounce the ten non-virtuous actions. But the Buddha also explained different types of vows which serve to strengthen the practice of virtue. Those vows which are designed to lead to liberation are known as Pratimoksha vows. There are Pratimoksha vows for lay people as well as for monks and nuns. A lay Buddhist, whether male or female, can take five vows for life: to abandon killing, to abandon stealing, to abandon sexual misconduct, to abandon lying, and to abandon intoxicants.

So a committed Buddhist can live a normal life, have a job, spouse, children, and home. These vows do not exclude any of the usual activities. Just because someone is a lay practitioner does not mean that he or she is not committed to the path of enlightenment. For people who already have so-called worldly responsibilities and commitments when becoming Buddhists, it is usually best for them to fulfill those responsibilities, and make them part of their practice. If one has no such commitments, then one is free to take monastic ordination as a monk or nun if one feels that this is appropriate.

Monastic vows are many, depending on one's lineage and sex. In general, fully ordained monks take over 200 vows; and fully ordained nuns take about 300 vows.

The practice of any of these types of Pratimoksha vows forms the basis of the path to liberation from conditioned existence. In order to achieve liberation one needs to accomplish three levels of practice: morality, meditative concentration, and wisdom. Without morality one cannot develop a very subtle or powerful meditative concentration, and without developing a particularly subtle and powerful meditative concentration one will not be able to focus one's mind single-pointedly on selflessness, so one will not be able to develop wisdom. Without developing the wisdom realizing selflessness, one will not be able to cut free of ego-grasping. So morality is absolutely necessary for spiritual development.

If one also wishes to help all other suffering beings to achieve enlightenment, one needs to practice stronger and more far-reaching methods than those needed to gain liberation for oneself alone. The basic practices for this higher path are known as the Six Perfections. They are: The Perfection of Giving, The Perfection of Morality, The Perfection of Patience, The Perfection of Joyful Effort, The Perfection of Concentration, The Perfection of Wisdom.

To develop the perfection of any one of these is in itself a vast practice, and altogether they constitute many lifetimes' work. The practices are not as simple as they look and to understand them one needs extensive teachings. Corresponding to this higher form of training is a higher set of vows known as bodhisattva vows. The practice of these vows, together with certain special meditation practices designed to transform the self-cherishing attitude into that of cherishing others, leads to the development of the intense and unshakeable compassionate attitude known as bodhicitta. The word literally means "mind of enlightenment." Generally it is understood to be the motivation to attain enlightenment for the sake of all other sentient beings. Once it has arisen fully, it pervades every moment of one's awareness and enables one to undergo any suffering for the sake of benefiting another being. Thus it is incredibly powerful. The practice of bodhicitta is the ultimate way of helping others. It is working to free them from the true causes of suffering, not only from the effects of their suffering nature.

Bodhisattva vows exist only within the Mahayana form of Buddhism, which is to be found in the traditions of Tibet, China, Korea, and Japan. The Hinayana form, which can be found in the traditions of Thailand, Sri Lanka, and Burma, have only the Pratimoksha vows and the Three Trainings mentioned earlier.

A Mahayana Buddhist seeks to develop what are known as the three principle aspects of the path: renunciation, bodhicitta, and emptiness. Without renunciation (the wish to free oneself from the true causes of suffering), one cannot develop bodhicitta (the wish to free others from the true causes of suffering). Emptiness refers to the non-inherent existence of the self and all phenomena. Meditation on emptiness is what actually frees us, and as such is the tool of renunciation and bodhicitta. As far as the actual practice of becoming enlightened is concerned, there are two main divisions of practice known as 'method' and 'wisdom.' Method refers to the first five of the six perfections mentioned earlier; wisdom refers to the sixth perfection. Method and wisdom are like the two wings of a bird. Just as a bird cannot fly to its destination with only one wing, so we cannot reach enlightenment with either wisdom or method alone.

Tibetan Buddhism is unique in that it has a living tradition of very powerful meditation practices known as Tantra, or Secret Mantra within which one also receives and practices correspondingly advanced and esoteric sets of vows. All the other practices that we have been discussing up until now are contained in the sutra system. Although all the sutra practices form part of the tantric path, there is a difference between sutra and tantra which can be characterized as follows: in Sutra the practices of method and wisdom are done separately. One practices wisdom by meditating on emptiness, but meditation on any other object, such as bodhicitta, or any form of practice that does not involve meditating on emptiness, is the practice of method. So at best they can be practiced alternately. By using the tantric path, however, one can practice both method and wisdom at the same time with the same moment of consciousness, so the end result can be one achieved much more quickly.

There are many symbolic representations of tantric achievements in the form of paintings of deities—often of a male and female deity in union. This represents the union of method and wisdom, the male symbolizing method and the female symbolizing wisdom. In the practice of highest yoga tantra, the subtle mind transforms into the deity, which realizes emptiness as its object. The manifestation as the mandala or holy body of the deity is the method practice and the realization of emptiness is the wisdom practice. The concentration that can be developed through the practice of highest yoga tantra is far more subtle and powerful than any level of concentration that can be attained through sutra practice alone, so it leads to a quicker result.

Devotion forms an integral part of Buddhist practice, and limitless gratitude is due to our teachers who show us and help us to practice the path to enlightenment. In the tantric path devotional practices are especially meaningful, and it is important to train one's mind to see the spiritual master, or lama, as the primordial Buddha. In this way one receives blessings from the Buddha to develop his qualities more easily. There are devotional practices, prayers, and ceremonies in all Buddhist traditions, and through these one can center one's awareness on the qualities of the Buddha, the teachings, and the spiritually realized beings. These three objects of devotion—the Buddha, the Dharma and the Sangha—are known as the Three Precious Jewels. Through prayers and devotional practices one can receive inspiration and spiritual nourishment, as well as create the causes for making progress along the path. One can also create formal bonds between oneself and the Three Jewels through the use of ceremonies. The various levels of vows are received through ordination ceremonies and initiations, some of which are very elaborate. There are also special ceremonies and methods for purifying any transgressions of these vows. In this way one maintains a direct link with the Buddha, Dharma, and Sangha which operates on a subtle level.

Spirituality in Monasticism

Receiving monastic ordination enables one to train in a relatively basic level of moral discipline which helps one to keep the higher sets of vows more purely. When one understands the great benefits of the vows, it seems that it is no great sacrifice to live within their limitations, for in fact they lead to true freedom. Constantly being under the influence of ego-grasping is itself the most gruesome kind of imprisonment. However, taking vows and practicing the Buddha-dharma does not instantaneously release one from this; one still has to tolerate the sufferings that are generated by ego-grasping. The difficulty is when some delusion arises very strongly and one cannot gain the temporary comfort of acting upon it. At such times one has to remember such things are impermanent: that this feeling or difficulty will pass. All experiences rise and cease. One can just observe its arising, its presence in the mind, and its departure, without grasping at it. This requires practice, but it certainly is possible to develop an awareness of the basic clarity of the mind, which then enables one not to be disturbed by whatever may arise and pass away within that inner space.

There are many other practices which help one to deal in a temporary way with the delusions, in which one actually analyzes the particular delusion that is present in the mind at that moment, and sees that there is no value in it, no good reason to act upon it, and indeed that it doesn't even exist in the way that it appears. Then one can try to cultivate the positive feeling or attitude which is its opposite. In this way one not only deals with the present situation, but lessens the power of the delusions themselves, so that gradually one's mind becomes more consistently peaceful.

A monastic lifestyle provides the ideal environment within which to study the mind and to practice meditation. It is very helpful to have a clear and simple way of life that does not encourage self-indulgence nor subject one to unconducive difficulties and complications. Even without the external support of a monastery or a nunnery, the vows themselves act as a very suitable framework within which to develop a constant awareness of one's mental states and so be able to transform them.

Being a monk or nun in itself by no means indicates whether or not one has developed renunciation in the Buddhist sense. True renunciation is indicative of an advanced level of spiritual development. Most of us who are monks and nuns are just working towards that. Our long, flowing robes and bald heads do not indicate that we have abandoned all worldly thoughts and wishes; rather they are a tool to help us abandon them. This change of one's appearance is really very effective and over a period of time one can concentrate one's energies more fully on the most meaningful things in life. Our human life is so short, and yet it gives us the precious opportunity to work for real freedom. It seems a tragic waste of time to use it only for fun and games and material comforts which themselves are so easily and certainly lost.

Things of beauty can open the heart and bring warmth into one's life, but when the beauty fades all too often the openness and warmth does also. One needs to develop openness and warmth in all situations and towards all beings, even the ugly and unpleasant ones. A monastic way of life helps one to develop an appreciation of a kind of beauty that flows from within the mind rather than that which appears to come from an external object. When the mind is at peace, all things can appear beautiful, even a pile of garbage. However, when the mind is agitated or upset, even a blazing sunset will seem uninteresting. So even 'external' beauty doesn't exist just by virtue of the object.

Although Buddhist practitioners, and particularly monks and nuns, often live in communities, the actual practice is a solitary one. No one else can be in your mind. You yourself have to deal with your own mental and emotional experiences. This does not mean that the monastic life is a lonely or selfish one. Loneliness is something that can be experienced in any situation, whether one is celibate or married with a family. People who are sincerely practicing a spiritual path are often less lonely than people who are not. We have close working relationships with our teachers and spiritual friends, and often such friendships reach much deeper levels than ordinary ones. One is also more easily able to get in touch with a certain 'something within oneself.' By developing deeper awareness one has access to greater reserves of energy, wisdom, and compassion. As such, one is able to give more, and to give more wisely, to others. So it is not at all selfish. One is trying first to develop the quality, and then the quantity, of what one can give.

As far as women are concerned, and particularly Western women, the Tibetan Buddhist monastic set-up is in many ways more suitable than that of other Buddhist traditions. The style of life is less formal, and monks and nuns have equal status—which is something that we Westerners feel quite strongly about. The Theravada tradition in particular takes a heavy view of women, and nuns are regarded as much lower in status than monks. In fact, I believe that in countries where Theravada Buddhism is traditional, they do not have any nuns, only female postulants or anagarikas. It is even believed that women cannot reach enlightenment at all but have to create the causes to be born as men in their next life so that they can make it next time round. This attitude is not usually held to be true by Western Theravada practitioners and certainly not by Tibetan Buddhists of whatever nationality.

In Britain, a new order of nuns has been established within the Thai Theravada tradition and the nuns here are given much more credibility than they would have in Thailand. I have friends among the nuns in this new order and know that although their status is more equal to the monks than it would be in Thailand, there are still quite a few differences. The nuns themselves cope admirably with their lower status. In fact this aspect of their life has proved to be a source of great strength to them; they really have to practice tolerance. On an external level their life is stricter than ours is within the Tibetan tradition. I maybe a nun and live on my own or with friends, not necessarily in a monastery or nunnery. I can get a job and earn money. For them this would be impossible. They cannot handle money nor own anything much other than their robes and bowl (which are in a sense monastic property anyway). So I still have quite a bit of freedom as a nun, and indeed do get jobs in the city from time to time, wear lay clothes, and grow my hair a little (so as not to shock my employers!). I find this very helpful. In any case, I have to do this sometimes, as within the Tibetan tradition there is no financial support for monks and nuns. Within the Theravada tradition the monks and nuns are 'alms mendicants' and live entirely on whatever the lay people offer to them. This is a very beautiful way of life and has a very powerful effect on those who live this way, as well as on those who give to it.

Although the external lifestyle within the Theravada tradition may be stricter than that within the Tibetan monastic tradition, the inner practice is no less strict. Within the Tibetan tradition there are several more sets of vows which relate to transforming one's feelings, thoughts, and energies. The monastic vows relate mainly to controlling one's actions of body and speech, and though these have a strong effect on one's thoughts, feelings, and energies, they more readily provide the basis for transforming them rather than functioning as a practice for that end. Our general training is geared to transform every moment of our daily experience and activities into the wish to remove the suffering of all living beings. At first one may feel squashed or crowded out by such all-pervading conceptual practices, but gradually the grasping for thought space for oneself subsides and one can motivate more and more of one's life for the benefit of others.

This kind of transformation seems to happen quite naturally when someone becomes a mother, though that intense feeling and concern is limited to her own family. In Tibetan Buddhist teaching many references are made to a mother's selfless love, and we try to develop that kind of love and concern for all living beings. Through an understanding of reincarnation we realize that we cannot point to any living being and say that this being has definitely never been a mother to me in a previous lifetime. Tibetan Buddhists are encouraged to view every living being as a mother from the past, as someone who has been very close to oneself and shown great kindness and self-sacrifice. In this way we can develop a real feeling for not wanting them to suffer, and the wish to free them from suffering as soon as possible.

In order to guide someone up the slippery mountain passes to liberation, one has to have the strength, the wisdom which knows the way—not only from maps but from experience—and the compassionate will to accomplish the task. Thus one works to develop these qualities within oneself so that one can act as a perfectly qualified guide for others. Although one can do much to help others in various ways throughout one's own long path of progress, it is when one's mind finally abides in the sphere of reality, completely free of all obscurations, that one can most fully and effectively help others to attain that lasting bliss—the perfect state of Buddahood.

Venerable Tenzin Dechen was born in England in 1955. After a traditional upbringing in an Anglican Church boarding school, she worked as an accounts clerk in London and Paris. For eleven years she was in the British Olympic Fencing Squad. In 1976 she went to London University to read philosophy, and in 1979 to Cambridge University to work on her Ph.D.

The study of philosophy and religion eventually led her to her first contact with Tibetan Buddhism. Realizing her attunement with Buddhism, she lived at a college of Buddhist studies in North England to continue her study and spiritual practices. In 1985-86 she visited Bodhgaya, India, and was ordained there as a novice nun in the Gelukpa tradition of Tibetan Buddhism by His Holiness the Dalai Lama.

At present Tenzin Dechen is studying Buddhist philosophy at a Tibetan monastery in India.

She who sows in tears will reap in joy.

P*SALM* 126

This is how love is:
So what if your head must roll,
What is there to cry about?

K*ABIR*

Suffering and Spirituality:
An Interview with

Irina Tweedie

he editor interviewed Irina Tweedie, Sufi mystic and spiritual guide, in her home in London.

Mrs. Tweedie, have you found that the spiritual path of women is different from that of men?

Yes, quite different. My teacher, whom I call Bhai Sahib (Elder Brother), said one day, "Men need many practices because the energy in men works entirely different from that in women. I give men many practices. Woman needs hardly any practices at all. She will reach reality because she is woman."

Just imagine how thrilled I was! I thought, "Aha!" but I didn't say anything. Suddenly he sharply turned to me and said, "Oh no, don't rejoice. It is just as difficult for everybody. It is only different."

You see, a woman has a special relationship to matter. We use matter to produce new life so we are made in a different way. We have to produce children out of our physical body, so our psyche and our bodies and our chakras (energy centers) and everything else are made entirely different from those of men. Man uses his creative energy, manifested as semen, to beget children. His energy is transmuted into something else and sent out of him, so it is rather difficult for him to reach a spiritual level. We women hold the creative energy of God in our chakras. We have it already and we keep it. Spiritually speaking, we don't need to get anything else.

For the sake of the children, however, we women need protection, we need warmth, we need comfort in order to procreate the human race. The woman is, therefore often much more attached to physical things. We need them. For our children we need security, money, food, shelter. These things are extremely important to us. The needs spring from our very nature as bearers of life.

Then the process of bearing and raising a child is important for a woman's spiritual growth?

Yes. Children are extremely important for spiritual development. For a woman to birth a child is a spiritual experience of the first magnitude. Children are very special; they are magic. And they are definitely an important spiritual experience.

What about women who do not bear children?

It doesn't matter. I never had children. I had two husbands (not at the same time!) but I never had children. They just didn't come. One can achieve the heights of spirituality without bearing children.

For some women to have no children is a terrible psychological suffering, because it is in woman's very nature to desire children. But because children are so important for a woman, they also present the greatest obstacle for her spiritual life. A swami in Dehradun, India, once told me that according to the philosophy of Vedanta, it is spiritually easier for a woman to have no children because children create such attachment. Children represent a tremendous attachment for a mother. How could it be otherwise? They are part of a woman. Then part of her spiritual work is to overcome this attachment.

It would seem, then, that women need a partner to progress spiritually.

I think man and woman both need partners. Bhai Sahib said to us, "I would like to take them together to God. They complement each other." More and more as I have to deal with people I see that human beings shouldn't be alone. We need each other. Women need men; men need women. Nobody is more; man is not more than woman and woman is not more than man. We are just different. Guruji used to say, "You all swim in the ocean. Who is nearer the shore? And which shore?" No one is higher or lower than another. We are all different, but we need each other.

What is the nature of personal relationship?

Relationship is based upon energy. The relationship between the two sexes (or between the same sex on the homosexual level), always has to do with the energy we call kundalini. Kundalini is very powerful; it is the same energy that is at the center of every atom. It is the earth energy, and it is traditionally considered to be feminine. When two people come together and there is love, or even not love but just sexual desire, what happens on the energy level? The energy forms a circuit, a closed circuit, between man and woman. They are enclosed in an energy grid which produces beautiful effects. But this circuit or grid can be so easily broken! The least little thing can break it. A tiny bit of hurt, a bit of pain inflicted by one upon the other, and it's gone. It is as if the chemistry wasn't all right. And sometimes the loveliest people leave each other in anger for quite small things.

But basically man and woman are really the same, and on one level of consciousness I often have difficulty distinguishing one from the other unless I pay close attention.

Then at the spiritual level men and women are basically the same reality?

Absolutely. For instance, my teacher said that in the moment of ecstasy, during sex, the experience is the same for man as for woman. He said that the feeling is the same, because it is an explosion of space. The one who is the real enjoyer is

Atman, our higher self. The body partakes only by reflection.

In order to be perfect we must have both the male and the female qualities. Psychologically in every woman there is also a man. Likewise in every man there exists a woman. We have both characteristics. No one is only male or only female. With spiritual progress, the man will not become effeminate, nor will the woman be masculine, but each will become whole, a perfect balance between the two qualities.

Why, then, did the creator make this division of the sexes?

In order to create the world, one had to become two and two had to be different and separate. It is as simple as that.

And once the two are different, the pursuit of spiritual life is to rejoin them?

Yes, quite right. And that will all happen in millions and millions of years when Brahman takes in the breath.

It appears that all the searching and seeking of life, all the desires and ambitions, all the achievements and hopes are, underneath the obvious, a striving for ultimate unity.

Yes. The whole of life, everything from a stone to a galaxy, searches for unity. If you look at nature, you see that everything looks like a human being. In trees you see the human form. Even in pebbles you see somehow a human form. Because we human beings are made in the image of God, we especially look for oneness. Sufis say that the human being is the crown of creation and seeks unity, unity, unity. We find this seeking in ourselves at every psychological level.

When we love someone we seek that oneness; we want to be of one mind with that person. Finally in the moment of ecstasy there is oneness. In union with God there is such fulfillment, such glory, that we never feel alone again.

Loneliness does seem to be a great problem for many women. Is there some reason for it? Does loneliness itself fit into our spiritual development in some ways?

I think that on the spiritual path loneliness is definitely a problem, not only for women, but also for men. What happens when we are seriously on the spiritual path? To be on the path, using the conventional words, is really—how shall I put it?—it is a great friction. It is a law of nature, like the tide, like day and night, like a pendulum swinging back and forth. There is nearness and there is separation. There is pain and there is joy. When we are in the state of nearness to that which we call God or That or Void or our Higher Self (which are all one and the same thing), then we are happy. When we are separated, the soul is crying. This very friction causes the purifying of the mind. You see, friction creates fire; fire is pain, suffering, and great loneliness. Nearness and separation keep altering, keep going backwards and forwards, move from pain to joy. That is how the mind will be purified.

In general, I find that women are more lonely than men because they have more longing. They are more aware of what is inside themselves, and of that which is missing. We bring into this world two qualities: the will to live, and the will to worship. The will to live is self-preservation. The will to worship is the love aspect embedded in the very texture of our soul. This love aspect is the very essence of God. It manifests itself in us as longing. Women seem to feel that longing very keenly.

We often feel an emptiness, a great yearning. There is always a place in the heart of a human being reserved for the divine. No mortal creature can fill it. We are made in God's image, the greatest lover, a jealous lover, who keeps a place there allowing nothing else to fill it. Longing is one of the messages which the soul sends to the human being: "Go home. We must go home to the Beloved."

Who is this Beloved?

The Beloved is a great emptiness! It is a void, terribly frightening to the mind, but responsive. It is at the same time absolute fullness, absolute light. It is the nothingness where everything is. It is the fullness where nothing exists. It is the fullness of love.

A woman doesn't want a friend; a woman wants a lover! The moment of union with God is the most intimate thing in the world. At that moment we are united with our Self, with our soul, the Atman, the personal God, the Creator, the constantly drunk one, drunk with his own creation. And that union is bought with suffering.

Must everyone experience spiritual suffering?

Yes, because there comes a time in spirituality when we have to find absolute happiness within ourselves. It is one stage on the path. This is a process that we all have to go through. People come and say, "Oh, I can't meditate. It is like a brick wall in front of me. I feel quite naked, suspended in the void and nothing is there. God is not there. I cannot pray. I can do nothing. All is dark." About this stage Swami Rama advised, "Get established in the darkness."

I remember one day when my teacher spoke to Lillian, the woman who introduced me to him. She was so happy that day; she was radiant and telling him all the wonderful things that had happened to her. Bhai Sahib very quietly turned to me and said, "And you?" I just shrugged because I was at that moment in the darkness. "Yes," he said, "union is good, but separation is better. When the human being is happy he doesn't do anything; he's just happy. But when you are alone, when you are forsaken, you are crying and you make an effort.

I asked, "Bhai Sahib, will that state last?"

He answered, "My dear, it will pass; it comes and goes. But don't tell it to pass. Just say, 'Oh beloved, it doesn't matter. I am still faithful. I am still true.' It will pass."

Then suffering cannot be avoided on the spiritual path?

It cannot be avoided. We have an idea of a spiritual life that is not true. We think it is all beautiful, with a master sitting in the Himalayas, and everything lovely and sweet. But it's not like that at all. The spiritual life and its training is hard and crude; it is rough and difficult. You are humiliated, thrown down; your face is rubbed in the dust and you are beaten to nothing.

After my training in India a friend asked me what my training was like. I replied, "Perhaps it is like a steam roller going over you. And what gets up is paper thin and transparent, and there is nothing left."

Of course, I think that women do suffer more. Psychologically, a woman is much more, I wouldn't say sensitive as that is too crude an expression, but I feel that we are hurt much easier than men. There is such a history of cruelty against women, perhaps we feel the suffering of all of them.

Long ago I read a beautiful poem that began, "We women bleed." We bear our children with suffering and blood. We bleed for our children; we bleed for our man. We bleed for all those we are connected to. We bleed in sympathy with other women. There is constant bleeding.

Very often just coming back from meditation or going into meditation, I remain half conscious and I feel women's suffering. Also, you see, being second class citizens we are constantly pushed down, down, down. There is suffering from all directions: physical and emotional and psychological and physiological and every possible way.

Can suffering be seen as good? Is it necessary for our development?

If it is good, I don't know, but I think it is the will of God. Spiritual growth should be like that, that's all. It is the drama of the soul.

Will there ever be an end to the loneliness and suffering?

I don't think so. But this is my personal opinion and should be accepted with a grain of salt. I think suffering is actually a very wonderful thing because suffering is also redeeming. Without suffering how will we know that there is no suffering? That there is joy? Suffering is fire; fire is purifying.

You know, we Sufis have written about this. It is actually in books, though I did not know it, and discovered it only afterwards. We have states, wonderful spiritual states, full of beauty and joy and peace. But after that there is a kind of depression. It is not an ordinary depression; it's something else: this world is oh, so difficult to bear because somewhere else is so much nicer!

How could I enjoy the other states if I didn't know that deep suffering afterwards? We have to accept that. You know, there comes a time when illness doesn't matter, pain doesn't matter, nothing matters anymore because there is this infinite joy that you can offer this suffering to someone, somewhere, and say, "Well, this terrible pain in me I offer to thee. It is a miserable flower, but it's all I have."

What is the role of the teacher in spirituality?

The whole spiritual life is getting rid of the ego. We have to get rid of the ego in order to get anywhere. Two masters cannot live in one heart. Either I or That; either the little self is there, or the divine is there. The role of the teacher is to get rid of this little ego. It is a very simple process, but it is very painful. The teacher must erase the ego and that is done through suffering. The master does nothing but his duty to help us get rid of it, but it is a painful thing. It is crucifixion, absolute crucifixion. The teacher's duty is to turn you inside out. After that you are never the same again.

     The goal of every yoga is to lead a guided life, to be able to listen. So the master must be able to reach the disciple and vice-versa. It's two-way process. (Either it is the master, or it is your higher self—they are the same thing). So spiritual training is really analysis, but much harder, much worse than any therapy and it's done with yogic power.

     Human beings want to run from such power and from such pain, but before a great teacher takes you in his hands and turns you inside out, he will give you something magnificent. He will show you what humans really are— what we look like somewhere where we are not human anymore, but divine. There is such greatness there; we are like a great fire! And from that moment you can never look at another human being without remembering that. From then on you will see each human being as part of the Beloved.

How does one find such a teacher?

There is a spiritual law which says, "When the disciple is ready the teacher will be there." So going out and looking for a teacher is grabbing the wrong end of the stick. If we aspire and if our torch is lit, in the darkness of the world somebody is bound to see it.

     Every one of us has only one teacher. Only someone who has deep karmas (spiritual relationships from the past lives) with you has the right to subject you to what a teacher subjects you to. Only one person in the world, the infinitely pure, disinterested one, can do that and not incur karma himself. The relationship with that teacher is a great grace from God based on mutual past karma. It is a great grace. It is not something we can accomplish.

Is meditation important for spiritual growth?

Yes. The feminine leads us to spirituality, to our deepest self. What is the feminine in spiritual practice? It is meditation.

Is a woman's approach to meditation different from a man's?

Very much so. I have to begin with love, because meditation belongs there. Love, like everything else in the world, has a positive and a negative aspect; in other words, a masculine and a feminine aspect. The masculine aspect in love is "I love you." The feminine aspect is "I'm waiting for you." Meditation is the feminine side of love. The feminine says to the divine, "I am a cup empty for you." That is meditation. "I am waiting for you. I am here. I surrender to you. I am waiting for grace."

For women, the spiritual life in one way is easier than for men. Only a certain temperament of man can surrender like women can surrender. And the essence of spiritual life is surrender. Bhai Sahib said, "Women are taken up through the path of love, for love is a feminine mystery." He said women do not need many spiritual practices, but need only to renounce. Renounce what? Renounce the world. Complete renunciation, which is the most difficult thing for women, is necessary. I had to do it—to give everything away. Bhai Sahib said to me, "You cannot say to the Beloved, 'Oh I love you, but this is mine, and I will go so far and no further.' You have to give everything away, including yourself, in complete surrender."

To whom do we surrender? We do not surrender to the teacher. That is rubbish! My teacher kept repeating, "You must surrender. You must surrender." And of course I presumed that he meant surrender to him. One really does want to surrender to the teacher, but one should not. One surrenders only to the light within oneself, to one's own highest self. Absolute surrender with love is necessary. You surrender to that eternal part within you; ancient, without beginning or end. That is an extraordinary thing. It is the thing that people do not know. I realized it in deep meditation. When we have self-realization, we do not realize anything else except ourselves. That is why it is called 'self-realization' or 'God-realization.' They are the same thing.

One day a young man told me something infinitely touching. He said, "When I am with my girlfriend, in that most supreme moment of sex, I have a tremendous desire to be one with her." I remember looking at him and feeling my heart full of compassion. Poor man. He was hoping to be united with somebody else. There is no such thing as somebody else. There is only you. The realization is always with oneself; it is never with anything or anyone else. It is the same thing as the first experience of the superconscious state. You find yourself in absolute omnipotence, in absolute light, in absolute magnificence, and there is no God to be found! It is a shattering experience. One brings only bits and pieces of memories from it; one tries to understand those states partially, little by little. It takes years. I have been thirty years at it and I still can't understand it well enough. But I know the more you meditate, the more silent you become. This is a fact. And what you have to say about that state you can say only in parables.

We start out, it seems, with a concept, an idea of God 'out there.' And then as we grow, and suffer, and struggle, and finally renounce our ideas and our concepts, we have the spiritual shock that the divine is not out there; it is within.

Yes. And it's here in this world, too. This life and the spiritual life are one and the same. But this is already a step on the path. At the beginning there is the world and there is something else to which we should aspire. But once we progress enough, we suddenly begin to realize that there are no such things as the world and the spiritual life, but that they are two sides of the same coin.

In *Zen Flesh, Zen Bones* there is a description of being thrown back into the marketplace. One is amongst the people; one buys and one sells. This life is then no different from the other. "Barefooted and naked of breast I mingle with the people of the world. My clothes are ragged and dust-laden, and I am ever blissful. I use no magic to extend my life. Now before me the trees become alive."

Great Sufis have always been shoemakers, tailors, potters; they lived among people. Guruji said that in our tradition we are not allowed to go to the monastery or the cave or the forest to meditate by ourselves. We have to live in this world and to realize God just the same as when the light is closing tightly around us. There is no difference; God is in the world, too.

What is the mystic joy you spoke about that comes after many trials, tears, and struggles and seems to surpass any other joy?

The state of the soul, the plane where the soul dwells, is pure joy. Joy is natural to our soul. When we reach a certain spiritual level, joy and tranquillity are ours. And here comes a great mystery: the first thing we all experience on the spiritual path is great peace. Joy comes afterwards. First you realize the self and then you realize God. First comes peace which surpasses understanding. Like the depth of the ocean where there are no waves, we realize absolute stillness. Only after that we realize God, which is a void, frightening to the mind. But this void is absolute fulfillment; it is full of love, absolute love, and unspeakable, absolute bliss.

And then after that nothing really matters. There is no man and no woman. There is no God. Everything is one.

Irina Tweedie was born in Russia in 1907. She was educated in Vienna and Paris, moving to England at her marriage. After her husband's untimely death she eventually married a naval officer. After his premature death in 1954, Irina was plunged into despair and profound spiritual crisis. A friend introduced her to the Theosophical Society where she began the journey which eventually brought her, at age 52, to India and to the Sufi master who was to completely transform her life. At his instruction she recorded her training in extensive diaries which were to become the inspiration for thousands of readers around the world. At the death of her master in 1966, Irina returned to England where she devoted all her time to teaching, lecturing and conducting workshops. She worked as librarian for the Theosophical Society where she also carried on the spiritual mission given her by her teacher. Until her eighty-fifth birthday, Mrs. Tweedie continued her travels to Germany, Switzerland and the United States, speaking to large audiences. She currently lives in North London where she continues to guide students. Parts of her diary were published as *The Chasm of Fire*; the complete diary is published under the title, *Daughter of Fire*.

Woman must come of age by herself.

ANNE MORROW LINDBERGH

For All the Secret Dancers

by

Virginia Haiden

*T*hey flew up one spring day
just as the oaks were beginning to bloom,
green and yellow warblers, filling the tree
with music and bright darting movements.
The mother and little girl stood outside
and marveled at the sight—
the mother's hand steadying her shoulder,
the child swayed backwards, closed her eyes,
opened her mouth, and swallowed the tree
like a spoonful of honey.
She tasted the sweet tasseling blossoms of oak,
felt the flickering wings,
the sway of the branches—swallowed it whole,
then opened her eyes, and breathed it out again.

But the tree had infiltrated her body
like iron in earth or smoke in wind,
like salt in water she became infused
with its quickening brightness.
She grew old listening to music,
she opened her mouth, and let it run in
until it came out her feet and fingertips,
the flickering motions of color and song,
as bright as jewels.

You can see her in the garden bending over the beds;
suddenly she lifts her face and smiles
as if she is drinking up the sunlight;
she sways above the bean-rows and marigolds,
weaving webs of light with long hands;
or in the morning when she sets the kettle on the stove,
turning in her shuffling slippers,
she lifts the shawl above her head,
and does again the dance of wings and branches.

Virginia Haiden was born and educated in Minneapolis. Her poetry, noted for its rich mythological references, has appeared in a variety of journals and anthologies. In 1989 she was a selected participant in the Squaw Valley Poets Conference, and in 1991 and 1992 she was runner up in the Loft-McKnight Mentor's Award and the Loft's Mentor Program.

Mother of four and grandmother of two, Virginia has served the community in the child protection field for the past seventeen years. She is also an avid rockhound whose interests extend into gardening, ethnic cooking, and jewelry design.

Notes

NOTES

King: What is Spirituality?

1. Gibran, Kahil. *The Prophet* (New York: Alfred A. Knopf, 1973) p. 13.
2. Frederick Franck in a lecture "Art as a Way" at the Marylebone Health Centre, London in March, 1987.
3. Mary Daly in *Beyond God the Father*; Carol Christ in *Diving Deep and Surfacing*; Mary Giles in *The Feminist Mystic*, among others.

Pare: Self-Image and Spirituality

1. Hutchinson, Marcia Germaine. *Transforming Body Image: Learning to Love the Body You Have* (Freedom, CA: Crossing Press, 1985) p. 20.
2. Lerner, Gerda. *The Creation of Patriarchy* (New York: Oxford University Press, 1986) p. 239.
3. Quotations taken from *Scholastica*, a booklet prepared by the Benedictine Committee for the General Chapter of the Federation of St. Scholastica, June, 1982 and from Feminist Connection Farewell, January, 1985.
4. Shepard, Chuck. "News of the Weird" Minneapolis Star Tribune, January 10, 1991, p. 6E.
5. Heise, Jori. "The Global War Against Women," *The Utne Reader*, Nov/Dec, 1989, p. 40.
6. Greenspan, Miriam. *A New Approach to Women and Therapy* (New York: McGraw-Hill, 1983) p. 303.
7. Lord, Audre. *The Sister Outsider* (Trumansburg, NY: Crossing Press, 1984).
8. Weber, Christin Lore. *Blessings—A Womanchrist Reflection on the Beatitudes* (New York: Harper & Row, 1991) p. 54.

Eagle: Nature and Spirituality

1. Drysdale, Vera Louise and Brown, Joseph Epes. *Gift of the Sacred Pipe* (Norman: University of Oklahoma, 1982), p. 6-7.
2. This true story is presented in Brooke's adult children's book, *The Naming* (Unpublished), p. 16-18.
3. Boone, J. Allen. *Kinship with All Life* (New York: Harper & Row, 1976).
4. Leslie, Robert Franklin. *In the Shadow of a Rainbow* (New York: New American Library, 1974).
5. For more information on this story see L. Taylor Hansen, *He Walked the Americas* (Amherst, WI: Amherst Press, 1963), and Brooke's article "Lineage of the Sun," in *The American Theosophist,* Spring, 1986.
6. From a letter of Chief Seattle of the Duwamish Tribe of the State of Washington to President Franklin Pierce in 1855. "This Land is Sacred" printed by Dale Jones of the Seattle office of Friends of the Earth.
7. For further information see Peter Tompkins and Christopher Bird, *Secret Life of*

Plants (New York: Harper & Row, 1973).

8. Drysdale and Brown, op. cit.

9. For a full description of this rite, see Drysdale and Brown, op. cit.

Young: Psychology and Spirituality

1. My goal here is not to give a complete discussion of the theories of Freud. Indeed, for the purposes of this paper, I've chosen Freud to symbolize that school of thought upon which traditional psychological theories of personality and development are based.

2. Also Colossians 3:18-24 and 1 Peter 2:18-3:7.

3. *New International Bible* Grand Rapids, MI: VonderVan Publishing House, 1984.

4. See Reuther, Rosemary Radford, ed. *Religion and Sexism: Images of Woman in the Jewish and Christian Traditions* (New York: Simon and Schuster, 1974).

5. See Judith Lewis Herman, *Father-Daughter Incest* (Cambridge: Harvard University Press, 1981).

6. I Peter 2:18-21, *New English Bible.*

7. Ruether, op cit., p. 9.

Eagger: Freedom and Spirituality

1. See also, King, Avrom E., "Right and Left Hemisphere Skills in Dentistry," in *Healing Currents, The Journal of the Whole Health Institute*, Vol. 10, No. 1, 1986.

2. Thompson, Clara, M. *On Women* (New York: Basic Books, 1964).

3. See also Dowling, Colette. *The Cinderella Complex* (New York: Fontana, 1982).

4. Bardwick, Judith. *The Psychology of Women* (Study of Biocultural Conflicts, 1971).

5. Horney, Karen. "The Overvaluation of Love, A Study of a Common Present-Day Feminine Type," *Psychoanalytical Quarterly*, Vol. 3, 1934. Also, *The Neurotic Need for Love* ed. by Harold Kelman. (New York: Norton, 1967).

6. Thompson, op. cit.

7. Douvan, Elizabeth, "Sex Differences in Adolescent Character Process," *Merrill-Palmer Quarterly*, 1957.

8. Laplanche, J., Pontalis, J.B. *The Language of Psychoanalysis* (London: Hogarth Press, 1983).

9. Harding, Esther. *Women's Mysteries: Ancient and Modern* (New York: Boston, 1973) p. 115-149.

Timmerman: Sex and Spirituality

1. These ideas have been developed at greater length in Joan Timmerman, *The Mardi Gras Syndrome: Rethinking Christian Sexuality* (New York: Crossroad,1984), and *Sexuality and Spiritual Growth* (New York: Crossroad, 1992).

2. Louis Monden, S.J. in *Sin, Liberty and Law* (Sheed and Ward, 1965) has written extensively about the three levels of ethics. See especially pp. 3-17.

3. For the best source of texts and interpretation from the first four centuries, see

Peter Brown. *The Body and Society: Men, Women, and Sexual Renunciation in Early Christianity* (New York: Columbia University Press, 1988).

4. Caroline Bynum. "Women Mystics and Eucharistic Devotion in the Thirteenth Century," *Women's Studies*, 1984, vol. 11, pp. 179-214.

5. Susan Sullivan and Matthew Kawiak. *Parents Talk Love: The Catholic Family Handbook About Sexuality* (New York: Paulist Press, 1985) p. 75.

6. Demaris Wehr. *Jung and Feminism: Liberating Archetypes* (Boston: Beacon, 1987) p. 17.

7. Dalma Heyn. "Body Hate" in *MS*, July/August, 1989, p. 36.

8. Lorna J. and Philip M. Sarrel. *Sexual Turning Points: The Seven Stages of Adult Sexuality* (New York: Macmillan, 1984) p. 9.

Qalbi: Motherhood and Spirituality

1. Allione, Tsultrim. *Women of Wisdom* (London: Routledge & Kegan Paul, 1984), introduction.

2. Hazart Inayat Khan. *The Complete Sayings* (New Lebanon, NY: Sufi Order Publications, 1978), p. 80.

3. Ibid., p. 128.

4. Swami Rama of the Himalayas in a public lecture in Chicago, Illinois, 1975.

5. Khan, op. cit., p. 29.

6. Pir Vilayat Inayat Khan. *Toward the One* (New York: Harper & Row, 1974),p. 1.

7. *New American Bible* I Corinthians, 13, p. 1353.

8. *Springs of Oriental Wisdom* (New York: Herder & Herder).

9. Rumi, Jelaluddin. *The Ruins of the Heart* trans. by Edmund Helminsi. (Putney: Threshold Books, 1960), p. 323.

10. Hazrat Inayat Khan, op. cit., p. 167.

11. Ibid., p. 115.

Robinson: Creativity and Spirituality

1. Miller, William. *The Creative Edge: Fostering Innovation Where You Work* (Reading, MA: Addison Wesley, Inc., 1987).

2. Frederick Franck. *The Zen of Seeing: Seeing/Drawing as Meditation* (New York: Vintage Books, 1973).

3. Herrmann, Ned. *The Creative Brain* (Lake Lure, NC: Brain Books, 1988).

4. The best and most lucid explanation of synchronicity I've found is in Jean Shinoda Bolen's little book, *The Tao of Psychology: Synchronicity and the Self* (New York: Harper & Row, 1982).

5. E. Paul Torrance. *The Search for Satori and Creativity* (New York: Creative Education Foundation Inc., in association with Bearly Limited, 1979).

Woodruff: Art and Spirituality

1. Fox, Matthew. *Original Blessing* (Santa Fe: Bear & Company, 1983).

2. Williamson, Cris "Waterfall" from *The Changer and Changed* (Oakland, CA: Olivia Records, 1975).

3. Woodruff, Sue. *Meditations with Mechteld of Magdeburg* (Santa Fe: Bear & Company, 1983), p. 92.

4. Doyle, Brendan. *Meditations with Julian of Norwich* (Santa Fe: Bear & Company, 1983), p. 84.

5. Sarton, May. "An Observation," *As Does New Hampshire* (New Hampshire: R.R. Smith, 1967), p. 30.

6. Ibid.

7. From Edith Warner's unpublished journal quoted in Peggy Pond Church, *The House at Otowi Bridge* (Albuquerque, NM: University of New Mexico Press, (1959), p. 18.

8. Woodruff, p. 126.

9. Woodruff, p. 69.

10. Rich, Adrienne. "Power," *The Dream of a Common Language: Poems 1974-1977* (New York: Norton, 1978), p. 3.

11. Houselander, Caryll. "Pastoral," *The Reed of God* (London: Sheed and Ward, (1944), p. 39.

12. Fox, op. cit., p. 208-219.

13. Williamson, Cris. "Wild Things," op. cit.

14. Sarton, May. "The Angels and The Furies," *A Durable Fire* (New York:Norton, 1972), p. 34.

15. Mechtilde of Magdeburg. *The Flowing Light of the Godhead* trans. by Lucy Menzies. (London: Longmans, Green and Co., 1952), p. 37.

16. Uhlein, Gabriele. *Medititations with Hildegarde of Bingen* (Santa Fe: Bear & Company, 1982), p. 39.

17. Ibid., p. 62.

18. Ibid., p. 123.

19. Lindberg, Anne Morrow. *Gift From the Sea* (New York: Random House, 1955), p.17.

20. Church, op. cit., p. 116.

21. Ibid., p. 117.

22. Woodruff, op. cit., p. 80.

23. Ibid, p. 74.

24. Ibid.

25. Ibid., p. 132.

26. Williamson, op. cit.

27. Ibid.

28. Woodruff, op. cit., p. 60-61

29. Uhlein, op. cit., p. 75.

30. Weil, Simone. *Gravity and Grace* (London: Routledge and Kegan Paul, 1952), p.10.

31. Dillard, Annie. *Holy the Firm* (New York: Bantam, 1977), p. 48.

32. Sarton, "The Autumn Sonnets," ADF, op. cit., p. 43.

33. Now published in Craighead, Meinrad. *The Mother's Songs* (New York: Paulist Press, 1986).

34. Day, Dorothy. *The Long Loneliness* (New York: Harper & Row, 1952), p. 134-5.

35. Woodruff, op. cit., p. 109.
36. Uhlein, op. cit., p. 124.
37. Cazden, Joanna. "The Hatching Song," *Hatching.*
38. Lindberg, op. cit., p. 56.
39. Williamson, "Sister," op. cit.
40. Littlebear, Naomi. "Like a Mountain," *Quiet Thunder* (Portland, OR: Riverbear Music, 1977).
41. Church, op. cit., p. 134.
42. Williamson, "Song of the Soul," op. cit.
43. Houselander, Caryll. *A Rocking Horse Catholic* (N Y: Sheed & Ward, 1955), p. 112.
44. Ibid, p. 137-38.
45. Near, Holly. "It Could Have Been Me," *Holly Near: A Live Album* (Ukiah, CA: Redwood Records, 1974.
46. Woodruff, op. cit., p. 117.

Giles: Prayer and Spirituality

1. Teresa of Avila. *Interior Castle* trans. by E. Allison Peers. (Garden City, NJ: Doubleday, 1961), p. 31-32.
2. Ibid., p. 85.
3. John of the Cross. *Ascent of Mount Carmel* trans. by E. Allison Peers. (Garden City, NJ: Doubleday, 1958).
4. Merton, Thomas. *Contemplative Prayer* (Garden City, NJ: Doubleday, 1971), p. 90.
5. John of the Cross. *Dark Night of the Soul* trans. by E Allison Peers. (Garden City, NJ: Doubleday, 1959), p. 119.
6. Teresa of Avila, op. cit., p. 154-155.
7. de Caussade, Jean-Pierre. *The Sacrament of the Present Moment* (San Francisco, CA: Harper & Row, 1989), p. 81.

Roberts: Introspection and Spirituality

1. Our defintion of religion as the revelation of the divine or Ultimate Truth to consciousness is the same used to define 'mysticism' in its broader sense.
   Although we prefer to define 'mysticism' in the Dionysian terms of a particular path , this definition is too narrow for our present purposes.
2. With Christ, the divine virtually put its stamp of approval on man's image-making relative way-of-knowing; Christ is the fulfillment of consciousness and its longing for a God like ourselves, with us. Because our passage through human existence is a passage through consciousness, Christ was the revelation of this passage.
3. Needless to say, the subject and object of consciousness are the same; the same mind bends back on itself. All awareness of consciousness, then, is subject-as-object. If this reflexive mechanism were suspended or put to rest, we could not speak of subject or object or speak of consciousness at all. Those who dispute this fact are only considering the conscious level of consciousness, whereas we are referring to the unconscious level of physiological functioning where the brain makes consciousness possible.

BIBLIOGRAPHY

ALLIONE, Tsultrim. *Women of Wisdom* (Boston: Rutledge & Kegan Paul, 1986).

ALSTON, A.J. *Devotional Poems of Mirabai* (New Delhi: Motilal Banarsidass, 1980).

ANDALSEN, Barbara Hilkert, et. al. (ed.) *Women's Consciousness, Women's Ethics* (San Francisco: Harper & Row, 1985).

AUROBINDO, Sri. *The Mother.* (Pondicherry, India: Sri Aurobindo Ashram, 1979).

BANKSON, Marjory Loet. *Braided Streams: Esther and a Woman's Way of Growing* (San Diego: Lura Media, 1985).

BELENKY, Mary Field, et. al. *Women's Ways of Knowing* (Basic Books, 1986).

BIANCHI, Eugene C. *Aging as a Spiritual Journey* (Crossroad, 1984).

BOLEN, Jean Shinoda. *Goddesses in Everywoman: A New Psychology of Women* (New York: Harper & Row, 1984).

BRUCHAC, Carol et. al., (ed) *The Stories We Hold Secret: Tales of Women's Spiritual Development* (New York: Greenfield Review Press, 1986).

BUDAPEST, Z. *Holy Book of Women's Mysteries* (Wingbow Press, 1989).

CADY, Susa, et. al. *Sophia: The Future of Feminist Spirituality* (San Francisco: Haper & Row, 1986).

CAMERON, Anne. *Daughters of Copper Woman* (Vancouver, BC: Press Gang Publishers, 1981).

CAMPBELL, Joseph and Charles Musé, eds. *In All Her Names: Explorations of the Feminine in Divinity* (San Francisco: Harper, 1991).

CANNON, Katie G. Black *Womanist Ethics* (Atlanta: Scholars Press, 1988).

CARR, Anne E. *Transforming Grace: Christian Tradition and Women's Experience* (Harper Collins, 1990).

CATHERINE OF SIENNA. *The Dialogues trans. Algar Thorold* (Rockford, IL: Tan Books, 1974).

CHERNIN, Kim. *Reinventing Eve: Modern Woman in Search of Herself* (New York: Times Books, 1987) *In My Mother's House: A Daughter's Story* (Harper Collins, 1984).

CHODOROW, Nancy. *The Reproduction of Mothering: Psychoanalysis and the Sociology of Gender* (Berkeley: University of California Press, 1978).

CHRIST, Carol. *Womanspirit Rising: A Feminist Reader in Religion edited by Judith Plaskow* (San Francisco: Harper & Row, 1979). *Diving Deep and Surfacing: Women Writers on Spriritual Quest* (Boston: Beacon Press, 1980). *Laugher of Aphrodite: Reflections on a Journey to the Goddess* (San Francisco: Harper & Row, 1987).

CLANTON, Jann Aldredge. *In Whose Image? God & Gender* (New York: Crossroad, 1990).

CLAREMONT DE CASTILLAJO, Irene. *Knowing Women: A Feminine Psychology* (Harper Collins, 1973).

COLLINS, Mary. *Women at Prayer* (Paulist, 1987).

DALY, Mary. *The Church and the Second Sex* (New York: Harper & Row, 1987). *Beyond God the Father* (Boston: Beacon Press, 1973. *Gyn/Ecology* (Boston: Beacon Press, 1978).

DINNERSTEIN, Dorothy. *The Mermaid and the Minotaur* (New York: Harper & Row, 1976).

DOWNING, Christine. *The Goddess: Mythological Images of the Feminine* (New York: Crossroad, 1984).

ECK, Diana L. and Devaki Jain, eds. *Speaking of Faith: Cross-cultural Perspectives on Women, Religion and Social Change* (London: The Woman's Press, 1986).

EHRENREICH, Barbara and Deirdre English. *Witches, Midwives, and Nurses* (Femininst Press, 1972).

EICHENBAUM, Louise and Susie Orbach. *Understanding Women: A Feminist Psychoanalytic Approach* (New York: Basic Books, 1983). *What Do Women Want: Exploding the Myth of Dependency* (New York: Basic Books, 1983).

EISLER, Riane. *The Chalice and the Blade* (Harper Collins, 1988).

ENGELSMAN, Joan Chamberlain. *The Feminine Dimension of the Divine* (Philadelphia: The Westminster Press, 1979).

FIORENZA, Elisabeth Schussler. *In Memory of Her: A Feminist Theological Reconstruction of Christian Origins* (New York: Crossroad, 1983).

GILES, Mary E. *The Feminist Mystic and Other Essays on Women and Spirituality* (New York: Crossroad, 1982) *When Each Leaf Shines: Voices of Women's Ministry* (Denville, NY: Dimension Books, 1986).

GILLIGAN, Carol. *In a Different Voice* (Cambridge, MA: Harvard University Press, 1982).

GOLDENBERG, Naomi. *Changing of the Gods* (Boston: Beacon Press, 1979).

GRAY, Elizabeth Dodson, ed. *Sacred Dimensions of Women's Experience* (Roundtable Press, 1988).

GREENSPAN, Miriam. *A New Approach to Women and Therapy* (McGraw Hill, 1983).

GRIFFIN, Susan. *Women and Nature* (New York: Harper & Row, 1978).

HALL, Nor. *The Moon and the Virgin: Reflections on the Archetypal Feminine* (New York: Harper & Row, 1980).

HESCHEL, S. *On Being a Jewish Feminist* (Jewish Publication Society, 1983).

HEYWARD, Isabel Carter. *Our Passion for Justice* (New York: The Pilgrim Press, 1984). *The Redemtion of God: A Theology of Mutual Relation* (Lanham, MD: University Press of America, Inc., 1982).

HILLESUM, Etty. *An Interrupted Life: Diaries of Etty Hillesum, 1941-1943* (New York: Pantheon Books, 1983).

HUNGRY WOLF, Beverly. *The Ways of My Grandmothers* (New York: William Morrow, 1980).

HURCOMBE, Linda. *Sex and God: Some Varieties of Women's Religious Experiences* (London: Routledge and Kegan Paul, 1987).

INAYAT, Taj. *The Chrystal Chalice* (Lebanon Springs, NY: Sufi Order Publications, 1980).

IYENGAR, Geeta. *Yoga: A Gem for Women* (Bombay: Allied, 1984).

JULIAN OF NORWICH. *Revelations of Divine Love* trans by James Walsh (St. Meinrad, IN: Abbey Press, 1975).

KENNETT, Roshi Jeiju. *The Wild, White Goose: The Diary of a Zen Trainee* (Mt. Shasta, CA: Shasta Abbey, 1977).

KINSLEY, David. *Hindu Goddesses: Visions of the Divine Feminine in the Hindu Religious Tradition* (Berkeley: University of California Press, 1986).

LAKOFF, Robin Talmach and Raqual L. Sherr. *Face Value: The Politics of Beauty* (London: Routledge & Kegan Paul, 1984).

LERNER, Harriet Goldhor. *The Dance of Anger: A Woman's Guide to Changing the Patterns of Intimate Relationships* (Harper & Row, 1985). *The Dance of Intimacy*

MAITLAND, Sara. *A Map of the New Country: Women and Christianity* (London: Routledge & Kegan Paul, 1983).

MAYORGA, Nancy Pope. *The Hunger of the Soul: A Spiritual Diary* (Los Angeles: Whitemarsh & Co., 1986).

MILLER, Jean Baker. *Toward a New Psychology of Women* (2nd ed.) (Beacon, 1986).

MOLLENKOTT, Virginia Ramey. *Women, Men and the Bible* (Nashville: Abingdon, 1977).

The Divine Feminine: The Biblical Imagery of God as Female (Crossroad, 1983).

MOLTMAN-WENDEN, Elizabeth. *Liberty, Equality and Sisterhood* trans. Ruth Gritsch (Philadelphia: Fortress, 1979). *A Land Flowing with Milk and Honey: Perspectives on Feminist Theology* (New York: Crossroad, 1986).

THE MUD FLOWER COLLECTIVE. *God's Fierce Whimsy* (New York: Pilgrim Press, 1985).

NURBAKHSH, Javad. *Sufi Women* (New York: Khankiquaki-Ni Matullahi Publishers, 1983).

OCHS, Carol. *Women and Spirituality* (Totowa, NY: Rowman and Allamheld, 1983).

ORBACH, Susie. *Fat is a Feminist Issue* (London: Paddington Press, 1977). *Hunger Strike: The Anorectic's Struggle as a Metaphor for Our Age* (NewYork: W.W. Norton, 1986).

OSIEK, Carolyn. *Beyond Anger: On Being a Feminist in the Church* (Paulist, 1986).

PAGELS, Elaine. *The Gnostic Gospels* (New York: Vintage, 1981).

PAPA, Mary Boder. *Christian Feminism: Completing the Subtotal Woman* (Chicago: Fides/Claretian, 1981).

PERERA, Sylvia Brinton. *Descent to the Goddess: A Way of Intiation for Women* (Toronto: Inner City Books, 1981).

PLASKOW, Judith and Carol Christ. *Weaving of Visions: New Patterns in Feminist Spirituality* (New York: Harper & Row, 1989).

RAY, Eleanor and Bernice Marie-Daly. *Created in Her Image: Models of the Feminine Divine* (New York: Crossroads, 1990).

REUTHER, Rosemary Radford. *Sexism and God-Talk* (Boston: Beacon Press 1983). *Womanguides* (Boston: Beacon Press, 1985) *Women of Spirit*, edited with Eleanor McLaughlin, 1979.

RIBIN, Lillian B. *Women of a Certain Age: The Midlife Search for Self* (Harper Collins, 1981).

RICH, Adrienne. *Of Woman Born* (Norton, 1986).

ROBERTS, Bernadette. *The Experience of No-Self: A Contemplative Journey* (Boulder, CO: Shambhala, 1984).

RUSSELL, Letty M. *Feminist Interpretation of the Bible* (Oxford: Blackwell,1985).

SANFORD, Linda Tschirhart and Mary Ellen Donovan. *Women and Self-Esteem* (Penguin, 1984).

SAYERS, Dorothy L. *Are Women Human?* (Grand Rapids: W.B. Eerdman's, 1971).

SCHAEF, Anne Wilson. *Women's Reality: An Emerging Female System in the White Male Society* (Minneapolis: Winston Press Inc., 1981).

SCHÜSSLER, Fiorenza, Elisabeth *Bread Not Stone: The Challenge of Feminisst Biblical Interpretation* (Beacon, 1984). *In Memory of Her: A Feminist Theological Reconstruction of Christian Origins* (Crossroad, 1983).

SEN, Ramprasad, Leonard Nathan and Clinton Seely, trans. *Grace and Mercy in Her Wild Hair: Selected Poems to the Mother Goddess* (Boulder, CO: Great Eastern, 1982).

SHARMA, Arvind. *Women in World Religions* (Albany: State University of New York Press, 1987).

SMITH, Margaret. *Rabia the Mystic and Her Fellow Saints in Islam* (Cambridge: Cambridge University Press, 1984).

SPRETNAK, Charlene. *The Politics of Women's Spirituality: Essays on the Rise of Spiritual Power within the Feminist Movement* (New York: Avelior Books, 1982).

STARHAWK. *The Spiral Dance* (San Francisco: Harper & Row, 1978). *Dreaming the Dark* (Boston: Beacon Press, 1982).

STONE, Merlin. *When God was a Woman* (New York: Dial Press,1976). *Ancient Mirrors of Womanhood* (Beacon Press, 1990).

TERESA OF AVILA. *Collected Works*, trans. Kavanough and Rodriguez, two volumes (Washington,

DC: ICS Publications, 1976, 1980).

THERESE OF LISIEUX. *Autobiography*, trans. John Clarke (Washington, DC: ICS Publications, 1975).

TRIBLE, Phyllis. *God and the Rhetoric of Sexuality* (Philadelphia, Fortress Press, 1978).

TWEEDIE, Irina. *Daughter of Fire: A Diary of a Spiritual Training with a Sufi Master* (Nevada City, CA: Blue Dolphin Press, 1986).

UNDERHILL, Evelyn. *Mysticism* (New York: New American Library, 1955).

WALKER, Barbara G. *The Woman's Encyclopedia of Myths and Secrets* (San Francisco: Harper & Row, 1983). *Woman's Dictionary of Symbols and Sacred Objects* (Harper Collins, 1988).

WARNER, Marina. *Alone of All Her Sex: Myth and Cult of the Virgin Mary* (New York: Alfred A. Knopf, 1976).

WILNER, Eleanor. *Shekhina* (Chicago: University of Chicago Press, 1984).

WOODMAN, Marion. *The Pregnant Virgin* (Inner City Books, 1985). *Addiction to Perfection* (Inner City Books, 1982). *Leaving My Father's House* (Shambhala, 1992).